ANDREW H. PLAKS

Archetype and Allegory in the *Dream of the Red Chamber*

PRINCETON UNIVERSITY PRESS

Publication of this book has been aided by grants from
the Princeton University Committee on Research
in the Humanities and Social Sciences and the
Andrew W. Mellon Foundation

Printed in the United States of America
by Princeton University Press at Princeton, New Jersey

Archetype and Allegory in the
Dream of the Red Chamber

CONTENTS

PREFACE

THIS book grows out of a close reading and structural analysis of the Ch'ing novel *Dream of the Red Chamber* with a view towards accounting for the widely acclaimed greatness of the work in terms that do justice both to its own narrative tradition and to recent advances in general literary theory. It is based on the assumption that the major works of Chinese narrative can, in fact, be meaningfully interpreted in accordance with critical concepts developed through the discipline of comparative literature—concepts derived primarily from Western literary models. The point is not that the specific aesthetic forms of European literature are to be applied in a normative sense to non-Western works, but, on the contrary, that those Western critical theories which aspire to universality cannot possibly be validated without reference to what is perhaps the major portion of the world's literary corpus. In the following discussions it may often appear that representatives of the Chinese and European traditions are accorded a particular privilege of neat, even antipodal, contrast. While broad comparisons of these two civilizations naturally arise within the context of Chinese studies in a Western milieu (and few other civilizations, for that matter, are comparable with respect to both antiquity and continuity), this is of course not meant to imply a two-party monopoly of cultural alternatives.

The reader whose interests lie primarily in the area of Chinese literary studies will notice that a considerable portion of this book is devoted to a lengthy discussion of several works of European allegory that seem to provide significant analogues and contrasts to the artistry of the *Dream of the Red Chamber*.

This approach is based on the conviction that comparative literary studies are most valid when critical attention is focused with equal earnestness on both sides of the comparison. It is hoped that these chapters may be of interest to readers in their own right, as well as providing a necessary link in the elucidation of the concept of allegorical composition as it applies to the Chinese text.

I wish to express my sincere appreciation to Professor Yu-kung Kao for his initial inspiration and continuous guidance of the preparation of this study, and to Professor Frederick W. Mote for his thoughtful reading of the manuscript and invaluable comments and corrections. Chapters v and vi were prepared with the specific encouragement of Professor Robert Fagles of the Department of Comparative Literature of Princeton University, who also offered valuable advice with respect to other sections of the text. In addition, I owe a debt of gratitude to the other·faculty members, librarians, administrative staff, and colleagues of the Department of East Asian Studies of Princeton University for their kind cooperation and support in the project. Finally, I wish to give thanks to the Council on International and Regional Studies of Princeton University for a summer grant that made possible the uninterrupted preparation of this manuscript, and to the Princeton University Committee on Research in the Humanities and Social Sciences and the Andrew W. Mellon Foundation for grants in support of publication.

Archetype and Allegory in the
Dream of the Red Chamber

INTRODUCTION

THIS book attempts to cover a good deal of territory. It begins and ends in the interpretation of a single Chinese narrative work, but its scope of inquiry necessitates extensive side-ventures into such diverse provinces as ancient mythology, logical method, European allegory, and garden aesthetics. Because of this somewhat circuitous—it is hoped, not circular—nature of the argument, it may be useful to set forth at the outset the path of reasoning to be pursued in the following pages.

The study takes its starting point in a consideration of the sense of encyclopedic fullness that emerges upon a reading of the Ch'ing novel *Dream of the Red Chamber*.[a] Since the actual mimetic level of the narrative is singularly lacking in epic breadth, this impression must be attributed to the author's ability to project a broader vision of the nature of existence, even as he recounts—much like Proust—the slow passing of days in the garden of his youth. In proceeding to investigate the

[a] By the time these pages come into print, the title of David Hawkes' masterful new translation of the first eighty chapters, *The Story of the Stone* (*Shih-t'ou Chi*, the common designation for this first section of the text), may have begun to replace *Dream of the Red Chamber* as the name of the book among the English-speaking audience. Since we are considering the novel *Hung-lou Meng* here in its relation to Chinese literature as a total system, rather than as a literary phenomenon *in vacuo*, we will refer throughout to the entire 120-chapter version generally ascribed to Ts'ao Hsüeh-ch'in and Kao E. Certainly it is this text which has established itself as a landmark of Chinese literary history and a treasured cultural possession of nearly two centuries of readers. The question of whether the work as we have it is the product of a single hand or the result of a variously appraised continuation will therefore not be relevant until we take up the problem of the ending of the narrative in Chapter IX.

specific contents of this vision, we turn to the two critical concepts set off by convenient alliteration in the subtitle of this book: archetype and allegory. In the case of both of these often-abused terms, what we are talking about is the manner in which the reduction of a broader framework of intelligibility into a limited narrative form tends to fall back upon patterns of literary structure that comprise homologies for the various formal models of conceptualization by which human experience is apprehended in different cultural spheres. The distinction between the two concepts comes in when we note that the presence of such patterns in a text is at some times simply implicit within a given linguistic and literary heritage, while at others they appear to be explicitly foregrounded and signposted—one might say *planted*—by the author in order to illuminate the nature of his own personal vision. The authors of *Dream of the Red Chamber*, at any rate, move freely back and forth between these two possibilities, now pushing hard at the meaning of their figures, now conveying levels of meaning of which they can hardly have been consciously aware. Since we can never presume to pin down the authors' original consciousness or lack of it—even the contemporaneous Chih-yen Chai commentary, to which we will turn for support at numerous points, cannot be said to speak with absolute authority on this issue—it is always the recognition of a range of possible meanings rather than the labelling of a given passage as archetypal or allegorical that will be pursued in the ensuing discussions.

In identifying the concept of literary archetype with the abiding structural patterns that underlie cultural forms of diverse period and genre, we must emphasize that what we are concerned with here is a particular rather than a universal tool of analysis. That is, we will not pursue the notion of archetype as an ultimate indicator of the pristine deep-structure of human thought, or even as a key to the "mind" of a single civilization, but simply as a recognizable unit of recurrence whose variation and transformation may provide an aid in the interpretation of the specific works of a given tradition. The fact that archetypes of structure are sharply conditioned by the cultural context in question becomes clearer when we turn to consider the area of mythology, the habitual stamping ground of archetypal critics. Here we find that the common conception of literary archetypes as patterns of narrative shape—the abstraction of *mythos* from myth—is not borne out in the corresponding Chinese materials. We observe that such mythical figures as Huang-ti, Kung Kung, and Hsi-ho are generally not treated through stories of human action, but are set into patterns of interrelation and sequence that reflect more the ritualizing than the mythologizing function of pre-literate culture: patterns that are no less archetypal for their apparent lack of narrative movement. Although we may not jump to the conclusion that archaic Chinese ritual provides a key to the entire civilization, the fact remains that the three-thousand-year literary tradition has consistently drawn upon non-narrative patterns of order and balance, patterns we tend to associate sooner with ritual than with myth, as its formal underpinnings.

Since the later text that comprises the object of this study opens with the mythical figure Nü-kua, the following chapter investigates the details of some of the earlier literary materials relating to this "goddess" and her consort Fu-hsi. It is suggested that the treatment of the conjugal relation between the two figures reflects archetypal patterns of mutual implication and cyclical recurrence that link the fragmentary mythological sources with the remainder of the tradition. The very fact that such patterns are expressed in terms of yin-yang dualism and five elements cosmology—the sort of formulas that mark out the sources of the study as examples of traditional "systematizing" rather than pristine mythic vision—serves to point up the common ground of formal continuity under consideration here.

In Chapter III the archetypal patterns traced in mythological fragments dealing with Nü-kua and Fu-hsi are reconsidered and restated within the broader context of Chinese philosophy. In order to emphasize the point that it is the formal patterns rather than the specific formulations that are at issue in the present study, the terms "complementary bipolarity" and "multiple periodicity" are introduced to refer to the logical relations underlying the yin-yang and five elements concepts. These archetypal relations are then further analyzed into four essential formal features: bipolar or cyclical arrangement of individual terms, ceaseless alternation from term to term, mutual implication of opposites, and infinite overlapping of axes or cycles. It is argued that in the Chinese tradition dual and five-term alternation is generally conceived of as a logical step from hypothetical unity to existential multiplicity, rather than the other way around, so that the "meaning" conveyed by the use of such patterns comes in only in the implication of a totalized vision within which all cycles complete themselves and all dual schemes hypothetically balance out. At certain points in the discussion it will be convenient to refer to this sort of overall vision as "spatialized" in the sense that it implies the simultaneous inclusion of all phases of temporal alternation, although admittedly this may lead to a certain amount of confusion with other usages of that term in recent criticism. In any event, the argument is that archetypal patterns of bipolar and sequential alternation are abiding ones underlying much of the literary tradition, not that they may account for all phases of the civilization.

In keeping with the pursuit of literary archetypes as a manageable tool of analysis for approaching difficult texts, the fourth chapter moves on to a close reading of the *Dream of the Red Chamber* in order to trace these formal patterns in the structure of the work. It is shown that ceaseless alternation along such axes as movement and stillness, union and separation, or prosperity and decline, goes to make up the overlapping web of narration that comprises the dense texture of the novel. Even more important, we observe the pains taken by the authors to structure the complex relations between characters in accordance with seasonal and elemental periodicity. It is suggested that this profuse overlapping of archetypal patterns in the novel adds up to something more than pseudo-philosophical ornamentation: that it evokes an all-inclusive vision of the totality of existence that underlies and sheds a measure of "meaning" upon the particular mimetic figures of the text. The fact that the characters in the novel most often fail to draw comfort from such a total vision (the same may be said for the authors and readers, at those points where vicarious identification outweighs literary detachment) serves to point up what we may call a "tragic" disjunction of vision between the time-bound perspective of mortal sensitivity and the detemporalized structure of intelligibility that is by definition beyond the scope of mimetic representation.

When we speak of the "intelligibility" that emerges from a close reading of the *Dream of the Red Chamber* we begin to pass over into the area of allegory, since the finely ordered correspondences between mimesis and meaning in the novel make the impression nearly inescapable that the authors were aware of and in control of at least some of these patterns of structure. This impression is supported, at any rate, by the traditional commentators on the novel, whose attempts to uncover the hidden meanings of the text often revolve around the sort of alternating sequences considered in the preceding chapter. Turning to a detailed inquiry into the nature of allegorical writing in the European tradition, with specific critical attention focused on the works of Dante, Chaucer, and Spenser, we find that the two-level ontological disjunction on which this mode is based in the West does not apply in the monistic universe of Chinese literature. But, by the same token, the most important of the various conceptual schemes by which Western thinkers have proposed to reconcile logically unbridgeable realms of existence (Platonic ideas and forms, Patristic incarnational aesthetics, Medieval figuralism etc.) do provide extremely significant contrasts with the approach to the problem of duality reflected in archetypal patterns of complementary bipolarity and multiple periodicity in the Chinese context. Such a distinction becomes even clearer when we note that the entire range of existential mutability—the object of the Chinese total vision of phenomenological flux—is represented in the Western allegorical texts as something noticeably less than the sum total of being: in the circumscribed dominion of Fortune, in one view, or in the realm of Nature hierarchically subordinated to the grace of its Maker in another. As a result, the essentially metaphorical relation between the European allegorist's fictive text and its immutable meaning must be distinguished from the manner in which the structural patterns woven into the *Dream of the Red Chamber* simply fall into, or add up to, the infinite totality of all such patterns (a relation that may be characterized as synecdochical).

This contrasting treatment of the problem of mutability is particularly relevant when we move on in Chapters VI and VII to a comparative study of the literary garden *topos*, an area of striking coincidence of concern between *Dream of the Red Chamber* and such works as the *Romance of the Rose*, the *Faerie Queene*, and *Paradise Lost*. Where the disjunction between being and becoming in the Western *locus amoenus* is expressed in terms of either a tropological choice between truth and falsity or a hierarchical ordering of lesser to greater degrees of perfection, the Chinese allegorical garden draws upon bipolar and multiple coordinates of perception to evoke a vision of the totality of existence in the given "natural" universe.

In Chapter VIII we return to the Ta-kuan Yüan garden, here rendered as the Garden of Total Vision (a translation that though somewhat forced does, I believe, convey the associations implicit in the term), and find the same "spatial" vision of totality evoked through archetypal patterns of bipolarity and periodicity. It is argued that the allegorical level of meaning behind the author's arrangement of the figures of his text lies in the sum total of all of its intelligible patterns, so that even the inexorable breakdown of the earthly paradise and the intense suffering that accompanies the expulsion of its inhabitants may be seen as forming, along with the rich plenitude of its earlier phases, yet another axis of complementary alternation within the total vision of the work. But since one of the principal logical underpinnings of this overall allegorical vision is the sheer endlessness of temporal change, this presents a particular critical problem in dealing with the literal ending of the narrative. In attempting to reconcile the sense of finality that accrues to Pao-yü's ultimate departure from the garden with the patterns of ceaseless alternation that keep rolling through to the final pages of the novel, we appeal once again to the aesthetics of complementarity. Given the essentially non-dialectical relation between finality and infinity within the authors' totalized vision, the title of our concluding chapter may reflect more the linguistic and academic milieu of the present study than the object of its critical focus.

CHAPTER I

ARCHETYPE AND MYTHOLOGY IN CHINESE LITERATURE

NEARLY all readers of the *Dream of the Red Chamber*—both native and foreign—come away with the impression that what they have experienced in the lengthy span from cover to cover is a comprehensive view of the entire civilization of Imperial China. This sense of cultural completeness may be largely attributed to the simple fact that the novel presents at exceedingly close range the day-to-day life of a bygone age of glory—and there is little doubt that this aspect is responsible for the degree of emotional attachment with which the work has been treasured by two centuries of readers. But for the purposes of this study we will focus attention on the fact that the *Dream of the Red Chamber* provides in one volume a summation of the three-thousand-year span of Chinese literary civilization. It contains within its pages a sampling of all of the major modes (poetry, drama, classical essay, vernacular fiction, etc.) and genres (*shih, tz'u, sao, fu,* etc.) of that tradition, and it takes up some of the central issues of its seminal thinkers (Lao Tzu, Chuang Tzu, Confucius, Mencius, and Ch'an masters). As a result, the work stands in its own cultural milieu as the major works of Homer, Virgil, Murasaki, Dante, Milton, Cervantes, Goethe, and more recently Proust and Joyce, do in theirs: as an encyclopedic compendium of an entire tradition in a form that itself serves as a model against which to judge works of less imposing stature.

It is on the basis of this role as an encyclopedic vessel of culture that we will justify speaking of the "archetypes" of the entire Chinese literary tradition within the scope of this one work. The conception of archetype, after all, has meaning only

11

within the context of a total *system* of knowledge, one in which recurring structural patterns both condition the formation of individual elements and are themselves modified by each new addition to the corpus. If it may be objected that the notion of systematization runs contrary to the spirit of literary expression, we may counter that it is precisely the existence of such a network of models, cross-references, and feedback that defines literature as a *tradition*, rather than simply an accumulation of finite works. In both the Chinese and the Western case, this system of literature must be seen as encompassing all verbal art, so that the distinction between history, philosophy, and what is commonly referred to as literature becomes one more of convenience than of substance. The fact that literature in this fuller sense has formed the basis of traditional education in the major civilizations further adds to this sense of the literary corpus as a self-contained system, a view that is particularly valid in the context of Chinese civilization, with its strong tradition of textual exegesis and its unique system of literary bureaucracy.

This is of course not to minimize the importance of the continuous development of styles and genres in literary history. On the contrary, it is precisely the fact of orderly development—from epic through romance to novel, from four-word poetry through *sao* and popular ballads to *shih*, *tz'u*, and *ch'ü*—that enables us to perceive the outlines of a unified system within literature. The abiding patterns of literary form to which we apply the term "archetype," then, stand out as the synchronic underpinnings that set off and render intelligible the diachronic dimension of historical modification within the system.

On the most immediate level one may note the recurrence of elements of content within a given literary system: particular character types, favored themes and motifs, conventional *topoi*. But what we are really concerned with here in connection with the notion of archetype are patterns of more generalized structure, since it is only on this subsurface level that we can perceive a common ground within the widely varying details of religious

12

belief, historical event, social milieu, and natural environment (and national language in the Western context) that occur over a span of millennia. Just as the spectrum of colors in painting and the tonal scales in music provide internal orders within the materials of artistic creation, so do archetypes of literary structure provide the ground of coherence, the aesthetic expectations, that may be fulfilled, subtly varied, or negatively transformed in a given work.

It must be added here that the sort of structural patterns we are talking about are nothing more than the cultural preferences shaped by a given tradition during the course of its literary history. This point must be emphasized, since in recent years the term "archetype" has often come to be a vague catchall for nearly any observable pattern of mental activity, with the corollary assumption that literary archetypes must provide a universal key to the infrastructure of the human mind.[a] In the following pages, however, we will attempt to keep our sights lowered to the specific aesthetic forms that recur throughout a given cultural tradition, and thus provide a tool of analysis for approaching its more complex literary works.

It is by now a commonplace of literary criticism that the archetypes of a given tradition may be studied within its ancient mythology. But while the association between depth of vision and chronological age of literary materials seems to arise naturally out of the central role of the Homeric epics and the Old Testament in Western culture, and is implicit in the work of such archetypalists as Frazer and Jung, and more recently Frye and Campbell, it should not go unquestioned here. Mythology, to be sure, is not the simplest or clearest form of literary expression. Nor is it more directly concerned with the ultimate questions of existence than other phases of literature such as, say, metaphysical poetry or the modern novel. We must be careful, in this regard, to avoid confusing the authors of the oral myths

[a] Cf. Jolande Jacobi, *Complex, Archetype, Symbol in the Psychology of C. G. Jung* (Princeton, 1971), p. 34: ". . . in time it was extended to all sorts of patterns, configurations, happenings, etc. . . . Ultimately it came to cover all psychic manifestations of a biological, psychobiological, or ideational character, provided they were more or less universal and typical."

that have found their way into writing with some sort of primeval seers at the dawn of human consciousness forging what Cassirer calls the "radical metaphors" of human experience.[1] Even if idealizations such as this may accurately reflect the origins of language and culture, this would have to be located far back along the time line of man's residence on the earth, while the mytho-poets who stand near the beginnings of the written traditions a mere handful of millennia removed from us cannot be said to be significantly closer to the pristine vision than we are today. Unfortunately, arguments based on this "pristine vision" fallacy occupy a good portion of contemporary discussions of ancient literature.

Perhaps the proper ground of mythological studies can be found if we agree to leave primitive man in the hands of the anthropologist and return literature to its proper sphere: the written record of civilization. Mythology may or may not provide a key to the secrets of the human mind, in the Jungian sense, but it can clarify our study of literature by roughly demarcating the starting point of the continuous tradition that we have, perhaps arbitrarily, roped off as a subject of inquiry. Taking the entire corpus of material from the *terminus a quo* up to the present as a total, self-perpetuating system, on the authority of tradition and education, we can proceed to uncover the recurrent formal relationships that pertain throughout the system. In this light, the term "mythology" may often indicate no more than the earliest body of literary materials in which the archetypes of the entire system are already evident. Frye seems to emphasize this chronological, rather than mystical, significance of mythology when he notes that it "provides the main outlines and the circumference of a verbal universe which is later occupied by literature as well."[2]

It seems significant that the specific patterns that critics have isolated within Western mythology, and further traced as archetypes of the Western literary tradition, fall primarily under the heading of narrative shape. The actual identification of these forms, of course, differs from author to author: some draw such categories as separation-initiation-return, while others

14

speak of patterns of expulsion and integration, fall and rise, confrontation and mortal combat, death and resurrection. In fact writers such as Frye and Campbell go on to outline total cycles of archetypal movement, of which each individual myth represents but a segment. What concerns us here is that these archetypes are nearly always conceived of in terms of action or movement, from the presentation of tension to its final resolution. Even more significant is the fact that such archetypal patterns of praxis are often abstracted from their narrative context and treated as cross-generic forms, such that the dialectical movement of drama, and even the progression of images in lyric, are thrown back upon archetypes of formal movement that are essentially narrative in shape. As a result, Frye's use of the Aristotelian term "mythos" in reference to such units of narrative shape tends to become synonymous with the concept of literary archetype as a whole. It is assumed in the present study, that, while this association of archetype with narrative "mythos" may be valid in describing the Western tradition, it need not necessarily hold true for other literatures as well.

In attempting to define the function of mythology within the system of Chinese literature, one is immediately struck by a singular lack of interest in preserving the specific details of pre-literary lore. Mythical figures appear only occasionally in later Chinese writings and almost never in a full recapitulation or reinterpretation of their deeds. Rarely do we find a later literary expansion of the battle between Huang-ti and Ch'ih-yu, a recounting of the hydraulic labors of Yü, or even, for that matter, an extended treatment of the careers of Yao or Shun.[b]

Part of the reason for the apparent deemphasis of mythology in the system of Chinese literature must lie in the fact that the aesthetic impulses underlying the tradition simply are not geared to the forward thrust of beginning, middle, and end that

---

[b]Such exceptions as the *pien-wen* tale of Shun's youth are conspicuous for their rarity. One might note the existence of the titles 大禹治水, 禹會塗山記, 盤古至唐虞傳, and 虞初小説, etc., but it can hardly be claimed that such works are central to the tradition (SunKài-ti, pp. 23f, 174f).

we naturally associate with patterns of narrative shape in other cultures. As a result of this, what is truly archetypal, in the sense described here, in the pre-literary lore recorded in China's early texts must be sought elsewhere, in the area of non-narrative qualities and relationships. Before we proceed to an investigation of the exact nature of these structural forms, however, it will be necessary to consider some of the issues that arise in connection with the sources employed in this study.

The problem in dealing with Chinese mythology is not, as has often been suggested, any lack of systematic compilations of mythical materials. The troublesome task of isolating and collecting Chinese myth, as described by Bodde—". . . these materials are usually so fragmentary and episodic that even the reconstruction from them of individual myths—let alone an integrated *system* of myths—is exceedingly difficult"[3]—is a problem encountered by mythologists of all cultures. Robert Graves, for example, voices a similar complaint with regard to his work with Greek mythology: ". . . genuine mythic elements may be found embedded in the least promising stories, and the fullest or most illuminating version of a given myth is seldom supplied by any one author."[4] Certainly the presence of any systematic treasury of mythology is the exception rather than the rule in human culture, and generally of quite late date. Moreover, the student of Chinese mythology soon becomes aware that the apparently chaotic proliferation of sources in fact revolves around a diminishing, manageable number of texts, primarily of the Han period. Such works as the *Huai-nan Tzu, Lun Heng, Shan-hai Ching*, and *Feng-su T'ung-i* are of course not intended to be exclusively mythological compilations. But what Han thinkers such as Wang Ch'ung and Ying Shao do seem to be trying to do is to construct a meaningful system of knowledge out of all the sources available to them, including what we now label mythology. In other words, they are indeed involved in analyzing and interpreting mythical materials. The fact that nearly all of the elements that characterize the mythologies of other cultures—personifications of natural phenomena, supernatural beasts, monumental battles, a golden age, a great deluge, and a schism between Heaven and Earth—are found in these materials leads to the conclusion that the difficulty of interpreting Chinese mythology is not a textual one. The reason that myth is not rearranged into an organized system in its own right is due primarily to the fact that it is treated as an integral part of human knowledge rather than a subdivision roped off by the attribution of divinity.

This last point brings us to the question of the nature of the actors in the mythological drama. The student of Chinese mythology soon observes that the common conception of myth in terms of a class of suprahuman actors engaged in the creation and destruction of worlds fails to describe the material at hand. Upon first sight, Maspero's explanation of the process as the euhemerization of supernatural beings of pre-literary lore into figures of strictly human proportions (e.g. the installation of such bizarre creatures as K'uei and Kung Kung as ministers at the court of Yao in the first chapter of the *Shu Ching* classic) seems to present a neat contrast to Frye's characterization of Western mythology as "the imitation of actions near or at the conceivable limits of desire."[5] Upon further examination, however, it becomes clear that the distinction implied by both of these writers between divine-oriented and human-oriented cultural forms must be sharply qualified. For one thing, we must recognize that the Olympian gods to whom Frye's remark refers are immortal only in the literal sense of invulnerability to death. In nearly all other respects they are quite subject to the desires, pain, and, most important, the frustrations of mortality. This is even more true of all the actors in the early books of the Old Testament save the Creator Himself. Clearly, it is not the attribution of omnipotence that sets the heroes of Western mythology off from their Chinese counterparts.

At the same time, the wealth of supernatural detail attached even to such euhemerized figures as Yao, Shun, and Yü shift them yet closer towards the barely immortal actors of Western myth, as Karlgren notes: "The divine nature and powers of those early heroes were ever present in the minds of all the writers of the last few Chou centuries, and in this sense, the tales about them are frankly mythological."[6] The resulting position of the Chinese sage-kings—somewhat beyond the monumental deeds of legend, yet somewhere on this side of the infinite potential of divinity—therefore cannot be cited as the factor responsible for the unique character of Chinese mythology.

With this qualification in mind, we must be extremely cautious in evaluating Bodde's observation that the Chinese have no creation myth.[7] It is certainly true that this fact accords well with the Chinese propensity to substitute human for divine patterns of authority, but we must note at the same time that the non-centrality of cosmogonic speculation applies to early Greek mythology as well (such that Hesiod's framing of a creation myth inspires suspicions as to importation from the Fertile Crescent), although this did not hinder the fusion of spiritual and temporal authority in the Classical and Christian traditions of the West. On the other hand, we do find tantalizing indications, both in textual fragments and in archaeological and anthropological findings, to the effect that pre-literate Chinese culture may have been rich in such elements as creation myths and anthropomorphic gods. What concerns us more in this study, however, is the manner, rather than the fact, of cosmic creation. Here we do find an interesting difference between the essentially autochthonous generation implied in the P'an Ku and Hun T'un fragments,[c] and the world-shaping will of creation *ex nihilo*.[d] In the final analysis, the question of cosmogony turns back upon the possibility of an absolute standard of judgement in human affairs: the ultimate accountability of man for his actions. It would be hasty to overlook, in this regard, the function of the conception

[c]Significantly, when the notion of a creator (*tsao-wu-che* 造物者) does appear, as in the "Ta-tsung Shih" 大宗師 chapter of the *Chuang Tzu*, its usage refers specifically to a molder of human forms, rarely to a Prime Mover of the universe itself.

[d]But, again, we also find the theme of spontaneous generation in many cultures, including ancient Greece, while the notion of creation *ex nihilo* has had rough going, to say the least, in Western theology.

of Heaven in early Chinese texts—for all its impersonality and spontaneity—as a backdrop of moral order against which to judge the deeds of mortal men. In any event, we can sidestep the issue of divinity in mythology by citing Lévi-Strauss' simple truism that mythology "refers to events alleged to have taken place . . . long ago."[8] In spite of their varying degrees of omnipotence, creativity, and hypothetical historicity, the Chinese figures who are generally classified as mythical share a common quality of high antiquity that sets them apart from latter-day heroes.

A second issue that has been raised with respect to the sources of studies in Chinese mythology—the fact that most of the texts are deliberate redactions of myth cited in defense or illustration of specific arguments—also should not impede us. Bodde's mention of this state of the sources: "All that we have are casual references and tantalizing fragments, widely scattered among texts of diverse date and ideological orientation,"[9] as well as Lu Hsün's complaint that Chinese mythology was deliberately expurgated by the Han Confucianists in the interests of philosophical coherence,[10] must again be read in conjunction with statements of similar difficulties on the part of mythologues of other cultures. Even in the case of myths recorded by anthropological field workers among non-literate peoples, for that matter, we should not overlook the centuries and millennia of *oral* redaction that have gone by in the interest of cultural demands external to "original" myth. Interesting as it would be to have them for comparison, any pursuit of the pristine forms of myth can be only pure speculation. With this in mind, Karlgren's careful distinction between "free" Chou texts and Han "systematizing" scholarship, "the products of scholars who deliberately tried to lay down laws or make a consistent whole of the ancient traditions and ritual ideas,"[11] seems perhaps to miss the point. For if the Han mythologues are guilty of imposing conceptual order upon mythical materials, the same evaluation must fall with nearly equal weight upon the Chou texts for their handling of traditions handed down from pre-literate times. For example,

19

Karlgren himself notes elsewhere in discussing a mythological passage in the *Tso Chuan* that "a fairly early systematizer . . . has tried to force some early, unsystematic cult phenomena to agree with the theory of the five elements."[12] It is always possible, of course, that all such passages may be passed off as later interpolations into the original texts, but to do so would necessitate the cutting of a good deal of canonic material, including for example such "systematized" chapters of the *Shu Ching* classic as "Yao Tien" (for its directional schemes), or "Lü Hsing" (for its mention of a schism between Heaven and Earth.[e]

At this point it must be emphasized that we are not considering myth here as a body of puzzling documents from which to reconstruct the earliest history of China, as in the admirable work of the authors of *Ku-shih Pien*, but rather as examples of verbal art that presumably predate the beginnings of the Chinese written tradition. It is the patterns into which the mythical figures are set in the literary texts, and not their chronological order or hypothetical authenticity, that concerns us. As a result, the feature cited as a fault by both Maspero, ". . . il est une élaboration littéraire des données légendaires, et ne peut servir à l'étude de celles-ci,"[13] and Karlgren, ". . . it has nothing to do with the history of early China, but only with the history of scholarship in medieval China,"[14] may be seen as precisely the subject of this study: the manner in which the Chinese tradition orders a mass of conflicting data into a meaningful structure. Since this impulse to systematization is clearly present, although perhaps on a pre-articulate level, in the Chou texts, it is maintained that such structural patterns as the Han compilers impose on their materials may be viewed as archetypal within the entire Chinese tradition, and not simply as characteristic of a single age. The argument that these very patterns which have determined the role of Chinese mythology in ensuing centuries are in some sense extraneous, or even alien to that tradition, would if carried to its logical conclusion be

[e]Ku Chieh-kang accepts these chapters as products of late and middle Chou, respectively (*Ku-shih Pien*, Taipei, 1960, Vol. I, p. 200f.).

tantamount to denying the Chinese-ness of Han learning. To do so would call much of Sung, Ming, and particularly Ch'ing scholarship into question,[f] and would certainly close the door on the present study.

It has already been suggested above that the literary archetypes perceived within Chinese mythology are in a sense non-narrative in nature. This would perhaps seem to be a contradiction in terms, since mythology, by very definition, comprises the earliest examples of narrative art. Nevertheless, the apparent lack, or at least meagerness, of narrative movement in Chinese mythology is inescapable. This may be partly blamed upon the fragmentary nature of our sources, but even in texts that treat the figures of myth in extensive detail we find the same non-narrative quality. Events, when they occur, are listed rather than recounted. Figures are described more in terms of their ultimate positions than through narrations of how they got there. Even combat is related by means of a cataloguing of stratagems and a statement of outcome, rather than by dwelling upon the moment of mortal confrontation.

As mentioned above, the earliest extant records of myth in Chinese literature, as elsewhere, are in fact removed by centuries or millennia from the original process of oral composition. But while it is impossible to determine exactly how far back into pre-history the tendency to deemphasize narration in the treatment of mythical lore may date, the striking fact remains that this tendency is a consistent feature of the Chinese written tradition—the subject of this investigation. In other words, the problem of dealing with Chinese mythology is nothing more or less than the problem of coming to terms with the unique aesthetics of the Chinese narrative tradition as a whole.

In order to propose an explanation for this generalization, let us recall the intimate connection between myth and ritual that is observed in all pre-literate societies. To judge from recent archaeological evidence concerning Shang civilization in ancient China—oracle-bone inscriptions, temple foundations,

[f] As Karlgren, indeed, concludes ("Legends and Cults in Ancient China," p. 345f).

pottery motifs, etc.[15] and generalizing on details that have survived in mythical texts, there is no need to assume that pre-Chou China was any different from other early or isolated cultures in this respect. Therefore, in view of the consistent deemphasis of myth in the three-thousand-year period of Chinese *literary history*, it will be suggested that this later relatively short span may be described in terms of a gradual emphasis of certain spatialized elements of ritual order and balance over the forms of temporal narration generally associated with mythology.

One clear symptom of this process may be observed in the steady elimination of what we may presume to have been a mythic content of ritual in Chinese life, a fact that may go a long way towards explaining the difficulty of isolating and defining religion in the Chinese context. This is not to say, of course, that the actual practice of ritual has ever dominated Chinese life (as in the ideal scheme of ritualized government in the "Yüeh Ling" chapter of the *Li Chi*), a fact noted with some chagrin by Confucius. The point is simply that the Chinese literary civilization has tended to draw upon formal patterns that we naturally associate with ritual—balanced forces, periodic rhythms, and cyclical sequences—as structural principles for artistic creation. When one views the sharp curtailment of mythological narrative already in the earliest texts of the tradition, it sometimes seems as if pre-existing myth were being, in a sense, deliberately ritualized, although of course it is only a question of relative emphasis. Such a conclusion, at any rate, may be drawn from the characteristic setting of mythical figures into formal patterns related to the cardinal directions and the seasonal cycle. The most extensive treatment of this type is found in the "Yüeh Ling" document, but even in less fully realized examples (e.g., Yao's appointment of Hsi and Ho to preside over the solar cycle at the opening of the *Shu Ching*, or the various figures mentioned in *Tso Chuan*, Duke Wen, 18) we may perceive the same principle at work. An even more extreme example of this tendency may be observed in the archetypal situations schematized in the hexagram commentaries of the *I Ching*. If we assume that the basic situations associated with the hexagrams were not originally derived from more fully fleshed narrative sequences,[g] the fact that the framers of the text deliberately avoid the recourse of myth in presenting patterns of temporal flux, choosing instead to retain a purely abstract format, cannot but be striking in this regard. We may note, by way of contrast, that one of the most well-known ancient Western treatments of the same problem of phenomenological metamorphosis takes the form of a mythological compendium. Without, of course, denying the importance of ritual in Western culture, we may point out here its consistent emphasis on the mythical content of ritual practice. Such examples as the dying-god treatment of seasonal change traced by Frazer in the Tammuz-Adonis-Osiris-Jesus myths, and the projection of the unilinear form of human life into narratives of cosmic creation, consciousness, fall, and redemption immediately come to mind.[h] Going one step further, one might explain the tendency towards unilinear narrative treatment of the figures of Mediterranean mythology as a reflection of the centrality of syntactic logic, and hence dialectical progression, to many of the most abiding forms of Western civilization.

While it must be acknowledged that such broad considerations as these are speculative at best, in the field of literature—and particularly with reference to the notion of archetype—the distinction does seem to hold true. We have already noted the essentially narrative character of the archetypes of Western literature traced by recent critics to the structural shape of Greek and Hebrew mythology. What concerns us here, however, is the direction in which the content of these mythologies is "displaced," to use Frye's term,[16] into cultural forms that are separated by time and self-consciousness from original

[g] Cf. Ku Chieh-kang's article: "Chou-i Kua-yao-tz'u chung ti Ku-shih" 周易卦爻辭中的故事, in *Ku-shih Pien*, Volume III, pp. 1–44.

[h] It is perhaps not accidental, therefore, that Western literary history has seen a recurrent tendency towards the re-mythicization of philosophical abstractions, as in the New Testament incarnation of Platonism, or the medieval allegorization of Scholasticism.

belief. In other words, the question here is how a literary tradition *uses* its pre-literary lore. As to the way in which Western literature uses its mythical materials, we immediately observe that such recurrent figures as Prometheus, Orpheus, and Adam reappear in later literature chiefly in order to relive the experiences associated with their names. Whether their actions are frustrated, fulfilled, or visited by dire consequences, it is what they do, rather than what they are, which reverberates through Western literary history. The case of a figure such as Oedipus might seem to present a contradiction to this point, but it is maintained that here too the primary emphasis is on acts and their consequences rather than on exploring a static relationship. When this emphasis on *praxis* is displaced beyond the direct recounting of deeds into the dimension of literary structure, a limited number of recurring patterns emerge, notably the "mythoi" of goal-oriented journey and antithetical struggle. The former shape in particular may be seen to underlie much of the literature that we have come to describe as epic, whether this involves a literal quest, a disaster-ridden return journey, or an internalized search for self-realization.[i]

Turning back to the Chinese literary tradition, we will suggest that the apparently non-narrative character of its most abiding forms may be explained by the fact that its archetypal structures are displacements of ritual relations rather than of mythical actions. We have already seen the tendency towards balanced systematization in the mythical materials recorded in China's earliest texts, and we will attempt to demonstrate in the following chapters that the recurrent use of schemes of order and balance associated with ritual remains a consistent aesthetic impulse of the entire tradition. We shall see below that such patterns are most often expressed in the language of yin-yang dualism and five elements cosmology—a fact that is often cited in order to discredit the authenticity of the mythical materials under consideration, but it will be maintained that

[i]Cf. Northrop Frye: "We have identified the central myth of literature, in its narrative aspect, with the quest myth" (*Fables of Identity*, New York, 1963, p. 18).

the formal method of ritual displacement implicit in such schemes both predates and underlies these specific formulations.

The essentially non-narrative use of myth in later Chinese literature may be seen on an explicit level in the fact that allusions to mythical figures generally refer to a specific quality or relation associated with them, rather than to any of the details of their deeds. For example, such often-used figures as Ch'ang-o (嫦娥) and Chih-nü (織女) may easily be traced to complete narratives in later compilations, but references to them in other works allude nearly without exception to static qualities—the cold loneliness of the moon, or the sadness of separation—rather than to the temporal process by which these states were reached. Similarly, the names of the sage-kings Yao, Shun, and Yü are generally invoked to emphasize the fact of transition from a state of primeval chaos to one of settled, governed society, but rarely are we led to envision the actual process of transformation. The case of Yü is perhaps most instructive, since his Herculean labors are almost never presented as anything resembling epic struggle.[j] Often, allusions to mythical personages or places seem intended to evoke a hypothetical state of ritual completeness which is entirely abstracted from the specific figures involved.

It has been proposed here that this emphasis on qualities, relations, and states of being as opposed to motivation, action, and consequences is directly related to the varying roles of myth and ritual in the Chinese and Western traditions. In this sense, when we speak of the archetypes of Chinese literature we must look beyond patterns of narrative action to what are essentially detemporalized forms of vision. By the same token, the apparent lack of logical development or dialectical progression must be reinterpreted with reference to an aesthetic system within which the poles of temporal opposition are contained as com-

---

[j]The *tz'u* poems "齊天樂，與馮深居登禹陵" by Wu Wen-ying and "生查子" by Hsin Ch'i-chi do project a kind of epic monumentality into their allusions to Yü, but, again, it is the quality rather than the act that is at issue.

plementary possibilities rather than antithetical forces. The distinction between these varying emphases on temporal and non-temporal (let us say "spatial") patterns in the archetypes of the two literary systems may perhaps explain the frequent application of critical concepts derived from music theory in the one tradition, and the complex interpenetration of the aesthetics of poetry and painting in the other. In any event, what we are talking about here is not a classification of the human race into two categories of mental activity, but rather a clarification of the *preferred* forms of the two traditions, as directed and shaped through the comparatively short span of cultural history. It is not the mythical materials themselves that lead us to such general conclusions, but how these materials are used in shaping a cultural mainstream. With this in mind, let us now consider in detail one figure of Chinese mythology—Nü-kua—with an eye towards the archetypal forms of Chinese verbal art that may aid us in interpreting a later work such as the *Dream of the Red Chamber*.

CHAPTER II

THE MARRIAGE OF NÜ-KUA
AND FU-HSI

THE reader of the *Dream of the Red Chamber* is confronted in the first chapter with the mythical figure Nü-kua 女媧[a] in her most well-known role as repairer of the heavens with many-colored stones. This passage introduces Pao-yü as an extra-human, if imperfect, being and serves as a frame of reference for the various supernatural episodes strategically placed throughout the novel, eventually justifying his ultimate exit from the world of red dust. Nü-kua herself, however, im-mediately passes from view only to return for a final bow in the last pages of the book. Aside from this incident of heavenly reconstruction, we get no further information in the novel as to her supposed nature as a mythical deity. Let us therefore consider some of the earlier materials relating to this figure in the Chinese tradition, with a view towards discerning certain archetypal patterns of significance that may shed light upon her later appearance in the novel.

The repute of Nü-kua as a figure in Chinese mythology centers primarily about two more or less well-known stories: the repair of heaven referred to in the *Dream of the Red Chamber* and the creation of mankind from handfuls of mud. The *locus classicus* of the first episode seems to be found in the Han philosophical tract known as *Huai-nan Tzu*:

往古之時，四極廢，九州裂，天不兼覆，地不周載，火爁炎而不滅，水浩洋而不息，猛獸食顓民，鷙鳥攫老弱．於是女媧鍊五色

---

[a]The choice of the reading *kua* over the variant *wa* for the character is based on the *fan-ch'ieh* spelling given in several sources (e.g. *Shuo-wen Chieh-tzu* (Taipei, 1965), 12 下, p. 8a).

27

石以補蒼天，斷鼇足以立四極，殺黑龍以濟冀州，積蘆灰以止淫水.

"In very ancient times, the four pillars (at the compass points) were broken down, the nine provinces (of the habitable world) were split apart, Heaven did not wholly cover (Earth), and Earth did not completely support (Heaven). Fires flamed without being extinguished, waters inundated without being stopped, fierce beasts ate the people, and birds of prey seized the old and weak in their claws. Thereupon Nü-kua fused together stones of the five colors with which she patched together azure Heaven. She cut off the feet of a turtle with which she set up the four pillars. She slaughtered the Black Dragon in order to save the province of Chi (the present Hopei and Shansi provinces in North China). She collected the ashes of reeds with which to check the wild waters."[1]

In this passage we read of a universal cataclysm upsetting the very foundations of the Earth and subjecting its inhabitants to the ravages of uncontrolled fire, water, and beasts. Our initial interest in the myth stems of course from Nü-kua's repair of the heavenly breach (補天), but we shall have cause to return to the giant tortoise,[b] the black dragon, and the reed-ashes in the following discussion. We should also take note of the word yin 淫 used to refer to the uncontrollable waters, an association with interesting echoes in the later novel, and we may point out the curious parallel between the spectral stone involved in the assuaging of this flood, and the rainbow that signals the renewed covenant after the Biblical deluge.[c]

It is significant that the presumably dramatic events leading up to such a cosmic upset are conspicuously omitted from the above passage (for that matter, the text seems to speak more

[b]The T'ien-wen section of the Ch'u Tz'u anthology (Taipei, 1962, pp. 10b, 12a) mentions this world-supporting tortoise, as well as the tilt of Heaven and Earth.

[c]Interestingly enough, the Sinicized Jewish community dating from Sung times in K'ai-feng chose the two characters of Nü-kua's name to transcribe the name of the hero of their own flood myth (Noah = Nü-wa).

of a disjunction between Heaven and Earth, than of any actual
breach in the vault of Heaven itself). Other sources lay the
blame for the cataclysm on Kung Kung 共工, an arch-demon
who appears repeatedly in Chinese mythology as a bearer of
floods and other ill-tidings.[d] In the course of combat with the
fire-god Chu Jung 祝融 (or, in other variants, with the "Emperors" Chuan Hsü 顓頊 or Kao Hsin 高辛), Kung Kung is
said to have collided with the north-west pillar of Heaven
formed by the peak of Pu Chou Shan 不周山 (cf. 地不周載,
above), causing the heavens to tilt towards the northwest and
the Earth to incline towards the southeast, hence the flow of
China's rivers.[2] Alternate versions place the burden of battle
on Nü-kua herself, with Kung Kung represented as a titan figure peevishly upsetting the world for his own evil designs,[3]
while the *Lieh Tzu* relates the struggle with Kung Kung as oc-
curring after the repair of Heaven.[4] But only in recent attempts
to reconstruct ancient Chinese mythology do we find anything
like a fully realized narration of Kung Kung's demonic deed
and Nü-kua's saving grace.[5]

The second aspect of Nü-kua's career is traced as far as extant sources permit to the Han compilation *Feng-su T'ung-I*:

俗說, 天地開闢, 未有人民, 女媧搏黃土作人, 務劇力不暇供,
乃引繩絚泥中, 舉以為人, 故富貴者, 黃土人也, 貧賤凡庸者,
人也.

"It is popularly said that when Heaven and Earth had
opened forth, but before there were human beings, Nü-kua
created men by patting yellow earth together. But the work
tasked her strength and left her no free time, so that she then
dragged a string through mud, thus heaping it up so as to
make it into men. Therefore the rich and the noble are those

[d]This evil cast does not prevent him from turning up in euhemerized
form as a functionary in charge of public works (evidently due to the
characters used to transcribe his name) in the Yao Tien text. One may
note the use of the expression *t'ao-t'ien* 滔天 by Yao in rejecting Kung-
kung as a possible successor, followed immediately by a description of
rampaging flood waters with the same words.

men of yellow earth, whereas the poor and the lowly—all ordinary people—are those cord-made men."[6]

In keeping with our earlier observation about the myths of creation in Chinese mythology, Nü-kua's fashioning of human beings—presumably in her own image—takes place only after the origin of Heaven and Earth (開闢). Like that of Chuang Tzu's *tsao-wu-che* mentioned above, the role of the goddess is significantly limited to the molding of corporeal forms. In other words, it is the phenomenon of regeneration rather than creation that is at issue here, or more accurately, it is the *continuous creation* of transient forms to which the myth refers.[e] This last association will be important in the following discussion of Nü-kua's role as an initiatory deity.

Outside of these two episodes, Nü-kua's appearance in the written sources of the Chinese tradition are limited to fragmentary items. Other sources mentioning her name include the following:

1. The "T'ien-wen" section of *Ch'u Tz'u* asks the following question: 女媧有體孰制匠之? ("Nü-kua had a body. Who formed and fashioned it?").[7] Karlgren interprets this as telling us no more than that Nü-kua had a "peculiar shape,"[8] but in view of her role as a creatrice it might perhaps be better explained as an occurrence of the perennial chicken-or-egg riddle. In any event, we see here an early reference to the fashioning of human forms that finds its way into the *Feng-su T'ung-i* passage cited above.

2. The "Shuo-lin Hsün" 説林訓 chapter of *Huai-nan Tzu* provides what seems to be the skeleton of a cooperative "creation" myth,[9] in which Huang Ti fashions the yin and the yang (presumably referring here to the reproductive organs), two deities known as Shang P'ien 上駢 and Sang Lin 桑林 (see below) create human eyes, ears, and hands, and Nü-kua is credited with "seventy transformations."[f] The precise meaning

---

[e] In the Ming novella *Hsi-yu Pu*, Nü-kua's repair work is also described as a continuous process rather than a one-time feat (Peking, 1955, ch. 5, p. 9a).

[f] Wen I-to notes that the number 70 in ancient Chinese texts may be

of this passage is unclear, but the association between the terms
"yin" and "yang" in the sexual sense and the hymeneal function of the figures Sang Lin and Nü-kua will be relevant to
the following discussion.

3. A capacity for extensive metamorphosis is also referred
to in the *Shuo-wen Chieh-tzu* entry cited above on the character
"kua": 故神聖女，化萬物者也 ("a former goddess, who
brought into existence the myriad things"), as well as in the
Shan Hai Ching, where Nü-kua's innards are metamorphosed
in a manner reminiscent of P'an Ku's generative dissolution:
腸化為神 ("intestines transformed into deities").[10]

4. Although one commentator explains her relative obscu-
rity among the god-emperors by her failure to produce many
inventions for the benefit of mankind,[11] Ying Shao cites her as
the originator of two musical instruments: the *sheng* 笙 and the
huang 簧,[12] while another source adds the five-stringed zither
and the hair ornament known as *chi* 笄 to her credit (see
below).[13]

5. Perhaps most important for our purposes, Nü-kua's
name is associated in a number of sources with various combinations of the character *mei* 禖 (= 媒, matchmaker)[g] as
either the inventor or the administrator of the institution of
human marriage. Exactly what this title seems to have signified
becomes clearer when we examine the description of the Mei
Shih 媒氏 ritual in the *Chou-li* text:

中春之月，令會男女，於是時也，奔者不禁，若無故而不用令者
罰之，司男女之無夫家者而會之.

"In the month of mid-spring men and women are brought
together. At this time license is not prohibited. Whoever
refuses to comply without reason is to be punished. All
unmarried men and women are mustered and brought together."[14]

---

interchangeable with 72, a figure familiar to all readers of *Shui-hu Chuan*
and *Hsi-yu Chi* (see "Ch'i-shih-erh" 七十二 in *Wen I-to Ch'üan-chi*,
Shanghai, 1948, pp. 207–220).
[g]Cf. 高禖, 神禖, 郊禖, etc.

According to the interpretations of Wen I-to and Marcel Granet, this passage describes an archaic ritual conducted at the time of the two equinoxes, when the youths and maidens of neighboring villages in ancient China assembled together in open country to perform a rite that consisted of the formal betrothal of couples followed by the public consummation of their unions. (Earlier in the same *Chou-li* section, the matchmaker figure responsible for this ritual is described in terms that sound like little more than a clerk for the registry of marriage data.)

Another text of interest to us here is found in the "Yüeh Ling"[h] under the second month of spring (again, the time of the equinox), where a court sacrifice is described in which the Emperor and his various consorts pray for male progeny before the figure Kao Mei, here seemingly a divine image rather than a human functionary. Wen I-to explains that each region of ancient China had its own Kao Mei cult under different appellations: Sang-lin (see above) in the state of Sung, and Nü-kua, Chien-ti 簡狄 (the ancestress of the Shang), Chiang-yüan 姜嫄 (the ancestress of the Chou), and T'u-shan-shih 塗山氏[i] in other areas, all of whom he relates to the temptress of the "Kao-t'ang Fu" 高唐賦.[16] We have already seen similar associations with the themes of initiation, marriage, and regeneration in other materials relating to the figure of Nü-kua.

6. Allusions to Nü-kua appear occasionally in the poetry of the Six Dynasties and T'ang periods, as in Ts'ao Chih's 女媧贊 ("Ode to Nü-kua"), and Lu T'ung's poem 與馬義結交詩 ("On Joining in Friendship with Ma-i") to be considered shortly.

7. Additional fragments variously identify the place of Nü-kua's death and the seat of her cult, and two short entries in the *T'ai-p'ing Kuang-chi* anthology relate her appearance as a river or storm deity.[17]

[h]This passage is absent from the *Huai-nan Tzu* version of the text (the "Shih Tse" 時則 chapter).

[i]A note on *Shih Chi* also makes the identification of Nü-kua with T'u-shan-shih,[15] and the mythical stories of this latter goddess' seduction of Yü during the course of his flood control (淫奔) resonate with several of our other sources concerning Nü-kua.

8. In contrast to her relative inconspicuousness in the earlier texts, Nü-kua does appear to have for some reason captured the imagination of the writers of vernacular fiction in the Ming and Ch'ing periods. In addition to the appearance in *Hsi-yu Pu* cited above (where the sexual connotations of the early sources are intensified by the context of Sun Wu-k'ung's visit to the proverbial *femmes fatales* Hsi-shih and Lü-chu within the author's allegorical vision of sensual illusion), we may also note the mention of her name in the late-Ming novel *Feng-shen Yen-i* (where King Chou's sexual arousal at the sight of a statue of Nü-kua leads directly to the elevation of Ta-chi and the fall of the Shang), and in the introduction to the Ch'ing military-domestic romance *Erh-nü Ying-hsiung Chuan*, which cites Nü-kua's repair of Heaven as the epitome of female heroism.[j]

These several citations seem to have little relation one to the other, and might lead one to conclude that they represent independent traditions with no intrinsic connection. The pieces do, however, fall together into a more meaningful cluster when we consider Nü-kua not as an independent entity, but as one term of a dual mythical construction in which she and Fu-hsi 伏羲 are intimately joined. Fu-hsi in his individual phase is quite well-known as a legendary emperor and supposed inventor of the *Pa-kua* trigrams from which the hexagrams of the *I Ching* are derived. The name of Fu-hsi is transcribed in various texts with an assortment of characters, presumably homophonous in archaic Chinese (伏, 庖, 炰, 包, 虙, etc, and 希, 戲, 犧, etc.). Ingenious commentators have distinguished among these various renderings, showing that the character 伏 describes his work as a domesticator (subduer) of animals, 包 refers to the all-inclusive nature of the *Pa-kua*, 庖 and 炰 to an association with the figure Sui-jen 燧人 as a tamer of fire and

[j]Nü-kua is somewhat conspicuous for her absence in the novel *Hsi-yu Chi*, where a number of figures of Chinese mythology (P'an Ku, Chü Ling 炬靈, Hsüan-wu 玄武, etc.) do appear alongside the more strictly Buddhist deities. On the other hand, the motif of the five-colored stone egg in Sun Wu-k'ung's autochthonous birth seems to reflect the type of materials with which we are dealing here.

inventor of cooking, 犧 to his domestication and subsequent slaughtering of animals, and 虙 or 宓 indicating his supposed relationship to the river-goddess Fu Fei 宓妃 who appears in the "Lo-shen Fu" 洛神賦.[18] He is also variously credited with the naming of earthly creatures (thus earning the sobriquet: "the Chinese Adam" in missionary scholarship), the practice of hunting, and the invention of rope and cord writing, fish nets, woven cloth, the bow and arrow, the five musical tones, the calendar, divination instruments, iron, and semi-annual sacrifices at the time of the two equinoxes.[k] More important, he is also recognized as an originator of the rules of matrimony, specifically inventing the archaic custom known as *li-p'i* 儷皮, in which animal skins are exchanged as some sort of wedding present, dowry, or mutual guarantee. It is this role as a god of marriage that now turns us back to Nü-kua and leads us to more interesting possibilities.

The exact relationship between Nü-kua and Fu-hsi is described in a variety of ways. Some sources place Nü-kua as an assistant or successor to Fu-hsi in his work, hence her appellation Nü-huang 女皇,[19] but most grant them a more intimate link as brother and sister. This trait of consanguinity is indicated by the variants P'ao-kua 庖媧 and Nü-hsi 女希 for Nü-kua's name, as well as by a common surname Feng 風, and a similar physical description consisting of a snake's body and a human head.[l] Another scholar suggests that the 女 of Nü-kua is a surname, and that she is in fact a male relative of Fu-hsi with the given name 媧.[20]

[k]In some sources Fu-hsi (Nü-kua in other versions) is credited with the invention of the *se* 瑟 zither, and the legend of splitting a fifty-stringed instrument into two twenty-five-stringed varieties is attributed to his name. Cf. a verse describing Fu Hsi in the popular *t'an-t'zu* genre (*Nien-wu-shih T'an-tz'u*, ed. Yang Sheng-an, Taipei, 1963): 通婚姻, 制琴瑟, 禮樂由興 ("He spread the institution of marriage, and created the lute and zither, thus giving rise to rites and music").

[l]Other variants give Fu-hsi a dragon's body, turtle teeth, a suit of animal skins or leaves, and long flowing hair, and to Nü-kua a cow's head, a tiger's muzzle, or a snail's body (cf. *kua* 蝸). Wen I-to (pp. 34ff.) identifies snake with dragon and sees the dragon motif as evidence of a totemic clan, hence the crawling-creature element 虫 in the clan name Feng 風 and the names of other mythical figures (e.g. Yü 禹, Chu-jung 祝融, etc.).

It comes as something of a surprise, therefore, that the T'ang poet Lu T'ung 盧仝 sings of Nü-kua as the wife of Fu-hsi.[21] At first sight this seems to be a slip of the poet's pen (quite consonant with the raving tone of the poem, with the result that one commentator suggests "sister" as an alternate reading). Upon examining some of the most well-known pictorial representations of Nü-kua and Fu-hsi (see Appendix I), however, we find the two deities, one male, one female, ranged side by side in stately robes with their serpentine tails intertwined. This last motif, of course, signifies much more than brotherly affection, and attests to the conjugal relation of the two figures. We should not, however, hasten to correct the numerous texts in which the two appear as brother and sister. This seeming contradiction should not only not disarm us, but indeed points the way to the archetypal pattern reflected in the treatment of the pair. The fact that the roles of sibling and spouse overlap here indicates that the Chinese literary tradition is interested more in the abstract relation of harmonious dual union than in the narrative depiction of the potentially dramatic causes or the precise circumstances of their conjugal conjunction. Before we go on to discuss the literary ramifications of this possibility, let us adduce more evidence that Nü-kua and Fu-hsi were conceived of in terms of such a relationship.

As we have seen, a necessary corollary of the notion of harmonious union is the promise of continuous creation that it affords. In an interesting passage reminiscent of the myth of Deucalion and Pyrrha in Ovid's *Metamorphoses* (Book I, l. 313 ff.), or that of Izanagi and Izanami in the *Kojiki* (Book I, section 4), the T'ang collection *Tu-i Chih* 獨異志 goes on beyond the cosmic marriage of Nü-kua and Fu-hsi to depict their roles as universal progenitors of mankind:

昔宇宙初開之時只有女媧兄妹二人在崑崙山，而天下未有人民．議以為夫妻又自羞耻．兄卽與其妹上崑崙山呪曰：天若遣我兄妹二人為夫妻而煙悉合，若不使，煙散．於煙卽合，其妹卽來就．

"Long ago, when the universe had first come into being, there were no people in the world, only Nü-kua and her brother on Mount Kun-lun. They considered becoming man and wife, but were stricken with shame. And so (Fu-hsi) and his sister went up on Kun-lun and (performed a sacrifice), vowing: 'If it is Heaven's wish that my sister and I become man and wife, let this smoke be intertwined. If not, let the smoke scatter,' whereupon the smoke was intertwined, and his sister did cleave unto him."[22]

The tenacity of this mythical tale in the Chinese tradition is demonstrated in a cycle of folktales recorded by anthropologists such as Jui I-fu 芮逸夫 in various localities in South and Southwest China (among both Han and minority ethnic groups). The composite story pieced together from local variants tells of a universal flood caused by the enraged Lord of Thunder 雷公. A brother and sister who have violated their father's warning and given aid to the thunder-dragon are saved from the flood by a magic gourd-boat, whereupon they face the task of repopulating the earth.[23][m]

Another version of this tale relates that the union of Nü-kua and Fu-hsi followed the Deluge, and first produced a strange formless offspring.[n] The parents are said to have wrapped the round mass of flesh in a cloth and attempted to carry it up a "ladder of Heaven" (see below), when it suddenly slipped from

[m]Certain details of this tale—the absentation of the father, the violation of his interdiction, the supernatural gift, etc.—conform precisely to Vladimir Propp's analysis of the folktale form (*Morphology of the Folktale*), and thus remind us that it is with this cultural phenomenon that we are dealing here. We may note, however, that other details of the story—the great deluge, the Lord of Thunder, etc.—reflect back to some of our more properly mythical sources. We may note that the flood-maker Kung Kung is described in several sources as a black dragon, while Nü-kua is in one place said to have concluded her role as a savior by riding in a dragon-drawn thunder-chariot.[24] The figure of the thunder-god also appears in the story of Fu-hsi's miraculous birth, in which his mother Hua-hsü-shih 華胥氏 conceives after treading a giant footprint in the Lord of Thunder's domain 雷澤.[25] Cf. other examples of footprint-conception, in the hymn to Hou-chi found in the "Sheng Min" ode in the *Shih Ching* classic, and even in legends concerning the birth of Confucius.

[n]The motif of the formless offspring is also a common element in the mythologies of various peoples: e.g. the "leech-child" (*hiru-go*) resulting from the marriage of Izanagi and Izanami cited above.

their grasp and fell to Earth, smashing into a myriad fragments that, in turn, developed into the human race.[26] The similarity of this formless mass to the well-known figure of Hun-t'un 混沌 (and his striking linguistic parallel Humpty Dumpty), as well as the analogy to P'an Ku's dissolution into the infinite phenomena of creation, reminds us of the "universal egg" motif appearing in mythical tales the world over. This motival similarity takes on a particular significance if we recognize the *hulu* gourd as a specific Chinese variant of this image of autochthonous generation. In a display of philological gymnastics, Wen I-to demonstrates that the name of P'an Ku may have been originally rendered with the characters 槃瓠, signifying the Chinese gourd. Even more striking, he goes on to trace the characters *p'ao* 庖 and *hsi* 戲 used in variants of the names of Nü-kua and Fu-hsi along the same etymological path back to the ideographs 匏 and 瓠, also signifying the *hulu* gourd; and notes that the musical instruments credited to Nü-kua were originally constructed from gourd shells.[27] In later chapters we shall see an interesting reflection of the *hulu* concept in the womb-like self-containment of the garden world in the *Dream of the Red Chamber*.

Let us now reconsider the various materials relating to the myth of Nü-kua and Fu-hsi with a view towards isolating the possible archetypal patterns of meaning obscured by a seeming confusion of details. As suggested above, the starting point of our discussion will be the theme of the cosmic marriage. We have seen that both Nü-kua and Fu-hsi in their individual phases have been acknowledged as instrumental in the institution of human matrimony: she in the role of Kao Mei 高禖, and he as the founder of the *li-p'i* betrothal practices. (It may also be noted here that Nü-kua's invention of the *chi* hair ornament, the donning of which at the age of fifteen signified the the marriageability of Chinese maidens, further affirms this specific function of the goddess.) Even more significant, we have adduced representational and folkloric evidence testifying to a compound image of the two figures as primordial husband and wife, and hence the universal parents of mankind. Signifi-

37

cantly, where the most well-known Western myths dealing with the human sexual relation are primarily presented in terms of dramatic *acts* of pursuit, ravishment, and refusal, the Chinese literary tradition has not felt constrained to describe the union of Nü-kua and Fu-hsi in narrative terms. (The *Tu-i Chih* passage cited above goes the furthest in the direction of turning a relation into a story, but, here again, the contrast between this fragment and similar myths in other cultures is instructive.)

What the traditional framers of Chinese myth seem to have perceived in the legendary materials relating to Nü-kua and Fu-hsi was not simply a document on the origin of marriage, or even on the origin of man, but, more important, the formal relation of harmonious dual union that we have proposed to function as an archetypal pattern of Chinese thought and art over the centuries. In other words, the marriage of Nü-kua and Fu-hsi emerges as a metaphysical one, not only providing for a contract of cooperation and a promise of continued creation, but in effect embodying the very structural and functional principles of an orderly universe.°

Noting that the Han commentator Kao Yu 高誘 identifies Nü-kua as the "Empress of Yin" (*Yin-ti* 陰帝) in a note on *Huai-nan Tzu* 6/7a, and that Pan Ku evaluates the effects of Fu-hsi's institution of marriage as follows in the *Po-hu T'ung*: "Only when husband and wife were joined, so that the five elements were regulated, did the Way of man become secure,"[28] we are reminded of the common use of the terminology of yin-yang and the five elements to refer to the notion of harmonious union in the Chinese tradition. We shall see however, in the following chapter, that it is not the simplistic conjunction of male and female principles that is at issue here, but rather a specific logical relation that may be entirely abstracted from the yin-yang formulation. As a result, the terms "yin" and "yang" may be replaced in various treatments of the same concept by such pairs as Heaven and Earth, the hexagrams *ch'ien* and *k'un*, or any other formula that bears the same

°The parallel in the Western conception of Natura will be explored in detail in Chapter v, below.

38

formal relation. In this light the significance of the carpenter's square and compass held by Nü-kua and Fu-hsi in the Wu-liang stone relief, tentatively ascribed by Bodde to Fu-hsi's construction activities,[29] clearly lies in the joining of Heaven (round) and Earth (square) to form the anthropocentric Chinese cosmos (see Appendix 1).[p]

The suggestion that the marriage of Nü-kua and Fu-hsi is to be interpreted as a metaphysical one, responsible for the endurance of the universe, may bring into clearer focus a number of details of the most well-known stories relating to the mythical couple. The repair of the dome of Heaven now emerges as the reestablishment of the harmony of the universe after a temporary loss of equilibrium (what Lévi-Strauss might call the restoration of continuity out of discontinuity). Similarly, the fusion of five-colored stones for this purpose must reflect the harmonious ordering of the five elements necessary for maintaining this equilibrium, much like the corresponding orderly sequence of the eight trigrams ascribed to Fu-hsi.

But the notion of the harmonious ordering of phenomenological change, such as we see implied in the conjugal union of Nü-kua and Fu-hsi, also bears the corollary imperative of the suppression of the forces of disorder, and thus the imposition of containing forms on the infinitude of mythological potential—the shrinking of "the conceivable limits of desire." This sense seems to be behind Nü-kua's variously conceived encounter with the titan-rebel Kung Kung, as well as the subdual and binding implied in Fu-hsi's contribution of fish-nets, iron, weapons, slaughter, and cooking. On a more abstract level, we may also perceive the impulse to order and control in Fu-hsi's invention of the calendar, musical tones, cord-writing, and certain sacrificial objects and rituals as well.

In this light, Chuang Tzu's conflicting references to Fu-hsi as an exemplar of pre-civilized communion with the Tao (Chapters 4, 6, and 10), yet already tainted by the will to order and control (Chapters 16 and 21),[30] place him precisely astride

[p]An alternate version, in which the two figures hold the moon and the sun respectively, also accords with this interpretation.

the boundary between divine freedom and human institutions. This transitional role is most clearly seen in the "Shan Hsing" (繕性) chapter:

逮德下衰，及燧人伏戲始為天下，是故順而不一.

"But as inner virtue began to deteriorate, by the time Sui-jen and Fu-hsi ruled the world there was compliance, but no longer unity."

Where Chuang Tzu views the crossing of this line as a mistake in human history, the *I Ching* seems to recognize the value of containment in the functioning of the universe: 範圍天地之化而不過 ("In it are included the forms and the scope of everything in the heavens and on earth, so that nothing escapes it").[31q]

This accommodation of limitation and death with the infinitude of spontaneous creation seems to be behind the association of Nü-kua's creation of human beings with her invention of marriage as a halfway measure to overcome the problem of mortality. The analogy between human marriage, aging, and reproduction and the functioning of the universe is, of course, an insight grasped by all myth-making peoples. Frazer notes how myth "explains the fluctuations of growth and decay, of reproduction and dissolution, by the marriage, the death, and the rebirth or revival of the gods. . . ."[32] It is perhaps significant, therefore, that the myth of Nü-kua and Fu-hsi insists on maintaining the dual separateness of the partners of the archetypal marriage, while other traditions have sought to unite them in a single image such as the virgin mother or the bisexual god. As we shall see, the Chinese cultural preference for the simultaneous presence of complementary forms (as in the emblematic representation of Nü-kua and Fu-hsi), rather than their absolute merging into one, remains an important logical underpinning of the archetypal form of dual union.

It has already been pointed out that this archetypal pattern

[q]An interesting corroboration of this citation may be seen in Tung Yüeh's choice of the same line to direct Sun Wu-k'ung towards enlightenment at the end of *Hsi-yu Pu*, 16/7.

within which the logical opposites perceived by the senses are joined in a generative partnership is roughly equivalent to the phase of Chinese thought commonly referred to by the terms "yin" and "yang." In the same way that the cycle of life and death in all cultural spheres immediately implies the annual cycle of seasons, this archetypal dualism in the Chinese context also leads directly to the four seasons, and by extension to the so-called theory of the five elements. Before proceeding to a fuller discussion of these two logical methods and their implications in Chinese literature, let us note the manner in which certain specific details of five-elements cosmology are worked into the literary treatment of the Nü-kua-Fu-hsi myth.

As early as the *Tso Chuan*, presumably predating any "Five Elements School" of geopolitics such as that associated with the name Tsou Yen 騶衍, Fu-hsi is identified under his appellation T'ai Hao 太昊[r] as a ruler by virtue of the element of wood 木德. As (temporary) master of the vegetative quarter, Fu-hsi is also acknowledged as Lord of the East 東公 and Master of Spring 春主, attributions that accord well with the generative aspect of his union with Nü-kua, and perhaps reflect the sense of life-force manifested in the serpentine or dragon-like form of their bodies. It may be noted that Fu-hsi is in places said to have had free access to a magical tree[33] (*chien-mu* 建木), which is elsewhere identified as the Ladder of Heaven (*t'ien-t'i* 天梯) by which the universal progenitors were seen to have climbed aloft in a passage mentioned earlier.[s]

In view of her intimate connection to Fu-hsi most sources also assign Nü-kua to the element of wood as well, a position that is borne out in references to water in connection with her supposed birth and parentage,[35] and in her identification with a scaly monster that emerges from the depths in the *T'ai-p'ing Kuang-chi* passages cited above. But other versions relegate

[r]Of course the identification of Fu-hsi with T'ai Hao is a perfect example of Han systematizing, but it is maintained that the specific structural scheme into which the different sets of figures are placed together is what is significant here.

[s]Cf. the similarity of this motif to a variety of sacred trees described by Frazer in different cultures.[34]

her to the sphere of metal in the West,[36] in keeping with her association with Hsi Wang Mu, the "queen mother" of the West, whose analogous conjugal relationship with Tung Wang Kung, "Lord of the East," carries our archetypal marriage into the realm of folklore.[37]t We have already noted the obvious association between Nü-kua's five-colored stone and the five elements, and we may see the same correspondences when the goddess combats Kung Kung's unleashed flood waters with the ashes of burnt reeds (fire and wood).u

Interesting as these correspondences may be, however, we should not look for a carefully schematized expression of the five-elements theory in the fragmentary mythical materials under investigation in this chapter. The point at issue, again, is the manner in which the Chinese tradition has "systematized" its mythology—the way in which later literary works order the mythical materials into an intelligible structure. Because the patterns used in systematizing the fragmentary items relating to Nü-kua and Fu-hsi do, in fact, coincide with structural patterns observable in later literary works—culminating in the *Dream of the Red Chamber*—we describe them as archetypal within the context of the tradition as a whole.

ᵗThese two figures appear together in the first chapter of the Ch'ing novel *Ching-hua Yüan*.
ᵘErkes claims that Pu-chou Shan is identical with yu-tu 幽都, the Northern, and hence watery, abode of what he calls the Han "God of Death."[38]

42

CHAPTER III

COMPLEMENTARY BIPOLARITY AND MULTIPLE PERIODICITY

IN the preceding chapter we have attempted to demonstrate that the treatment of the marriage of Nü-kua and Fu-hsi in the sources of Chinese mythology reflects a pattern of conceptualization that may be considered archetypal within the system of Chinese literature. Specifically, it has been suggested that the cluster of associations evoked by certain details of the mythical fragments, as well as the tendency to work yin-yang and five-elements terminology into the representation of the two figures, leads to the conclusion that it is the abstract formal pattern of dual interrelation that finds expression in the texts under investigation. But since the notion of "dual union" might apply just as well to a variety of other modes of conceptualization—from the "binary opposition" isolated by Lévi-Strauss in primitive thought to the dialectical method seen to underlie much of Western civilization—it will be necessary at this point to go beyond this oversimplification in order to distinguish between the specific formal relation embodied in the yin-yang formula and the philosophical solutions to the problem of duality in other cultural spheres.

In speaking of the "dualism" in Chinese thought, we must make it clear at the outset that we are not referring to an absolute categorization of all phases of existence into two distinct classes of phenomena, or even to a relative distribution along a single continuum ranging between the two hypothetical poles of yin and yang. Instead, what we have is a whole *series* of axes, or continua, along which the myriad phenomena of existence may be ranged according to the degree of intensity, or presence, of various qualities. These axes include such polar pairs of

43

sensory perception as hot and cold, light and dark, solid and empty, moist and dry, and clear and turbid, as well as abstract correlatives such as true and false, elegant and profane, substantial and illusory, or active and static. When we use the terms "yin" and "yang" as a shorthand for referring to this entire range of polar conceptualizations, we must be careful not to assume that all these paired concepts can theoretically be lined up in parallel fashion such that the two sets of poles form two logical categories of experience. In fact, the many sets of conceptual polarities, which serve as frames of reference for the perception of reality, are *overlapping* schemes not reducible to a final two-term analysis.

On first sight, the definition of yin and yang given in many general works on Chinese philosophy as two total categories containing, respectively, the subheadings: female, passive, cool, dark, wet, turbid, etc., and male, active, warm, light, dry, clear, etc., seems to be valid. But upon further investigation, it soon becomes evident that the individual terms grouped under each of the two categories often bear no intrinsic relationship to one another. For example, in the two conceptual pairs hot-cold and dry-wet, the former terms are classified as yang and the latter terms as yin, although there is in actuality no logical connection between hot and dry or cold and wet. When we turn to such abstract correlatives as joy and sorrow, harmony and conflict, order and disorder, or modernity and antiquity, the difficulty is compounded, since such pairs do not even correspond clearly to the conception of male-active versus female-passive, no less to one another.

Given the complex interrelation of qualities that underlies the dualism designated by the terms "yin" and "yang," the simple assignment of existential phenomena to the one or the other camp can be of little value as a tool of analysis, particularly as far as literature is concerned. At the risk of confusing the issue, I would therefore like to introduce the term "complementary bipolarity" into the present discussion, in order to emphasize the fact that it is the abstract logical relation rather than the specific formulation that is at issue here.

Turning back to the series of conceptual polarities described above, let us attempt to isolate some of the formal characteristics that all of these pairs bear in common.

The most obvious point of similarity, of course, is the form of bipolarity already mentioned. In practice, what this means is that the apprehension of experience is realized in terms of the relative presence or absence of opposites rather than absolute states, or in Erkes' formulation: "Jeder Begriff ist ihr nur dadurch erfassbar, dass er einen Gegenbegriff hat . . . Jedes Ding vermag nur dadurch zu existieren, dass es ein Korrelat hat."[1] Since the poles that determine the bipolar form in the first place are in all cases hypothetical, there can never be any question of a literal "balance" between them, but simply a sense of the *pairing* of all possible qualities and concepts. The fact that the pairing of concepts constitutes in itself an abiding feature of logical method in the Chinese tradition is immediately obvious to all those familiar with the culture.

A second formal feature, of yin-yang dualism, one implicit in the description of the Chinese world-view as an "organismic"[2] cosmos, is the fact that phenomenological change is conceived of in terms of regular and ceaseless alternation towards and away from the hypothetical poles of each duality. This alternation may perhaps be termed "cyclical" in the sense of recurrence within a closed system, but the notion of circularity should not be allowed to obscure its essentially bipolar form. The *Lieh Tzu* seems to refer to this feature of closed-circuit alternation in the following passage:

故天地之道，非陰則陽，聖人之敎，非仁則義，萬物之宜，非柔則剛，此皆隨所宜而不能出所位者也.

"Therefore, given the totality of Heaven and Earth, if it is not yin then it is yang; as to the teaching of the Sage, if it is not humane, then it is just; within the proper sequence of the myriad phenomena, if it is not yielding then it is firm. All these follow their proper order, and cannot move out of their sequential position."[3]

45

The important implication of absolute ceaselessness of alternation leads directly to a third point of common form among the various polarities of Chinese thought: the fact that, given the inevitability of continuous alternation, the ascendance of one term immediately implies its own subsequent diminution. In other words, as one term is generated and grows, it nourishes by its own essence the seed of the opposite term, until the seed ultimately supersedes and reduces to (approach) zero the "parent" term, whereupon the process reverses itself. This results in the apparent paradox that a quality is often perceived to be stronger, or more enduring, at the moment of its own suppression and the ascendancy of its opposite. Such a notion is most often expressed in a variety of formulas of presence within absence, or more accurately, of the presence of one quality within its opposite: e.g. stillness within movement (動中靜), being within non-being (無中有), etc.

Finally, an important corollary of the cluster of formal assumptions underlying the yin-yang pattern is that the potentially infinite number of axes of alternation in the world of experience can never be expected to line up like iron filings into two overall fields of intelligibility. Instead, the endless overlapping of axes of change—at varying angles and intervals of intersection—manifests what is on the surface a random chaos, but what eventually adds up to a convincing illusion of plenitude, and hence the perception of reality. In the Appendices to the *I Ching*, we find a clear statement of this positive generation of "reality" through ceaseless alternation:

日往則月來，月往則日來，日月相推而明生焉，寒往則暑來，暑往則寒來，寒暑相推，而歲成焉.

"As the sun goes the moon comes, as the moon goes the sun comes, the sun and moon displace one another, giving rise to (a continuity of) brightness. As the cold goes the heat comes, as the heat goes the cold comes; the cold and heat displace one another, forming (the continuity of) the yearly cycle."[4]

The four formal characteristics of the Chinese logical method for dealing with the problem of duality may now be summarized as follows: (1) Bipolarity. (2) Ceaseless alternation. (3) Presence within absence. (4) Infinite overlapping. In the following chapter we will attempt to demonstrate that these formal patterns can serve as a key to the structure of the *Dream of the Red Chamber*, and we will hypothesize that they are equally basic to a major portion of the Chinese literary tradition. It must be repeated at this point that what we are interested in here are archetypal patterns underlying cultural forms of diverse period and genre, and not the particular philosophical doctrines of any specific school of thought. Although general studies of Chinese philosophy often attribute this sort of conceptual patterns to the cosmology of a "Yin-Yang School," to Han and Six Dynasties Neo-Taoism, or to Sung Neo-Confucianism, it would not take much documentation to demonstrate that the formal relation of complementary bipolarity comprises the logical underpinning of many other phases of the civilization.

It will be useful for our purposes to distinguish here between two possible lines of argument associated with the idea of cosmic duality: what have been described as the reduction of the Many into the One and the derivation of the Many out of the One. Although these two logical directions may both be seen as expressions of the same fundamental perception of unity within diversity, it is argued that the distinction between converging focus and diverging manifestation is indeed significant, particularly as far as literature is concerned. Returning to our discussion of bipolar form in the Chinese tradition, we find that although the central position of duality between unity and multiplicity can conceivably lead in either of these directions, its significance as an archetypal pattern is clearly of a derivational nature. As seen in the following passages, the dual conceptualization of yin and yang is generally cited as an intermediate step *from* nothingness *to* totality, rather than the other way around:

天地之氣，合而為一，分為陰陽，判為四時，列為五行.

"The breath of Heaven and Earth, when combined forms

47

one, when divided forms yin and yang, when distinguished forms the four seasons, and when set in sequence forms the five elements."[5]

是故易有太極，是生兩儀，兩儀生四象，四象生八卦.

"Therefore change bears in itself the great ultimate, this gives rise to the two modes; the two modes then give rise to the four images, the four images give rise to the eight trigrams. . . ."[6]

道生一，一生二，二生三，三生萬物.

"Tao gives rise to one, one gives rise to two, two gives rise to three, three gives rise to the myriad things."[7]

While the dualism in Chinese thought carries an implication of unity, it is generally not *talking* about unity. Even when we are told that "the myriad things revert to unity" (萬物歸一), it is the sheer infinitude of existence—its all-ness—that brings us around full-circle to the idea of one-ness.

Recalling the materials examined in the last chapter, we can see how the logic of myth leads us from the unity of the universal egg-gourd, the common womb of brother and sister, to a marriage that while essentially a union is quintessentially dual. It is the separateness between male and female rather than their merging into one that makes the union fruitful and results in the harmonious continuity of creation. As in the pictorial emblem of Nü-kua and Fu-hsi, the polar pairs of the Chinese dualism are not fused into one figure, but are ranged side by side, rooted at the base yet pulling in opposite directions. This formal quality of separateness within union, as opposed to unity within diversity, seems to find expression in the *t'uan* commentary on Hexagram 38 of the *I Ching*:

天地睽而其事同也，男女睽而其志通也，萬物睽而其事類也.

"Heaven and Earth are opposites, but their action is concerted. Man and woman are opposites, but they strive for union. All beings stand in opposition to one another: what they do takes on order thereby."[8]

48

The importance of this separateness of polar terms, here signified by the character *k'uei* 睽, cannot be overemphasized. Since the conceptual scheme as a whole is based on ceaseless bipolar alternation, the paired concepts of the Chinese system by very definition can never reach an ultimate synthesis, as Erkes claims, evidently led astray by his own use of the term "dialectic" for the dual interrelation we are considering.[9] Instead, the polarities of Chinese thought remain forever distinct, producing and destroying each other in a ceaseless process of mutual displacement.

The notion of ultimate unity comes into the picture only when we consider the various opposing terms of duality as complementary aspects of a single overall view of the universe of experience. Whereas the hypothetical poles of each pair of concepts never achieve any union vis-a-vis one another, they are united—in the sense of "joined" rather than "fused"—as integral parts of one total ground of being. With this point in mind, we may use the term "spatial vision" to describe the sum total of all possible patterns of existential alternation, with the understanding that the terms contained simultaneously within a totalized frame of reference must still appear mutually contradictory, and occasionally even hostile, when apprehended from the perspective of any given individual, time-bound element within the system. What is here termed the "spatial" character of this total vision may be distinguished from the essentially temporal frame of the boundless vision attributed to God and approached by poet-seers in the literary tradition of the West, in that in the former case it is the *simultaneous* inclusion of all human experience rather than the inexorable unilinearity of universal history that is at issue.[a]

This outward thrust of the Chinese counterpart to the dialectical method in the Western context may become clearer when we consider the five-elements theory as another intermediate

[a]Of course, when we speak of temporality, what we often have in mind is a sense of logical progression, *from* one state *to* the next, not necessarily a pattern of change in time. The Great Chain of Being concept, for example, carries a strong implication of unilinearity without any ostensible temporal dimension.

step in the logical procession from zero to infinity. As soon as we take notice that these five elements, or elemental powers, are linked up with the five directions (four cardinal points and center), the five seasons (derived through various schemes of intercalation), the five musical tones of the Chinese scale, the five legendary emperors, five colors, five tastes, five limbs, five grains, five organs, five planets, five beasts, and so on, it becomes evident that we are dealing here with "fiveness" as a form, rather than with the actual terms of each pentad. (Whether the efficacy of the number five in Chinese culture is the cause or the effect of such formulations need not concern us here.) Moreover, when such five-term classifications of reality are brought into alignment with similar conceptualizations involving 6, 8, 10, 12, 24, or even 64 terms, the number five becomes nothing more than a cipher for the entire concept of multiplicity. With this in mind, I would like to introduce one more mouth-filling term, "multiple periodicity," to refer to the logical relation of ceaseless closed-circuit alternation of five or more terms, corresponding to that of complementary bipolarity on the level of conceptual pairs.

Because what we are talking about is the generalized concept of multiplicity rather than any specific number scheme, the introduction of five-term sequences into the context of the dualism described above functions to perform the same conceptual leap from primary distinction to infinite manifestation that we find in the famous passage from the *Tao Te Ching* quoted earlier in this chapter. It embodies both the logical result of the step from 1 to 2, and the generation of multiform phenomena that are not readily reducible to a two-term analysis. As a structural principle in Chinese literature, we shall see, it allows a far greater flexibility than simple duality (greater by a proportion larger than 5:2) in structuring the innumerable details of full-length allegorical narrative.

The complex possibilities for interlocking relationships within the framework of the five-elements scheme are immediately apparent if we take a look at a simple diagram of the sequence of terms:

The first observation we may make is that the actual direction of alternation may be either clockwise or counter-clockwise,[b] with the result that the influence of each term may be seen as extending to both of its neighboring terms. In addition, the precise position of the element earth, here placed in the center, remains a variable factor. Particularly when it is the seasonal cycle or some other intrinsically four-term scheme that is at issue, the absence of a conceptual "center" necessitates the interpolation of an extra, intercalary term somewhere in the middle of the sequence of the other terms. As a result, the element earth, though essentially inert, paradoxically has the greatest range of possibilities of interaction with the other elements. Finally, we may note that the five-term scheme also entails a number of two-term oppositions within its own framework. Not only can each term interact with its two neighboring terms and the center, but in addition it may fall into a relation of mutual displacement with the term located diametrically opposite in the cycle of elements. This last possibility—the seemingly dialectical yet somehow complementary juxtaposition of fire and water, or wood and metal—is a particularly favored pattern for literary structure. It accounts for a great many lines of subtle parallelism in regulated verse poetry, as well as the majority of the memorable episodes in the late-Ming allegory *Hsi-yu Chi*; and, as we shall see, it comprises the central structural device around which the plot of *Dream of the Red Chamber* is woven.

Recalling the four formal characteristics distilled from the concept of yin-yang dualism in Chinese thought, we may now modify them as follows to apply to the five-term scheme:

[b]In the context of the sixty-four hexagram cycle, the question of the direction of alternation brings in the extremely complex philosophical and mathematical issue of the *hsien-t'ien* and *hou-t'ien* sequences.

1.   The periodic alternation becomes more truly cyclical, in the sense of the cycle of seasons.

2.   The alternation is again necessarily ceaseless, but the greater number of terms means a relatively longer period of latency between the recession and the renewed dominance of each term.

3.   The process of mutual displacement (*wu hsing hsiang sheng, wu hsing hsiang sheng* 五行相生, 五行相勝) is seen as inevitable, so that the presence of a term is implied by its own absence.

4.   Periodicities overlap in infinite profusion (the diurnal cycle, the lunar cycle, the solar cycle, the cycle of human life and death, the dynastic cycle, etc.).

Examining the circular representation of the five elements, as elaborated in Chou Tun-i's *T'ai-chi T'u*, we can conceive more clearly the possibility of a total simultaneous perception of all time and space, as discussed above. We should be careful, however, to avoid confusing the schematic circularity of such diagrams with the contemplation of the circle as a perfect form, as for example in Medieval Christianity.[10] The circle here appears to be a representational convenience for studying the *multiple* relationships among phenomena, rather than a reduction of all things to symbolic oneness.

As was stated earlier in connection with yin-yang dualism, it is maintained here that the archetypal pattern of multiple periodicity also predates its later formulation into the specific theory of the five elements. The most striking early examples of this cluster of formal relations are to be found in the "Yüeh Ling" text (presumably originating much earlier than its incorporation into the *Li Chi, Lü-shih Ch'un-ch'iu*, or *Huai-nan Tzu* compilations of the Han period), and the "Hung Fan" chapter of the *Shu Ching* classic. In addition, we have already seen an example of the use of five-elements geopolitics in the *Tso Chuan*, and several other passages in that work record speeches that apply the framework of cyclical periodicity to sequences of monsters or deities. Since the present study is concerned more with the continuity of these patterns in the tradition than with their actual antiquity or hypothetical origins,[c] the possibility that such examples are either forgeries or interpolations dating from the Han period does not substantially affect the argument. The fact remains that perhaps the most sophisticated treatment of the archetypal form of periodic alternation dates back to near the beginnings of the entire tradition: to the *I Ching* classic. Again, the precise dating of the various strata of this text is irrelevant, because the very conception of the hexagram sequence already embodies the four formal features of multiple periodicity described above.

Before moving on to the other end of the Chinese literary tradition, to demonstrate the presence of these archetypal patterns in the Ch'ing novel *Dream of the Red Chamber*, let us repeat that the structural forms isolated here are not proposed to be a master key to the entire civilization of traditional China. The argument is simply that complementary bipolarity and multiple periodicity are, among other possible patterns, abiding aesthetic forms that lend consistency and continuity to the system of Chinese literature.

[c]Since it is a logical method that is at issue, an inquiry into its origins would have to consider the linguistic logic of Early Chinese. Cf. Chmielewski's discussion of "double implication" in this context.[11]

CHAPTER IV

THE ARCHETYPAL STRUCTURE OF
DREAM OF THE RED CHAMBER

THE authors of the *Dream of the Red Chamber* demonstrate in the first pages of the novel at least a superficial familiarity with certain details of the mythical lore of ancient China. In addition to Nü-kua's two appearances cited above, we find mention of her lord Fu-hsi in Chapter 102[a] (as one of four "sages" invoked in the ritual exorcism of the Ta-kuan Yüan garden), as well as of the demon Kung Kung in Chapter 2 (I, 20, as an example of the arch-villains of the tradition). Moreover, the motif of the multicolored stone in Pao-yü's miraculous birth also harks back to mythological sources such as the story of Chien-ti's conception of Hsieh 契 after consuming a five-colored swallow's egg, T'u-shan-shih's birth of a son from stone, and various instances of unusual children born with jade in their mouths.[1] In spite of such evidence, however, it will not be argued here that the authors of the novel were necessarily aware of the mythical details relating to Nü-kua and Fu-hsi, particularly as far as their cosmic marriage is concerned. Nor will the point be stressed that as educated members of the Ch'ing literati they must have been familiar with at least some of the many philosophical treatises in which yin-yang dualism and five-elements cosmology are discussed at length, although we do find explicit treatment of the concept of bipolarity in Chapter 2 (I, 20, in Chia Yü-ts'un's somewhat dialectical discussion of the pair *cheng* 正 and *hsieh* 邪 with Leng Tzu-hsing)

---

[a]Ts'ao Hsüeh-ch'in (and Kao E), *Hung-lou Meng* (*Dream of the Red Chamber*), Peking, Jen-min Wen-hsüeh Ch'u-pan-she, 1972, Volume IV, p. 1303. All citations from the text of the novel will refer to this readily available new edition.

and Chapter 31 (II, 378f., Shih Hsiang-yün's explanation of yin and yang to the maid Ts'ui-lü). We might also mention repeated medical diagnoses couched in the terminology of five-elements alternation, as in Chapters 10 (I, 123f.) and 83 (III, 1076). The point is, however, that to the extent that complementary bipolarity and multiple periodicity comprise archetypal patterns of the literary system inherited and advanced by the authors of the *Dream of the Red Chamber*, their functioning must be observed more in the dimension of structure than in that of explicit reference. In the following pages, therefore, we will attempt to trace such structural patterns of two- and five-term alternation within the narrative arrangement of the novel.

It will be recalled that in the preceding chapter the formal relation underlying the characteristic Chinese approach to the problem of duality was defined in terms of four specific features: bipolarity of perceptual and conceptual qualities, ceaseless alternation from pole to pole, presence within absence or weakness within strength, and multiple overlapping of polar schemes. In tracing these four relationships as structural principles within the novel, we have isolated a limited number of paired concepts for closer investigation. These are: movement and stillness 動靜, elegance and baseness 雅俗, joy and sorrow 悲喜, union and separation 離合, harmony and conflict 和怒, and, finally, prosperity and decline 盛衰.

The incessant process of ebb and flow, advance and return, waxing and waning along the axes of these and other polar pairs leads to a difficult critical problem. Since the sense of incessant alternation within a closed system results in the blunting of moments of intensity—in effect the rapid defusing of points of potential climax—an impression may tend to arise that is perilously close to monotony. It seems significant, in this regard, that Western translations of the novel have generally attempted to break this chain of inevitable recurrence by retaining scenes of relative action or intensity, and omitting passages of static inactivity. In the present study, however, it will be argued that it is precisely this resultant sense of endlessness, or pointlessness—the fact that the processes of existential alternation never roll on to a final end-point—that is largely responsible for the rich totality of vision that arises within the sheltered confines of the Chia family compound. The Chih-yen Chai commentator,[b] at any rate, seems to acknowledge this fact when he condemns as forced and mechanistic in lesser novels "the stereotyped treatment of alternating union and separation or joy and sorrow" (離合悲歡窠旧 [sic]),[2] the same sort of patterns of alternation to which he elsewhere ascribes the greatness of *Dream of the Red Chamber*.[3]

Since it will be impossible to trace here, even in one or two of these polar pairs, the entire cycle of alternation through the 120 chapters of the huge novel, we will consider only briefly several examples of this type of structural alternation. The reader with a taste for the schematic will find a complete table of the relative presence or absence of these opposing qualities attached as Appendix II at the end of this study. Of course, the precise judgment of how to characterize a given passage is in all cases a subjective one, but it is hoped that such a table may be useful in considering the overall pattern—or lack of one— that emerges in a reading of the novel as a whole.

The method of alternation of scenes is immediately evident to the reader in the early chapters of the novel. Lin Tai-yü's arrival in Chapter 3 and her introduction to the grandeur of the Chia family—and to the strange temperament of its primary heir—are followed directly by an account of kidnapping, murder, and corrupt justice in Chapter 4. In Chapter 5 we are transported to the world of dream and prophetic vision, only

[b]For the purposes of this study, we will take the Chih-yen Chai commentator at his own word and assume that he is a close personal acquaintance of the author, inserting reflections and critical comments into the margins of the text during the course of several re-readings contemporaneous with the actual composition and revision of the novel. For a review of the involved arguments regarding the identification of the writer of the commentary, the reader is referred to Wu Shih-ch'ang, *On the Red Chamber Dream*, Chapters VI, VII, and VIII, and C. T. Hsia, *The Classic Chinese Novel*, pp. 249–255. Citations below are taken from the *keng-ch'en* 庚辰 manuscript (1760, Wu's "Version 3"), and the *chia-hsü* 甲戌 manuscript (1754, Wu's "Version 1").

to return abruptly to the petty concerns of poor relatives and crafty servants in Chapter 6. In Chapter 7 Pao-yü is introduced to Hsüeh Pao-ch'ai and to his alterego Ch'in Chung, after which the rivalry of the two girls begins to take shape in Chapter 8. The schoolroom brawl in Chapter 9 gives way to the silent brewing of antagonism and the steady advance of Ch'in K'o-ch'ing's illness in Chapter 10, followed by the extravagant birthday feast in Chapter 11, resulting in the venomous thwarting of Chia Jui's lust in Chapter 12, and so on through the remaining 108 chapters of the novel.

In some cases, particularly in the earlier sections of the novel, such alternation seems to coincide roughly with the chapters of the traditional text. But most often the sense of polar reversal is to be perceived in smaller units of narration: in the episodes that break up and cut across chapter divisions.[c] For example, one may recall the manner in which we are turned away from an uproarious scene of Liu Lao-lao's overindulgence in liquor to witness a quiet visit to Miao-yü's retreat and a sampling of the rarest of teas in Chapter 41. Similarly, in Chapter 85 we see Pao-yü's visit to the palace of Pei-ching Chün-wang and his father's auspicious promotion immediately followed up by news of the arrest of Hsüeh P'an for murder, while conversely the description of unsuccessful bribery attempts in the next chapter is cut short for a quiet view of Tai-yü playing on the elegant *ch'in* lute. In a supplementary note to Chapter 22, the commentator Hu-hua Chu-jen 護花主人 (Wang Hsi-lien 王希廉) interestingly suggests that the abrupt turn-about from a joyous celebration to somber prophecies pregnant with Ch'anist implications in that chapter is analogous to the "birth" of the yin-phase of the seasonal cycle out of the most intense heat of summer.[5]

---

[c]Chih-yen Chai notes that each chapter (*hui* 回) of the novel, as expected, breaks down into two episodes (*tuan* 段), but that the number of incidents that goes into each episode-unit, and the interconnection with preceding and subsequent chapters is subtly varied in the course of the novel.[4] (It should be pointed out here that the chapter divisions of the traditional text do not necessarily accurately reflect the arrangement of earlier manuscripts.)

On another level the same pattern of structural alternation may be observed in larger units of the novel as well. For instance, the substantial section devoted to the dramatic story of the Yu sisters from Chapters 64 to 69 follows on the heels of the slow-paced period of the elders' absence for a court funeral from Chapters 58 to 63, during which time the lack of parental authority gives rise to numerous petty quarrels among the maids and makes possible Pao-yü's midnight birthday party.

The simple alternation of such contrasts of experience, of course, is not in any sense unique to the *Dream of the Red Chamber*, but is basic to extended narrative in all traditions. The important point here is that the bipolarity of narrative form described above is specifically complementary rather than dialectical in nature: that is, it conforms in most respects to the four formal relations analyzed in the preceding chapter. We can therefore anchor our discussion in the particular forms of the Chinese tradition if we return now to the second, third, and fourth features of this archetypal pattern: those which describe the complex interpenetration and overlapping of bipolar schemes.

We have already seen that the ceaselessness of alternation that has served as an obstacle to the meaningful translation of the novel into Western languages is carefully framed as an endless process, one that never moves on to a final conclusion or synthesis. A good example of what we are talking about may be seen in Chen Shih-yin's verse gloss on the cryptic *Hao-liao Ko* 好了歌 revealed to him in Chapter 1 (I, 12): 昨日黄土隴頭埋白骨，今宵紅綃帳底臥鴛鴦 ("Yesterday you buried your white bones in a mound of yellow earth; tonight you sleep in conjugal bliss behind curtains of red silk"). Taken out of context this line might be interpreted as referring to an end to temporal suffering, but within the framework of the novel as a whole it can only describe the ceaseless cycle of rise and fall, joy and sorrow, that we immediately witness in Chen's own life story, and that continues to roll on through the remaining chapters of the work. Even in Chapter 120, as we shall see, the continuer keeps the ball rolling by contriving to qualify the sense of finality that naturally accrues to the end of the book.[d]

Perhaps the most interesting feature of complementary bipolarity in narrative structure is that of mutual implication, whereby qualities of experience are often perceived to be most essentially present at the time of their nominal absence. This formal pattern emerges with particular relevance in *Dream of the Red Chamber* in the authors' use of subtle variations along the continuum of movement and stillness (in conformance with the common formula *tung-chung-ching, ching-chung-tung* 動中靜, 靜中動), although it applies in the other polar pairs as well. We have already cited an example of this technique in Chapter 42, where we are turned aside from a scene of excitement and gaiety to visit a remote corner of the garden. In fact, nearly all of the joyous or contrived celebrations staged by the Chia elders throughout the novel are either interrupted or closely followed by smaller, calmer gatherings often producing poetry or philosophical discussion. The obverse, of course, is also true, as we see various forms of excitement—both pleasurable and painful—arise spontaneously out of the sequestered quietude of the garden world.

This interpenetration between excitement (*je-nao* 熱鬧) and ennui (*wu-liao* 無聊) marks out a major thematic dimension of the novel, and draws numerous comments from Chih-yen Chai and other traditional readers.[6] In particular, Pao-yü's life in his earthly paradise falls into an alternating pattern of buoyancy and depression, as in this passage: (II, 267) 誰想靜中生動, 忽一日不自在起來, 這也不好, 那也不好, 出來進去只是發悶 ("But, strange as it may seem, excitement arose in the midst of calm; on some days he would all of a sudden become uneasy, he would get upset by this or that, and whether he went outside or stayed at home he could not help but feel depressed"). In fact, Pao-yü's propensity to arouse ripples on the

---

[d]Cf. Hsüeh I-ma's comment on Pao-ch'ai's final consolation in Chapter 120 (IV, 1513): 他頭裡的苦算吃盡的了, 如今的甜來 ("The bitterness she has suffered until now may be considered to have reached its limit, so that now this sweetness has come").

surface of calm earns him the nickname: Wu-shih Mang 無事忙, "busy-for-no-reason." Chih-yen Chai picks up this interpenetration of activity and idleness in the portrayal of Pao-yü and cites it as a major structural device of the novel as a whole, for which he uses the term *mang-chung-hsien-pi* 忙中閒筆.[7] Often when commentators on *Dream of the Red Chamber* and other traditional Chinese novels speak of the interrelation of heat and cold[e] (e.g. Chih-yen Chai's exegesis of the name Leng Tzu-hsing),[8] what they are really talking about is the interpenetration of movement and stillness we are considering here.

Another pair of concepts within which this relation of interpenetration is most readily observable is that of joy and sorrow. Examples of the arising of sadness in the midst of happiness, or joy at a time of sorrow, are extremely numerous in the novel. This pattern is immediately manifest in the counterpoint of changing moods among the residents of the garden, and is perhaps most poignantly expressed in the fleeting visit of Yüan-ch'un, now an imperial concubine imprisoned by the walls of wealth and honor, to her beloved parents and family in Chapter 18. We shall return below to the axis of interpenetration of truth and falsity (*chen-chia* 真假) underlying the surnames Chen and Chia in both the prologue and the body of the novel, in order to elucidate the nature of the allegorical vision projected in the Ta-kuan Yüan garden. On the level of images, the aesthetic sense of the presence of qualities within their opposites is realized in Chapter 76 (III, 987), when a snow-white crane suddenly emerges from the shadows of a dark pool, and in Chapter 49 (II, 608), as the children roast a deer against the background of a snow-covered landscape.[f]

As discussed earlier, an integral feature of the structural pattern of complementary bipolarity in Chinese narrative lies

[e]Mao Tsung-kang uses the expression *han-ping p'o-je* 寒冰破熱 ("cold ice cuts through the heat") for the alternation of active and static passages in *San-kuo-chih Yen-i*, and Chang Chu-p'o also speaks of the heat and cold in *Chin P'ing Mei* with this sort of narrative pattern in mind.
[f]Chih-yen Chai notes the juxtaposition of elegant purity and pungent odor in this scene.[9]

in the overlapping of various schemes of alternation that go to make up the perceived texture of manifold reality. This over-lapping of polar pairs prevents the respective poles from falling into an overall dialectical line-up of active versus passive, or desirable versus undesirable. As a result, where we might expect the alternation of joy and sadness to coincide with that of harmony and conflict, while calm might seem to imply elegance, we find that this is not the case. Instead, calm quietude often coincides with bitter quarrels, sublime elegance may be accompanied by deep sadness, or illness and decline may give rise to harmony and friendship, as we see in the reconciliation of Tai-yü and Pao-ch'ai in Chapter 45. Here the difference noted by Chih-yen Chai between the pattern of bipolar alternation in *Dream of the Red Chamber* and the mechanistic scene-switching in many popular novels may become clearer. The fact that the various schemes of alternation do not fall into converging patterns of overall significance, far from indicating a lack of control on the authors' part, in fact demonstrates the consummate skill necessary in *keeping apart* the strands that make up the dense weave of the novel. It is in this sense that the archetypal pattern of complementary bi-polarity in the Chinese literary system has been described as a step in the derivation of a welter of detail, rather than as a means of focusing in on the central oneness of existence. At this point, therefore, let us pass on to the next stage in the derivational process: the multiple correspondences of cyclical periodicity.

Every maid in the garden is well aware of the identification of Lin Tai-yü with wood and Hsüeh Pao-ch'ai with metal; and even the obtuse Hsüeh P'an and the notoriously unpoetic Wang Hsi-feng have noticed that Pao-yü, whose elementary essence hangs about his neck for all to see, stands midway between the virtues of the two girls. The question of whether the stone will finally unite with the wood or the metal—which girl Pao-yü will marry—of course sums up the plot of this weighty novel in a nutshell. Upon closer investigation, however, we shall see that the structural use of this five-term frame of reference is far more complex than a simple assignment of characters to this or that position in the diagram.

Tai-yü's surname Lin ("forest") immediately places her in the eastern quarter, the sphere of wood, and indeed we are first introduced to her as a heavenly plant: *chiang-chu hsien-ts'ao* 絳珠仙草, watered by Pao-yü's spiritual stone in paradise. Her vegetable nature is further indicated by her birthday in the second lunar month, the height of spring, and by the name of her apartments in the garden: Hsiao-hsiang Kuan 瀟湘舘, evoking associations of luxuriant bamboos, which in fact grow in her yard. Tai-yü herself clearly acknowledges her elemental identity in a bitter comment in Chapter 28 (I, 339): 比不得 寳姑娘什麼金哪玉的, 我們不過是個草木人兒罷了 ("How can I compare with Pao-ch'ai's gold and jade? I am nothing but a maid of grass and wood"). As we have indicated, however, the simple identification of Tai-yü with the power of wood would be meaningless if we did not go on to consider the interaction of this element with the preceding and subsequent terms. We have already noted the generative effect of water on wood with regard to the watering of the heavenly plant in Chapter 1, and the origin of wood in water may also be behind the name of her father, Lin Ju-hai ("hai" = sea),[8] as well as the river journey that brings her to and ultimately away from the capital.

As the novel progresses, however, it becomes increasingly clear that Tai-yü's association with the plant world is more as a frail blossom than as a hardy tree. After the famous scene in Chapter 23 in which she takes pity on the fallen petals of spring, she continues to identify with the hopeless delicacy of spring flowers in Chapter 26, and then goes on to her elegy to the fallen blossoms in Chapter 27 (I, 323), ending with the line: 花落人 亡兩不知 ("The falling of flowers and the passing of men, both are equally unfathomable"). The association of her wooden

---

[8]One commentator notes this correspondence, and goes on to speak of Tai-yü as the principle of yang.[10] Chih-yen Chai explains the name on the basis of the expression 學海文林.[11]

nature with fading beauty and approaching death is further advanced by the identification of the "humour of wood" (木氣) as the cause of her illness in Chapter 83, and by her own mournful plaint in Chapter 86 (III, 1123): 只恐似那花柳殘春, 怎禁得風催雨送 ("I can't help but worry how the flowers and willows in late spring will withstand the blowing wind and driving rain"). Similarly, a joke by the servant Hsing-erh (興兒) at the end of Chapter 65 (III, 848) suggests that "Miss Forest's" frail constitution could not withstand a puff of wind.

Having traced the origin of wood in water and the fleeting passage of spring, we must continue on around the seasonal cycle into summer, where fire consumes wood and turns it to ashes. Thus Tai-yü returns consistently in her poems as well as in her needless quarrels with Pao-yü to images of ash and smoke as an expression of her inevitable outcome. For example, Pao-yü advocates "blocking off Tai-yü's perceptive insight with ashes" (灰黛玉之靈竅) in his essay inspired by Chuang Tzu's "Ch'ü Ch'ieh" (胠篋) chapter, and soon thereafter she herself produces a lantern riddle describing a type of incense burned to mark the passing hours (keng hsiang 更香). In effect, we may observe that Tai-yü's identification with the power of wood in fact traces one half of the circle of elements, rising in water, passing through the springtime stages of growth and rapid decay, and finally ending in dissolution through fire: a course that coincides precisely with the waxing and waning of yang in the cycle of seasons.

The association of Hsüeh Pao-ch'ai with the element of metal, on the basis of her name ("ch'ai" = metal hairpin) and the golden locket of mysterious origins whose inscription seems to match that on Pao-yü's magical stone, must also be examined in greater detail. The rich whiteness of Pao-ch'ai's skin, which disarms Pao-yü in Chapter 28 and again when he lifts her marriage veil in Chapter 97, as well as her particular beauty in mourning white in Chapter 110, clearly place her in the western quarter of autumn. Her lantern riddle in Chapter 22 (I, 260), containing the line: 恩愛夫妻不到冬 ("the loving couple will not reach the winter")[h] further foregrounds her association with the season of advancing mortality. The identification of her name as a homophone for "snow" (in her couplet in the Red Chamber Dream prophecies in Chapter 5 (I, 57) is further echoed in the description of the cold simplicity of her rooms, "like a snowy cave," in Chapter 40 (II, 490). Now a snowscape in the Chinese tradition, of course, is rendered complete by the addition of plum blossoms, and indeed Pao-ch'ai is likened to the "pure whiteness and clear fragrance" (潔白清香) of the plum in Chapter 110 (IV, 1399). The *heng-wu* 蘅蕪 flower, by which her quarters in the garden are known, seems to be reminiscent of the plum blossom, opening in winter with a purplish hue. Her autumnal station is again indicated by the cold incense (*leng hsiang* 冷香) and other cool-sounding ingredients of her daily medicine enumerated in Chapter 7 (I, 81), while the same joke by Hsing-erh reminds us that warm winds must in the end melt the snows of winter.

The southern quarter of the cycle of elements is clearly occupied by Wang Hsi-feng. In addition to the common use of the phoenix in her name as an emblem of the South in five-elements lore, her spicy-hot temper indicated as early as Chapter 3 also refers her to the sphere of fire. Moreover, the searing heat of her indignation in Chapter 11, her jealous rage in Chapter 44, and her cruel revenge in Chapters 68 and 69 betoken the venomous heat of summer. (The association of venom and summer is later sealed in the death by poison of Hsia 夏 Chin-kuei.)[i] Her suffering of the same scalding curse as Pao-yü in Chapter 25, following immediately after Pao-yü's literal scalding at the hands of Chia Huan, also reveals her association with fire. Finally, the profuse flow of blood at various stages of her illness in Chapters 55 and 110 con-

[h]The *keng-ch'en* edition of Chih-yen Chai's annotated text does not give a lantern riddle for Pao-ch'ai, although a supplementary note to the chapter signed by Chi-hu Sou 畸笏叟 (see Wu Shih-ch'ang, *op. cit.*) claims to fill in the missing lines with an alternate riddle.[12]

[i]Chi-yen Chai notes the incongruity of summer (夏) and cassia (桂) in the name of this figure.[13]

nects Wang Hsi-feng with the heraldic color of the South.

In accordance with the common diagram of the five elements, Pao-yü's spiritual stone places him in the central position of the element earth. Although earth in itself is essentially inert, the fact of its centrality allows for its interaction with each of the other four elements (see above). Thus we see Pao-yü throughout the first half of the novel flitting about the garden like a bee from flower to flower, able to communicate with all of the girls regardless of their varying temperaments.[j] Perhaps it is to this all-reflecting quality that the association of Pao-yü with a mirror, in the hall of mirrors in his apartments and in his lantern riddle in Chapter 22, refers. The unresolved issue of his future marriage seems to indicate that he can conceivably go either way: as a stone he can (presumably through the medium of soil) unite with plant life in a generative union such as we have seen in Chapter 1, while as a precious jewel he seems destined for the cold embrace of wrought gold. In spite of many readers' sympathies to the contrary, the rightness of the latter course is indicated by numerous references to Pao-yü's lack of hardness, an attribution that makes his conjunction with metal more suitable than with wood.[k] In any event, in the course of the novel Pao-yü is fatefully connected with each of the major heroines: with Wang Hsi-feng in Chapter 25, with Tai-yü until Chapter 97, and with Pao-ch'ai from their marriage in Chapter 119. (An extremely interesting Ch'ing source informs us that Pao-yü was originally intended to meet Shih Hsiang-yün again after the death of Pao-ch'ai and Hsiang-yün's husband, and then to reenter the red dust to become her mate.)[l]

Interesting as it would be to work out the five-elements correspondences behind the various other characters in the

[j]Chih-yen Chai describes Pao-yü's role as "the thread which runs through all of the 12 lovely maidens" (諸艷之貫).[14]

[k]One commentator gets around the problem by positing an inner-outer distinction: 內木石而外金玉.[15]

[l]*Hsü Yüeh-wei Ts'ao-t'ang Pi-chi*, quoted in K'ung Ling-ching, *Chung-kuo Hsiao-shuo Shih-liao*.[16] Perhaps Hsiang-yün is the missing term of the North, as the "cloud" in her name suggests.

novel—using numerous clues in their names, residences, poems, lantern riddles, and flower-cards, as well as the murky prophecies in Chapters 5 and 116—we must repeat that it is the formal relationship between terms, rather than the identification of figures as one term or another, that concerns us here. Recalling the archetypal pattern by which the ascendancy of each term immediately implies its own disappearance and the rise of its "opposite," let us reconsider now the relationship between Tai-yü and Pao-ch'ai in the novel.

We have seen that Lin Tai-yü occupies the eastern or springtime phase of the seasonal cycle, while Hsüeh Pao-ch'ai represents the metallic barrenness of autumn at the onset of winter. Tai-yü, however, is anything but a lighthearted maid of spring. True, her capacity for depth of feeling (ch'ing 情) associates her with the exuberant growth of the springtime months, yet her very position as a denizen of this vital quarter immediately shuttles our vision forward into the phases of decay and death. In other words, within the structural pattern of cyclical alternation discussed above an image of renewed life may be the surest possible sign of approaching death, so that Tai-yü's association with such images makes her a clear figure for the opposite range of meaning. In the course of the novel we see Tai-yü orphaned, bedridden, and increasingly preoccupied with the hopelessness of her own situation. Her beauty is that of Hsi-shih 西施, accentuated by her illness,[m] and her thoughts and poems turn consistently upon the theme of her own death. Ultimately, we see her revived in Pao-yü's dream in Chapter 116 as Hsiao-hsiang Fei-tzu 瀟湘妃子, reminding us of the legend of luxuriant bamboos watered by tears of bereavement. This latter phase of Tai-yü's characterization,[17] however, need not cancel out the many scenes in which we see her in a warm, sympathetic mood, without her usual cynicism. The point is that Tai-yü represents a whole range of movement, from generation through growth to decay, so that while she

[m]Hence her somewhat teasing nickname: A-p'in 阿顰 (or P'in-erh 顰兒), that by which Chih-yen Chai refers to her in most notes.

always signifies the dissolution of life into death, she need not
be characterized by death alone.

Turning now to Hsüeh Pao-ch'ai, we find the same kind of
implication of opposites, though this time with the poles re-
versed. As we have seen, Pao-ch'ai is associated in the novel
with images of autumn and, consequently, death. Where Tai-yü
acts upon impulse and feeling, Pao-ch'ai is guided by restraint
and self-control. Yet, in the same way that Tai-yü's springtime
passion implies its own destruction, Pao-ch'ai's cool demeanor
implies its own thaw. As a result, Pao-ch'ai ultimately survives
(at least in the 120-chapter version we are dealing with), and in
her pregnancy bears the seed of the coming spring. Her
identification with the plum blossom or *heng wu* flower may
also be considered to be such an expression of growth and
renewal within the barren coldness of winter. Even Pao-
ch'ai's obedient restraint, seemingly indicating a lack of feeling (*wu-ch'ing* 無情), comes to take on the opposite significance as she recites the line: 任是無情也動人 ("Even though it
is without feeling, it can still move the beholder") in Chapter
63 (III, 806). We may remember Pao-yü's momentary enchant-
ment with Pao-ch'ai's physical charm in Chapter 28 (I, 340),[n]
as well as her association with Yang Kuei-fei, as examples of
this warmth within coldness. Chih-yen Chai seems to pay
particular attention to this sort of presence within absence in
the portrayal of the two girls. In a note to Chapter 4 he speaks
of "Pao-ch'ai's warmth,"[18] and later he indicates that Tai-yü's
use of "warm-incense" medicine (煖香), as jokingly suggested
by Pao-yü, would serve to remedy a deficiency in her body-

[n]In most later versions of the novel it is the snow-white plumpness of
Pao-ch'ai's arms that sets Pao-yü daydreaming of the possibility of
combining Tai-yü's spirit with Pao-ch'ai's Yang Kuei-fei-like physical
allurements. The earliest extant version of the text (*chia-hsü*, 1754),
however, tells us that Pao-yü caught a glimpse of his cousin's "creamy
back" (酥背). The latter character may perhaps be a copyist's error for
the character 臂 ("arm"), as indeed the *keng-ch'en* (1760) manuscript
corrects the usage, but in any event the mildly erotic overtones of the
passage—coming immediately after the ribaldry of Hsüeh P'an's birthday
party—seem inescapable.

67

temperature, thus implying a corresponding surfeit of warmth to be counteracted by Pao-ch'ai's "cold incense."[19] In another place, he characterizes Pao-ch'ai's deceptive warmth as "nearness within distance," as opposed to Tai-yü's "distance within nearness,"[20] in their relations with Pao-yü.

This sort of symmetrical implication of opposites reminds us that the formal relation underlying five-elements correspondences begins to take on an intelligible pattern only when the separate phases are viewed from the perspective of a single, continuous cycle. Thus the very fact that Pao-ch'ai and Tai-yü imply and tend towards the qualities initially represented by the other leads us to consider them not as logical opposites, but rather as complementary aspects of a single construction. Their names, of course, each containing one character of Pao-yü's two, immediately alert us to this possibility. At the start of the novel, we see them both as semi-orphan grand-children of unusual literary ability who arrive at the Chia household at nearly the same time (the fact that Pao-ch'ai is one step removed in relation, and arrives second, may reflect the following of autumn after spring). In any event, the mutual implication of the girls is sealed as early as Chapter 5, when they share a single verse in the Red Chamber Dream vision revealed to Pao-yü in the chamber of Ch'in K'o-ch'ing, whose childhood name Chien-mei (兼美 "combined virtues") clearly reflects the ideal composite figure formed by the two girls.[o]

Soon the two guests disclose similar ailments and tell similar stories of their destinies foretold by mendicant priests: Tai-yü

[o]The combination of the two images flower and snow in this verse is paralleled in a description of Yu Erh-chieh shortly before her suicide: 花為腸肚, 雪作肌膚 ("Insides made of flowers, and skin made of snow," III, 893). In any event, the yoked characterization of opposite types is quite common in the treatment of female figures in Chinese fiction preceding *Dream of the Red Chamber*. For example, one may note the juxtaposition of the plump Yang Kuei-fei with the wan Mei-fei 梅妃 in literary treatments of T'ang Ming-huang's court (e.g. *Sui-T'ang Yen-i*), as well as a similar arrangement of the beauties in *Chin P'ing-mei*. Such a sense of complementary balance is clearly present in the use of the names Yang Kuei-fei and Chao Fei-yen (the "swallow-waisted") to refer to Pao-ch'ai and Tai-yü in the title of Chapter 27.

doomed to an early death and Pao-ch'ai fated to marry the bearer of jade. After a brief period of rivalry, culminating in their use of verses from the plays *The Peony Pavilion* (*Mu-tan T'ing* 牡丹亭) and *The Romance of the Western Chamber* (*Hsi-hsiang Chi* 西廂記) to taunt one another, they realize by Chapter 42 that their common knowledge and experience in fact unite rather than divide them, as Pao-ch'ai argues in Chapter 45 (II, 554) 我也是和你一樣 ("I am just like you"). From this time on the two rivals appear more as intimate friends—whose deep mutual understanding and appreciation[p] approaches the level of *chih-chi* 知己—than as bitter enemies, and indeed Pao-ch'ai's mother Hsüeh I-ma begins to treat Tai-yü as her own daughter, particularly in Chapters 57 and 58. This sympathy between the two is preserved throughout the next forty or fifty chapters of the novel, until Tai-yü's chronic illness and Hsi-feng's fiery will combine to provide for the realization of the destined union of jade and gold. The fact that Tai-yü's life is extinguished at precisely the start of Pao-ch'ai's short-lived ascendancy reminds us of the logic of alternation that binds the girls together.[q]

This type of mutual implication we have outlined above in relation to Lin Tai-yü and Hsüeh Pao-ch'ai is also repeated among various other pairs or sets of characters in the novel. The similarity of form shared by Tai-yü and Pao-ch'ai may immediately be expanded to include Shih Hsiang-yün (cf. the Hsiang 湘 in her name), another orphaned grandchild (this time thrice-removed) of unusual talent, whose ultimate fate as a quasi-widow nursing her hopelessly consumptive husband (or a full widow in earlier manuscripts) combines elements of the destinies of both of the major heroines. In addition, several commentators have noted that the central trio of the novel's

[p]Cf. Chih-yen Chai's comment on the reconciliation of the two girls in Chapter 45.[21]

[q]Cf. Chih-yen Chai's introductory note to Chapter 42: 釵玉名雖二個人 却一身. 此幻筆也 ("The gold [Pao-ch'ai] and the jade [Tai-yü] are two in name, but in fact they are one person. This is a stroke of literary imagination."),[22] and Hu-hua Chu-jen's use of the expression 比肩 ("parallel figures") to describe this relation.

plot: Pao-yü, Tai-yü, and Pao-ch'ai, may be properly considered as a single composite entity: 三人一体.[23r]

The fact that it is the form of bipolar and multiple interrelation rather than the assignment of specific terms that is of major importance here becomes clearer when we note that the same sort of mutual implication and complementary balance is carried over into the characterization of many of the lesser figures of the novel as well. For example, the complementary form behind the portrayal of Pao-ch'ai and Tai-yü is clearly reflected in the depiction of the two maids Hsi-jen and Ch'ing-wen.[s] The resemblance between Pao-ch'ai and Hsi-jen, indicated by their common advice to Pao-yü throughout the novel, is brought into relief in Chapter 36 (II, 433) when Pao-ch'ai takes the place of the maid in Pao-yü's room and is discovered by Tai-yü. In the end, of course, they share for a short while a dubious honor as the two "wives" of an absent Pao-yü. This formal similarity between mistress and maid is also evident in the case of Tai-yü and Ch'ing-wen. These two recipients of Pao-yü's love possess the same trait of single-mindedness to the detriment of their own health, and are recalled by Pao-yü in a single vision in Chapter 116. The nearly identical outcome of Li Wan and Pao-ch'ai, as husbandless mothers of the sons of rising fortune (Chapter 119), is also quite clearly a construction of this sort, as Li Wan's drawing of the plum-blossom card in Chapter 63 reminds us. In this sense, one is reminded of a whole range of sets of characters bound together by common names, appearances, birthdays, and attributes. Examples of this last group include the recurrent types of the orphaned maid (Hsiang-ling, P'ing Erh, Yüan-yang), the elegant young man (Ch'in Chung, Liu Hsiang-lien, Pei-ching Chün-wang, Chiang Yü-han),[t] the lustful rake (Hsüeh P'an, Chia Jui, Chia Ch'in, Chia Ch'iang, and later

[r]In another place Chih-yen Chai uses the geopolitical term *ting-li* 鼎立 to refer to the tripartite form at issue here.[24]
[s]Cf. Chih-yen Chai's comment on Chapter 8: 晴有林風, 襲乃釵副 ("Ch'ing has the spirit of Lin, Hsi is Ch'ai's double.")
[t]Pao-yü might also be placed in this category. For example, Chih-yen Chai associates Ch'in Chung's name with the character 玉 Yü.[26]

Chia Huan), and the suicide (Chin-ch'uan, Chang Chin-ko, Pao Erh's wife, Yu Erh-chieh, Yu San-chieh, Ssu-ch'i). Of particular interest is the chain of female figures who initiate Pao-yü into the ways of the world: Ch'in K'o-ch'ing, Yüan-ch'un, the Goddess of Disillusionment, and Tai-yü in the form of Hsiao-hsiang Fei-tzu in Chapter 116, all of which reflect back to the initiatory deity Nü-kua with whom the novel opens.[u]

It is a major contention of this study that the overlapping of such schemes of bipolar and multiple alternation is responsible for the rich texture of the novel, and hence the plenitude of vision realized within it. But while the conception of a "spatial vision of totality" was rather easy to embrace in discursive terms in the preceding chapter, and in fact may be diagrammatically represented in such schemes as the *T'ai-chi-t'u*, its presentation is quite another story in the novel form, where the reader's attention must be occupied by the illusory linearity of time sequence and the specificity of detail. Since the great length of the work precludes its apprehension in a single sitting, the authors must resort to a wide range of devices to constantly remind the reader of the totality of vision encompassed by the outer binding of the book. Let us consider, then, some of the specific signs by which the authors direct our attention to the possibility of an overall frame of reference within which the temporal oppositions of the plot may at least hypothetically balance out.

The most immediate technique is the use of the prologue section to give away at the outset something of the final picture we can expect from the novel as a whole. In *Dream of the Red Chamber* the prologue device goes beyond its use as a stock feature of the colloquial fiction tradition to allow for the reappearance of the prologue characters at various points in the body of the novel proper, thus minimizing the impression of an introductory section. In fact, one might say that there are

[u] Ch'in K'o-ch'ing seals this association when she calls herself the "younger sister of the Goddess of Disillusionment" (警幻之妹) in Chapter 111 (IV, 1402).

several overlapping layers of prologues in the first few chapters of the book, a subtle device that further results in integrating the abstract pattern of the overview with the concrete particularity of the mimetic characters. The prologue section, of course, serves to explain Pao-yü's entry into and exit from the world of red dust, as well as the tearfulness of his relationship with Tai-yü. But, even more important, we find in Chapters 1 and 2 a model of simultaneous rise and fall, joy and sorrow, integration and detachment in the parallel careers of Chen Shih-yin and Chia Yü-ts'un. The fact that the one's ruin coincides exactly with the other's ascendance, added to the sheer number of turnabouts of fortune contained within a limited number of pages (cf. Chen Shih-yin (I, 12): 你方唱罷我登場 "As soon as you finish singing, I go up on the stage"), establishes in the opening chapters of the novel the pattern of mutual displacement that pertains throughout the work.

A further device for calling attention to the bipolar alternation of the novel's structure may be seen in the parallel couplets that serve as both title and summary of each chapter of the book. Although some of these couplets may be read as single descriptive sentences, the majority contribute to the sense of dual alternation by juxtaposing quite neatly some of the polar concepts treated in the chapter. For example, we may note the following opening couplets: "At the Ti-ts'ui Pavilion Yang Kuei-fei sports with butterflies; by the mound of buried flowers Chao Fei-yen weeps for fallen petals" (滴翠亭楊妃戲彩蝶, 埋香塚飛燕泣殘紅, Chapter 27),ᵛ "A birthday celebration in the Yi-hung Hall; a bevy of maidens holds a midnight feast; Death through gold and cinnabar, a single beauty runs her parent's funeral" (壽怡紅羣芳開夜宴, 死金丹獨艷理親喪, Chapter 63), and "The maid Yüan-yang, a martyr for her master, ascends to the Ultimate Void; A dog of a rascal, cheating Heaven, invites

ᵛIn this case the carefully contrived parallelism of the two lines seems to overlay a subtle pseudo-parallelism, in that the lighthearted tone of Pao-ch'ai's half of the couplet is undercut by the fact that she overhears a startling conversation in the course of her butterfly chase. Wu Shih-ch'ang (p. 197) demonstrates that in one chapter at least (75) the chapter title does not necessarily coincide with the contents of the section.

a gang of thieves" (鴛鴦女殉主登太虛, 狗彘奴欺天招夥盜, Chapter 111). Within the text itself, this ceaseless alternation within conceptual pairs is further intimated through the constant repetition of such formulas as: "sadness turned to joy" 轉悲為喜, "both startled and pleased" 又驚又喜, "ready to cry, ready to laugh" 似哭似笑, or "sadness and joy intermingled" 悲喜交集, both in dialogue and in narrative.

This impression of fullness of vision evoked by constant reference to patterns of cyclical alternation is further enhanced by the sheer fullness of life within the Chia compound: the innumerable details of clothing, food, and architecture that dot the authors' broad canvas. Specifically, we may note the plenitude of Chinese literati culture displayed in the course of the work. Although we can observe the advent of outside influence at several points in the text (cf. Pao-ch'in's acquaintance with a European merchant's daughter and Pao-yü's Russian cloak mentioned in Chapter 52),[w] the integrity of Chinese civilization as the totality of human culture is certainly unquestioned here. The cultural bouquet presented in the novel includes the four elegant arts: chess (Chapters 87, 92, and 101), the lute (Chapters 86 and 87), calligraphy, and painting,[x] as well as the entire range of Chinese literature: history, philosophy, poetry, fiction, and drama. Even in the numerous riddles, jokes, stories, and drinking games that occupy much of the static phases of life in the garden (e.g. Chapters 19, 54, 62, 75, and 117) we may perceive the same sort of bipolar aesthetics at work. But by far the most memorable figure of plenitude—and perhaps the master stroke of the author's creativity—is of course the Ta-kuan Yüan garden within which the total vision of the narrative takes shape. We will return to consider the significance of the garden *topos* below in our discussion of the allegorical dimension of the novel, since it is in this figure that

[w]Mention of foreign goods is made no less than 33 times in the course of the novel. Chih-yen Chai also notes Wang Hsi-feng's particular weakness for foreign goods.[27]

[x]In a note to Chapter 7 in the *chia-hsü* edition Chih-yen Chai notes the use of the four arts in the names of the four maids: Ssu-ch'i 司棋, Tai-shu 待書, Ju-hua 入畫, and Pao-ch'in 抱琴.[28]

the author's conscious manipulation of form and meaning is most evident.

In the same sense that the reader's apprehension of the totality of vision evoked by two- and five-term alternation cannot be sustained throughout the time-consuming process of reading—so that numerous devices must be employed to continually point towards the entire picture—so are the characters by definition unable to know the complete story in which they figure. While the more spiritually perceptive (*ling* 靈) among them may experience moments of poetic insight, more often the fact of their own mortality obscures their vision of the totality within which their own suffering is but a faint ripple. Paradoxically, it is precisely this quality of insight which prompts the rejected stone in Heaven, and his cousins on Earth, to enter into the mortal web of entangling distinctions, as the monk and priest tell him in Chapter 25 (I, 298): 只因鍛煉通靈後，便向人間惹是非 ("Only after it was fused and tempered with boundless insight did it [the stone] stir up right and wrong in the world of men"). As a result, the inhabitants of the garden paradise consistently fail to see what is conveyed to the reader through devices of explicit reference and implicit structure.

The thickness of this blockage is perhaps clearest in the theme of forgetfulness, which is introduced obliquely in the profound doggerel of the *Hao-liao Ko* 好了歌 in Chapter 1 and repeated in nearly every chapter of the novel. The instances of faulty memory range from simple oversight on the part of servants and costly absent-mindedness among the masters (cf. Liu Lao-lao's proverbial remark: 貴人多忘事 "rich people are always forgetting things" in Chapter 6, I, 71),[y] to occurrences of *déjà-vu* and Pao-yü's inability to recall the fateful revelations of the Red-Chamber Dream in Chapter 5. Significantly enough, after Pao-yü's return to his dream in Chapter 116 his memory improves and he is able to recall what he has learned there, though, again, he refrains from divulging the information.

[y]In Chapter 101 the surname Wang is jokingly associated with the word *wang* ("forget" 忘).

By way of contrast, Pao-ch'ai is described at several points (e.g. Chapter 29, I, 350) as having an exceptionally good memory.

A further dimension of this forgetfulness is evinced in the recurrent theme of loss. Throughout the novel masters and servants alike are continually losing objects in the garden, as well as losing their way along its winding paths. The most monumental loss occurs in Chapter 119 when Chia Lan, in his own expression, "loses" Pao-yü after the Palace Examination in which they have both achieved honors: 二叔丟了 (IV, 1501). The two themes of loss and forgetfulness come together in Pao-yü's recurrent loss of his spiritual stone, which in turn brings on his loss of consciousness. The total vision presumably available to the Taoist priest and Buddhist monk who accompany Pao-yü at a distance through his sojourn in the world has been forgotten by the foolish stone—hence the tragic events of the second half of the novel.

An inevitable consequences of this "loss" of vision of the entire picture is the tendency towards ill-advised reliance on the one or the other pole of its alternating axes of experience, with the resulting upset of the harmony of the system as a whole. The act of upsetting, or at least denying, the hypothetical harmony of the whole seems to be conveyed in the novel by the repeated use of the character *yin* 淫, which we have seen to bear this range of significance in the sources of Chinese mythology. In view of the use of the term in connection with the flood waters in the stories of Nü-kua and Kung Kung, it may be less than accidental that the progressive decline of the Chia family fortunes (Chapter 53), as well as the prolongation of Chia Cheng's absence from home (Chapter 89), are attributed to widespread flooding in the provincial countryside.

In view of this understanding of the concept of *yin* as the destructive one-sidedness of insistence on individual fulfillment, the emphasis on individual feeling (*ch'ing* 情) in the treatment of Pao-yü's life in the Ta-kuan Yüan garden must be carefully reconsidered. The fact that we are told in Chapter 1 that the entire story has been transmitted by a "monk of feeling" (情僧) and that the object of Pao-yü's deepest emotional involvement is designated as *ch'ing ch'ing* 情情 in numerous Chih-yen Chai comments referring to a non-extant chapter in which the Goddess of Disillusionment is to have published a list of those who evince the deepest emotion in the novel (*ch'ing-pang* 情榜), seem to indicate a positive emphasis on this particular aspect of existence.[z] This emphasis, of course, accords well with the frequent allusions to the late-Ming drama *Mu-tan T'ing* throughout the text. But at a number of points in the novel we are reminded (by the Goddess of Disillusionment in Chapter 5, by Ch'in K'o-ch'ing in Chapter 111, and by Chen Shih-yin in Chapter 120) that when human feeling is not held in proper measure consonant with the harmony of the universe, it is easily distorted into *yin*, so that the as yet sexually uninitiated Pao-yü may be labelled "the world's greatest profligate of all time" (天下古今第一淫人也) in Chapter 5 (I, 64). Significantly, both Pao-yü and Yüan-yang (in Chapter 111) protest that their feelings are innocent of sensual excess, and both are sharply reminded that any excess of feeling, no matter how chaste, is tantamount to *yin* by the very fact of its excess. If Pao-yü had in fact been reading the *Four Books* instead of a popular romance[aa] as he protests to Tai-yü in Chapter 23 (I, 268), he should have reviewed the central passage in the *Chung-yung* text:

喜怒哀樂之未發謂之中，發而皆中節謂之和.

"Before the (feelings of) joy, anger, grief, and delight have taken on (concrete) manifestation, they may be said to be in a state of (latent) equilibrium. If they become manifest yet

[z] Many commentators have pointed out that the pun on *ch'ing* in the name Ch'in marks out Ch'in K'o-ch'ing and her brother Ch'in Chung as particularly involved in this aspect of experience. Significantly, in both of these cases we see *ch'ing* shade over into *yin*—in Ch'in Chung's behavior in the Man-t'ou nunnery and in the chapter to have been entitled "Ch'in K'o-ch'ing Dies a Licentious Death in the Tower of Heavenly Fragrance" (秦可卿淫喪天香樓), which, according to Chih-yen Chai's note at the end of Chapter 13, was mercifully excised to save her name.

[aa] 古今小說並那飛燕, 合德, 則天, 玉環的外傳與那傳奇角本 ("fiction of various periods, as well as apocryphal biographies [of the famous beauties] Fei-yen, Ho-te, Tse-t'ien, and Yü-huan, and drama scripts").

(remain) in a state of ordered equilibrium, they may be said to be in a state of harmony."

The possibility held out in this passage of some sort of harmonious integration of individual sensitivity within a broader view of existence contrasts sharply with the disequilibrium which characterizes life in the garden.

Pao-yü would of course counter with the late-Ming Ch'anist position that one may attain enlightenment by passing through sensual desire: 自色悟空, the message announced at the start of the work (I, 4). But to the very end of his sojourn in the red dust Pao-yü's career betrays a degree of emotional intensity that often belies his protestations of equanimity.[ab] Chih-yen Chai acknowledges the principle of enlightenment-through-sensuality (以情悟道), and even goes as far as asserting that the gross sensuality of Hsüeh P'an may mask a degree of spiritual detachment, but he also notes in Chapter 21 that at the moment at which Pao-yü conceives of his ultimate withdrawal he is still held back by the "poison of human feeling" (情極之毒).[29]

As a result of this distorted focus on individual sensitivity at the expense of the sort of balanced perspective held out in the *Chung-yung* passage cited above, Pao-yü's existence on Earth—and hence the existence portrayed in the novel as a whole—is characterized more by frustration and suffering than by the plenitude of the garden world. The reader will perhaps have taken note of the use of the expression "tragic" in the preceding discussion to describe this cleavage between mortal, time-bound perception, and the possibility of a total vision of phenomenological flux. While we of course cannot expect the configurations of mortality in *Dream of the Red Chamber* to conform to either the Aristotelian or the post-Romantic definitions of tragedy as a literary mode, the sheer intensity of feeling—the pity and fear—with which the novel has been received by two centuries of readers suggests that we are dealing here with an aspect of the Chinese tradition functioning

---

[ab]The presumed equanimity that earns him the title *ch'ing-pu-ch'ing* 情不情 in the missing *ch'ing-pang* 情榜 section.

on the level of the tragic vision of the West. In this case, however, it is a block in perception rather than a failure of action or a weakness of will that gives rise to the tragic situation. Paradoxically, while the concept of a total vision within which life and death, joy and sorrow, may balance out would seem to obviate the possibility of a fully realized tragic sense, at the same time the very totality of its scope necessitates the inclusion of those aspects of experience generally covered by tragic literature. Thus, Pao-yü may see through the illusory nature of suffering on one level of vision, and still *suffer* himself on the level of individual sensitivity, as he admits in Chapter 100 (IV, 1288): 我却明白, 但只是心裡鬧得慌 ("I do understand, but my heart is still driven to distraction").

Having traced the archetypes of complementary bipolarity and multiple periodicity from ancient Chinese mythology to the *Dream of the Red Chamber*, let us return now to the original myth with which we started. It will be recalled that the compound figure of Nü-kua and Fu-hsi was seen as a cosmic marriage of opposites through which the harmonious functioning of the universe is both generated and preserved. It was noted that the two deities appear both as brother and sister, presumably enjoying a degree of god-like freedom, and as a dignified pair of conjugal rulers responsible for matrimony and other institutions of social organization and control. The famous story cited in the novel in which Nü-kua repairs the dome of heaven with five-colored stones was interpreted as a further expression of the generative interplay of elemental forces in the orderly cosmos.

By now the similarity between this myth and the story of Pao-yü, Tai-yü, and Pao-ch'ai in the Ta-kuan Yüan garden is quite evident. In the early stages of the novel, Pao-yü and his cousins live as brother and sisters in their enclosed garden of earthly delights. Particularly towards Tai-yü, the hero displays the uninhibited intimacy of siblings from a common womb, as we see in Chapter 5 (I, 51): 就是寶玉黛玉二人的親密友愛, 也較別人不同, 日則同行同坐, 夜則同止同息, 真是言和意順似漆如膠 ("Even the friendly intimacy between Pao-yü and Tai-yü marked them as different from other people: in the daytime they walked and sat together, in the evenings they stopped and rested together. It was truly a case of speaking in harmony and thinking in accord; they were as inseparable as lacquer and glue.") Although several slips of the tongue call their absolute innocence into question (cf. Pao-yü's jest about sharing Tai-yü's conjugal couch in Chapter 26, I, 306), their union is essentially one of the spirit. As we are told in Chapter 29 (I, 353), "the two of them were essentially of one heart" (兩個人原是一個心), or in other words they fall into the *topos* of mutual appreciation (*chih-chi* 知己) that is taken up explicitly in the text soon thereafter in Chapter 32 (II, 385). As a result, the concourse between Pao-yü and Tai-yü remains that of siblings (she is his cousin on his father's side, and thus his "sister" within the semantic range of Chinese kinship terms), such that the recurrent intimations of future codification and consummation emerge as somehow anomalous, somehow not in keeping with the unripe prefecundity of the passing spring.

Pao-ch'ai, of course, is also Pao-yü's first cousin (on his mother's side), and though their formal union receives the sanction and blessing of the Chia elders, it is not wholly free of the taint of in-breeding (*ch'in-shang tso-ch'in* 親上作親). But Pao-ch'ai's steady association in the course of the novel with five-elements correspondences and poetic images of autumn and cold mortality renders the ultimate alliance of gold and jade increasingly inevitable as the cycles of alternation roll on. It should not be overlooked that Pao-ch'ai does succeed in winning over a certain amount of Pao-yü's love for Tai-yü, a turn that has brought condemnation upon the continuer of the text, but that is well foreshadowed in the first eighty chapters. Almost immediately after their marriage, we are told that: 又見寶釵舉動溫柔, 就也漸漸的將愛慕黛玉的心腸略移在寶釵身上 ("Seeing the mild compliance of Pao-ch'ai's behavior, his deep longing for Tai-yü was gradually transferred to Pao-ch'ai's person," IV, 1263). In succeeding chapters the new wife is shown at several points to truly understand (*chih-chi*) Pao-yü, and in Chapter 109 we witness a scene of warm consummation inconceivable with the earlier heroine.

What is most significant here is the precise coincidence of the marriage of Pao-yü and Pao-ch'ai with the death of Tai-yü, which, along with the fact that the wedding is rushed through during the mourning period for Yüan-ch'un,[ac] highlights the intersection of youth and death in the hymeneal ritual. We have already considered the accommodation of the aspects of love and death within the experience of life in connection with the mythical complex of Nü-kua and Fu-hsi. This understanding of marriage as a submission to order, restraint, and mortality, yet at the same time a fertile compact of Heaven and Earth is clearly expressed in the *t'uan* commentary on Hexagram 54 of the *I Ching*:[30]

歸妹天地之大義也，天地不交，而萬物不興，歸妹人之終始也.

"The MARRYING MAIDEN describes the great meaning of heaven and earth. If heaven and earth do not unite, all creatures fail to prosper. The MARRYING MAIDEN means the end and beginning of humanity."

While Pao-yü's marriage to Pao-ch'ai entails the ritual murder of Tai-yü's springtime spontaneity, it also provides at the same time a promise of future life: it brings together what Campbell calls "the womb and the tomb."[31ad]

Finally, before going on to consider the allegorical meaning that may be present in the structural patterning of the *Dream of the Red Chamber*, let us pause to consider one more example of the sort of overlapping focus of ancient mythology and

[ac]Yüan-ch'un's death on the day after the start of spring (*li-ch'un* 立春) reflects the same sort of conjunction of events.

[ad]Interestingly enough, the traditional commentary on this hexagram notes the fact that the two constituent trigrams: *chen* (the eldest son) and *tui* (the youngest daughter) indicate a union in which it is the submissiveness of the concubine rather than the generative compatibility of the wife that is more appropriate. The fact that the line commentaries are replete with images of lameness, deformity, and infertility further reflects the sort of nexus of associations to which Campbell's neat slogan refers.

recent fiction for which the term archetype seems most appropriate. It may be recalled that the five-colored aspect of the magic stone—the link between the Pao-yü of Ch'ing fiction and the breached vault of Nü-kua's Heaven—was interpreted above as reflecting Pao-yü's central role in the five elements scheme, conjoining, as it were, the other four terms of the cycle. Although as we have seen it is the sequential alternation rather than the actual union of separate phases that is at issue in the archetypal pattern of multiple periodicity, the use of five-elements correspondences does serve to evoke a vision of harmonious unity within the phenomenological system as a whole.

But Pao-yü's existence in the Ta-kuan Yüan garden can scarcely be characterized in terms of harmonious union. If anything, the events that make up the text of the novel must be described as tragic sooner than idyllic. Where, then, is the amalgam of elements that seems to be symbolized in the five-colored stone? Why, instead, the emphasis on disunity, suffering, and the inexorable dissolution of the garden world?

Of course, it may be suggested that Pao-yü's stone was explicitly rejected from use in Nü-kua's repair of heaven on the grounds that it was for some reason lacking in the quality of five-elements harmony necessary for the task. But there also seems to be another possible range of meaning here that comes into clearer focus when we consider the spectral unity of Pao-yü's stone as a particular variation of the image of the rainbow. In his structural studies of the mythology of Amazon tribes, Lévi-Strauss notes that the image of the rainbow may convey the sense of both a "normal beneficent conjunction" (the generative confluence of sky and earth through the medium of rain) and an "abnormal, maleficent one" (the reappearance of the disjunction of Heaven and Earth after the end of rainfall, and hence associations with disease, poison, and death).[32] He further interprets the conjunction of these two opposite ranges of significance in a single image in terms of a deeper pattern of conceptualization, whereby the rainbow may represent what he calls "the residue of a wrecked continuum," a phenomenon in which "the continuous contains the discontinuous and even gives rise to it."[33] Most interesting for our purposes, he goes on to apply this radically bivalent pattern of conceptualization in a discussion of the wedding ritual in a number of tribal myths. We have already noted a similar conjunction of the "continuous" and the "discontinuous" in the treatment of the problem of marriage in Chinese mythology, and Lévi-Strauss' discussion of the association between the spectral unity of the rainbow and concepts of disease and death strikes a resonant chord in the context of the story of Pao-yü's maturation from sibling to spouse.

One might immediately shy away from attempting to apply the brilliant excesses of Lévi-Strauss in the context of Chinese civilization, but interestingly enough the equally brilliant scholarship of the anthropologist Wen I-to arrives at strikingly similar conclusions in a study of some of the texts of Chinese mythology. Using certain details of Sung Yü's "Kao-t'ang Fu" (高唐賦) as a key to the interpretation of a number of puzzling lines in the *Shih-Ching*[ae] and elsewhere, Wen demonstrates that the rainbow image implies a harmonious confluence of Heaven and Earth, yin and yang, and particularly clouds and rain, which bears in the Chinese tradition as well a taint of what Lévi-Strauss calls "reprehensible unions."[34] The same phenomenological conjunction that gives rise to a sense of generative union on the abstract level of nature as a whole also seems to inspire intimations of excessive, even taboo unions on the level of human individuality.[af] Without going as far as to say that the authors of *Dream of the Red Chamber* may have had this range of meaning in mind, we may note that their work is also deeply concerned with the "continuous" and the "dis-

[ae]Cf. the association between the rainbow and sexual desire in the *Ti-tung* 蝃蝀 and *Hou-jen* 候人 odes. Granet presents an interesting discussion of this association in Appendix II to his *Festivals and Songs in Ancient China* (London, 1932), although he goes perhaps too far in relating this particular confluence of yin and yang to his own theory of the origin of the *Shih Ching*.

[af]The same association seems to be present in the fact that the promise of renewed life in the post-deluge Biblical rainbow turns immediately sour in the story of Noah's drunken nakedness.

continuous" in the area of human relations. In its simplest terms, the novel may be described as the story of the sexual initiation of the rainbow-stone, from the puberty rites of Chapters 5 and 6 to the conjunction of marriage and death in Chapter 97. Despite the rich plenitude of life in the garden evoked through overlapping patterns of ceaseless alternation, a sense of uneasiness also hovers over the vague impropriety of Pao-yü's residence among the girls, the faint echoes of taboo in the practice of cousin-marriage, and particularly the emotional excess of Pao-yü's relation with Tai-yü. As a result, the hypothetical continuum of existence mimetically portrayed in the Ta-kuan Yüan "contains . . . and gives rise to" a manifest discontinuity that is ultimately problematical, and even tragic in tone.

CHAPTER V

ALLEGORY IN CHINESE AND WESTERN LITERATURE

MANY modern readers of the *Dream of the Red Chamber* have come away with the impression that the work is, in some uncertain sense, designed to be read in an allegorical manner. The life-giving stone hung about Pao-yü's neck, the thinly veiled significances of the names of the major figures,[a] the symmetry of correspondences between natural and human events, and the mythological frame that reappears at several key points in the novel, all add to the conclusion that we are dealing here with a mode of literature quite familiar in the Western tradition. Beyond the simple recognition of this fact, however, recent critics have been unwilling to go on and set forth a full allegorical interpretation of the text. This may be explained partly by the absence of an articulated concept of allegory as a distinguishable mode in Chinese literary theory,[b] but the problem ultimately lies in the fact that the *Dream of the Red Chamber* simply does not lend itself to the type of allegorical reading to which we have been redirected by Twentieth Century medievalists.

Yet it will be argued here that the *Dream of the Red Chamber* is indeed composed in a mode to which we may justly apply the general term "allegory," once the specific nature of that mode and its varying uses in China and the West have been defined. The principal justification for this position may be

[a] The traditional commentators evince a particular enjoyment in the exegesis of the names of people and places in the text. Viz. the introductory essay entitled "Tu-fa" (讀法), p. 3, and Chih-yen Chai, *passim.*[1]
[b] The nearest equivalent term, *yü-yen* 寓言, refers sooner to the use of parables or *exempla* in texts such as the *Chuang Tzu*, not to the sustained manipulation of structure we will consider below.

84

found in the fact that many of the traditional commentators on this masterwork do, in fact, show a marked concern for a critical dimension that conforms in many respects to the aesthetic premises of allegory in Western literature. When Chih-yen Chai speaks repeatedly of the "hidden meaning" (寓意) or the "deep significance" (深意) of certain passages in the novel, he is sometimes simply referring to personal details of which he alone is aware, but in other places he clearly has in mind a level of meaning that goes beyond the autobiographical level of the text. The title does, after all, present the work as a dream vision, and like the Red Chamber dream-sequence viewed by Pao-yü in Chapters 5 and 116 the text as a whole is thus marked out for allegorical interpretation.[c]

In order to arrive at an understanding of the nature of the allegorical mode of Western literature that may illumine, by contrast, the scheme of *Dream of the Red Chamber*, the following two chapters will examine in detail the structural forms and thematic contents of the mode in some of its greatest examples in the European tradition. Specifically, we will consider *The Romance of the Rose*, the poems of Chaucer, *The Divine Comedy*, *The Faerie Queene*, and *Paradise Lost*. The inclusion of Milton's expansive epic in spite of the fact that it can scarcely be categorized under the rubric of allegory is based on the fact that it does take up within its pages some of the structural devices and conventional *topoi* that are most characteristic of the allegorical tradition.

In attempting to reduce over two thousand years of Western literary history into a workable set of hypotheses for application in the Chinese context, we must apologize at the outset for the oversimplification necessarily involved in the enterprise. Certainly the term allegory has been used to refer to a wide

[c]Such a possibility is made explicit in the comment (sometimes attributed to the author's younger brother Ts'ao T'ang-ts'un) on the very first page of the most common text of the novel: 更於篇中間用夢幻等字, 却是此書本旨, 兼寓提醒閱者之意 ("... and moreover, he uses words like 'dream' and 'illusion' in the chapter, which in this case signify the underlying meaning of the book, while also conveying a hidden intention of awakening the reader").

range of cultural phenomena that we can hardly expect to fall neatly into a single conceptual entity. As a method of scriptural reading and exegesis, allegory traces its roots to the Platonic and Stoic interpretations of the Homeric epics, and thence through Philo of Alexandria's apologetic Hellenization of the Old Testament to the hermeneutical method developed by such early Church Fathers as Origen, Augustine, and Jerome. At the same time, however, the term also refers to a purely secular element of classical rhetoric, and it is from here that it seems to have been borrowed and extended to its Patristic usage.[2] A crucial role in the transition of allegory from a rhetorical device or an exegetical method to the category of monumental literary works we are dealing with in the present chapter seems to have been played by late-Classical poets such as Prudentius and Martianus Capella. Their experiments with personification allegory in the *Psychomachia* and *De Nuptiis Philologiae et Mercurii* open up the possibility of moving from the static use of allegorical reference as a rhetorical device to the creation of fictional texts in which the dynamic *interaction* of allegorical figures projects correspondingly complex relations on the philosophical level.

In the Middle Ages, where our own study of Western allegory begins, the term continues to refer to a specific aspect of scriptural reading (Dante's "allegory of the theologians"), but for our purposes it may be taken more to indicate a particular mode of writing (Dante's "allegory of the poets") in which purely literary narrative forms—epic, romance, troubadour ballads, etc.—are put to work as a means of conveying truths of a transcendental nature. Even here, recent scholarship has differed on whether it is the aesthetic patterning of the fictional text or the heuristic value of its projected meaning that is of primary importance in works such as *The Romance of the Rose* and *The Faerie Queene*; and critics have debated whether it is Chaucer's manipulation of iconographical detail or Dante's "figural typology" that is more representative of allegory as a general concept.

The fact that the *Dream of the Red Chamber* still seems somehow comparable to works such as *The Divine Comedy* and *The Faerie Queene,* in spite of the extreme difficulty of pinning down allegory as a specific literary mode, may perhaps be explained in terms of the quality of encyclopedic expansiveness discussed earlier in this study. In both the Chinese and the Western masterworks, what we observe is an attempt to create in a single volume a mimesis of an entire system of knowledge. In doing so, both the authors of *Dream of the Red Chamber* and the European poets to be treated below turn to an allegorical projection from traditional models of literary structure to patterns of intelligibility that are not subject to direct mimetic presentation. In the following pages, therefore, we will consider the manner in which some of the leading Western allegorists structure their literary universes, before returning to an interpretation of the allegorical projection in the Chinese work.

It has been found in this study that the common ground underlying the various definitions of allegory in Western theory and practice lies in the predication of a literary universe that is, despite all protestations of unity, essentially dual. Philosophers and theologians at various points in the Western tradition may claim to have reconciled, harmonized, or synthesized the opposites of sensory experience, but the duality of existence that originally called forth such attempts remains the dominant structural principle of the mimesis of existence in literature. In encyclopedic allegory, the bipolarity of form perceived within finite creation is projected into an ontological dimension, such that the sum total of the visibilia of this world (including both the perceptible and the conceivable) is set against an invisible dimension that is absolutely other.[d] In more strictly literary terms, meaning is seen as something essentially separate from, or at least more than, surface texture. Sense implies *sententia.* The function of allegory in this system, then, is to define the multiple links, or correspondences, by means of

[d] Cf. Kenneth Burke, *A Grammar of Motives* (New York, 1945): ". . . The most thoroughgoing dialectical opposition, however, centers in that key pair: Being and Not-Being."[3]

which events and relations within one plane are made intelligible on the basis of analogous relations known to hold in the second: "They are so completely two that analogies naturally arise between them: hence comes a strange reduplication of experience."[4] It should be noted that this dual structural framework is implicitly present in all Western allegory, even when mimetic attention is primarily focused on one plane (Chaucer and *The Romance of the Rose*) or the other (Dante and Milton).

This emphasis on a two-level structure of literary intelligibility may be seen in some of the earliest definitions of allegory, such as that of Heraclitus: "a figure which speaks of one thing while meaning something completely different,"[5] and Quintilian: "*aut aliud verbis aliud sensu ostendit aut etiam interim contrarium.*"[6] By the same token, a review of several definitions of the mode offered by recent scholars shows a recurrent focus on the element of ontological dualism:

1. "... start with an immaterial fact, ... and then invent *visibilia* to express them."[7]

2. "... a vision, an explicit act of spirit which transforms but does not vaporize the image of concrete reality."[8]

3. "... reference to man's ultimate destiny or meaning, perhaps his relations to supernatural Being—usually in some ancient similitude or element accustomed to bear this burden of reference."[9]

4. "This tradition of allegory is, in religious terms, the spirit of gnosticism, in which the objects of perception have value only as they lead us toward the ineffable, toward salvation through wisdom—as they are clues to the spiritualized, nontangible, abstract essence of the universe."[10]

5. "... aspects of a very real order of being beneath the material surface of things."[11]

6. "... to make you feel that two levels of being correspond to one another in detail, and indeed that there is some underlying reality, something in the nature of things, which makes this happen."[12]

7. "... the reality of the relations which prevail between separate orders of existence."[13]

8. "A writer is being allegorical whenever it is clear that he is saying 'by this I *also* (*allos*) mean that.' "[14]
What all these definitions have in common, of course, is the concept of ontological dualism discussed above. The last example, neatly enough, brings us back to the term *alienoloquium* in the definition of allegory by Isidore of Seville that seems to have been among the most current in the Middle Ages.

One source of confusion in discussions of allegory in European literature has been the conflicting use of the medieval concept of "four-fold" allegory in critical writings. Tuve, for example specifies that true allegory refers only to the anagogic level of the polysemous scheme, while Hollander argues that the term should be primarily reserved for the *quid credas* section of the well-known schoolboy's rhyme. For the purposes of this study, however, we will follow Dante's lead and reduce the four-fold scheme to an essentially twofold one: "And although these mystic senses have each their special denominations, they may all in general be called allegorical, since they differ from the literal and historical; for *allegory* is derived from *alleon*, in Greek, which means the same as the Latin *alienum* or *diversum*."[15] In other words, what we are talking about in allegory is the relation between the literal text and its other meaning. The precise relation being described at any one moment, or in any one figure, may be either allegorical (in the *quid credas* sense), tropological, or anagogical, but in all cases it is a two-level correspondence between surface and depth. Perhaps the most convincing argument for this point lies in the fact that even in scriptural exegesis, the proper home of four-fold allegory, the specific significances sorted out between the three mystical senses for any given figura vary widely from Father to Father, and even from occurrence to occurrence. It may be useful to note, in this regard, the efforts of many modern medievalists to turn the attention of readers "back to" the literal sense.[e] While such arguments are generally

[e] E.g. Rosemond Tuve, *Allegorical Imagery* (Princeton, 1966), p. 48; Erich Auerbach, *Mimesis* (Princeton, 1953), p. 200; Robert Hollander, *Allegory in Dante's Commedia* (Princeton, 1969), p. 52.

4444444444444

supported by the incarnational aesthetics of the Christian Fathers, they may perhaps be more intelligible when viewed in the light of the preoccupation with surface texture in recent Western critical theory, than as a response to any actual neglect of the literal level in the past. In any event, the instincts of such critics in calling attention to the poetic surface as inseparable from its conceptual meaning reaffirm the dual structure of allegory described here.

At this point, it will be necessary to confront the confusion in terms between allegory and symbolism that has perhaps resulted in widening the readership of medieval literature in recent years, but has left the precise nature of the allegorical mode in doubt. Much of the problem lies in the fact that discussions of symbolism and allegory are often quite indistinguishable. For example, the following discussions of symbolism might just as well have been added to the list provided above in connection with allegory:

1. "The poem is allegorical *and* symbolical *and* analogical. Each and all of these dimensions of the poem involve it in more than a literal meaning, each is a dimension of 'otherness.' "[16]

2. "The symbolic imagination conducts an action through analogy, of the human to the divine, of the natural to the supernatural, of the low to the high, of time to eternity."[17]

Most attempts to draw a distinction between the two concepts, unfortunately, offer little help. The most common solution, for example, that offered by Lewis, Huppé, and Frye,[18] argues that it is the direction of movement between the two levels that differentiates them. That is, the symbolist begins with a concrete sign and moves toward an abstract idea, while the allegorist begins with a bare idea that he then clothes in concretized flesh. Such an explanation has the advantage of symmetry, such as we expect from Lewis and Frye, but it seems to involve a confusion of the processes of allegorical composition and allegorical reading. It seems idle, for example, to speculate whether Dante used his celestial rose as a springboard to mystical insight, or rather employed its image to "realize" a previously held conception of the City of God. Another explanation,[19] proposing that symbolism is characterized by a metaphorical relation involving vehicles of this world, with the opposite true of allegory, also seems to fall short of accuracy, since all metaphoric vehicles must be presented in images, or concepts, drawn from the world of experience. Here as elsewhere we must be careful to avoid the pitfall of associating the concrete with this world and the abstract with the other, or of misreading a concrete figure on the basis of its abstract name (as in personification allegory). For example, Milton's Sin and Death are nominally pure abstractions, but their description and functioning as allegorical figures are all too concrete. Such particularized figures as the Redcross Knight or Britomart, on the other hand, remain for all their bleeding primarily disembodied virtues.

In the light of our above discussion of the dynamic interaction between figures that is characteristic of the sort of allegorical texts we are interested in here,[f] it may be more useful to define symbol as a single element of text with external reference,[g] and to reserve the term allegory for larger chunks of narrative in which structural patterns woven into the text refer obliquely to patterns of intelligibility not directly presented. In other words, in allegory we are dealing with the "horizontal" relations that hold and develop among a number of symbols or signs in a fictional narrative. In terms of the two-level literary universe discussed above, the allegorical pattern that takes shape among symbolic figures on one level points, in its overall configurations, to an analogous pattern on the unseen level of truth.[h]

[f] Cf. Marc-René Jung, "Études sur le poème allégorique en France au moyen age" (*Romanica Helvetica*, Vol. 82, 1971): "Les poémes allégoriques se distinguent par ce que nous appelerons l'*allégorie dynamique*. La *narratio* elle-même (voyage, bataille, siège, etc.) contient le *sensus allegoricus*."[20]

[g] Cf. Frye's definition of symbol as: "any unit of any literary structure that can be isolated for critical attention."[21]

[h] At least this distinction between allegory and symbol would also allow for the most recent literary phenomenon to which the term symbolism has been applied. Modern symbolism, however, largely abandons the horizontal allegorical structure by which intelligibility was projected into the realm of invisibilia, and concentrates on particularized symbols in isolation, with the result that potential truth relations on the referential level remain undefined and beyond the grasp of conceptualization.

ALLEGORY

Such a definition, of course, accords special importance to
the trope of metaphor in describing the dimension of "vertical"
reference implicit in both individual symbols and the allegorical
structure as a whole. One may note that Cicero speaks of the
rhetorical device of allegory as continuous metaphor.[22] The
exact role of metaphor in lending cohesion to an allegorical
structure, however, is subject to the same overlapping of
terminology we have seen with regard to symbolism. Thus
most definitions of metaphor in critical writings, to the extent
that it is a literary rather than a psycholinguistic phenomenon
that is at issue, are more or less descriptive of allegory in
general,[i] while conversely, the traditional explanation of
alienoloquium—saying one thing and meaning another—is
variously applied to allegory, symbolism, metaphor, or irony.
For the remainder of this essay, therefore, the term metaphor
will be employed to refer specifically to the relation of analogy
that holds between the figures and larger structural patterns
presented in an allegorical fiction on one plane, and the configurations of truth to which they point on the level of invisibilia. In speaking of analogy, however, we must hasten to
note that similarity of form plays only a minor part in the
functioning of the metaphoric relation. More often, at least to
the extent that a given metaphor is indeed more than an implicit simile, the impact of the trope is to emphasize the disjunction, rather than the likeness, between sign and referent.[j] For
example, the metaphorical relation by which Dante's celestial
rose refers to the true City of God functions less on the basis
of similarity of attributes (color, fragrance, circularity, loss of
innocence) than by the absolute disparity between the fading

[i]E.g. C. S. Lewis, *The Allegory of Love* (Oxford, 1936), ". . . every
metaphor is an allegory in little";[23] C. K. Ogden and I. A. Richards,
The Meaning of Meaning (New York, 1948), "Metaphor . . . the use of one
reference to a group of things between which a given relationship holds,
for the purpose of facilitating the discrimination of an analogous relationship in another group";[24] Northrop Frye, *Anatomy of Criticism*
(Princeton, 1957), "the unit of relationship between two symbols."[25]
[j]Cf. W. K. Wimsatt and Monroe Beardsley, *The Verbal Icon* (Kentucky, 1954): "Metaphor proceeds from likeness and disparity."[26]

image, whose associations with incarnation and martyrdom further bind it to the world of passing shapes, and the eternal truth to which it points. Rather than analyze the precise proportions of similarity and difference present in every metaphorical figure, however, let us simply state that the trope functions to establish the equipoise by which the coordinates of the dual structure of allegory are defined.

Without becoming too involved in rhetorical theory, we may now return to the functioning of allegory. We have seen that when we speak of allegory in the Western context we mean the creation of a two-level literary universe (in mimesis of an ontologically dual cosmos) by means of the projection into a hypothetical plane of structural patterns actually presented in the images and actions of narrative (the author's fiction). For further precision, we might apply the term symbol to the individual figures that evoke the possibility of external reference, and allegory to the manner in which the syntagmatic relation between symbols on the literal level points to an analogous relation on the referential level. Such horizontal patterns of intelligibility may take the form of actions (*A* defeats *B* in battle) or static relationships (*X* dwells in a chamber in the house of *Y*). Thus, for example, Dante's Griffin, taken in isolation, is a symbol, but when it binds its chariot-pole to the tree of knowledge, it is functioning allegorically. In the same way, as long as Spenser's Mammon is alone in his cave he remains a symbol, but as soon as he tempts Guyon he enters the allegorical structure.

This gives primary importance to the author's fiction—the *narratio*—for it is here, in the intricacies of plot and characterization that remain largely the product of the individual artist's ingenuity, that the transcendent truths to which his figures point take on a dimension of temporal development. Theoretically, the possible configurations of such fictional patterns would be limited only by the bounds of a poet's imagination, but of course we find that they are in fact reducible to a small and recurrent number. "There are not very many such great public images (quest, pilgrimage, marriage, death, birth, purgation, for example) and not very many such metaphysical problems."[27]

It may be noticed that the notion of "great public images" taken over as models for narrative shape tends to overlap considerably with the concept of archetype introduced in preceding chapters. We must repeat here, therefore, the distinction drawn earlier between archetype and allegory as tools of analysis in dealing with complex literary structures. Where archetypal patterns of form remain semi-conscious, implicit elements of a literary tradition, the presence of "meaning" in allegory necessarily indicates actual authorial intention,[k] not simply possible signification or accessibility to interpretation. Thus, while nearly any narrative work of comprehensive scope or sufficiently puzzling surface texture may be interpreted so as to evince an entire range of "meanings," it is only in those works where the author explicitly directs the reader to look beyond his fictional narration that we are justified in speaking of allegory. When such patterns of intelligibility emerge in narrative seemingly without the author's conscious intention, we must fall back upon the notion of psychological or literary archetypes to account for them.[1]

In speaking of the ontological dualism seen to underlie the allegorical mode of writing in the Western context—and particularly mimeses of the totality of existence in encyclopedic allegory—we must hasten to add that it is not our aim to reduce the entire history of that civilization to a simple duality of warring opposites of the sort often ascribed to the Manichaeans. On the contrary, European poets as well as theologians have consistently sought to *resolve* the "binary oppositions" of sensory experience into some scheme of unity, or at least balance.

---

[k] Cf. Marc-René Jung: "Il fallut l'intervention de la volonté des auteurs pour créer cette autre chose qu'est le poème allégorique."[28]

[1] In relating the functional feature of allegory to archetype, we may note the similarity between Max Black's definition of archetype and the concept of allegory presented here: "By an *archetype* I mean a systematic repertoire of ideas by means of which a given thinker describes, by *analogical extension*, some domain to which those ideas do not immediately and literally apply."[29]

But it will be maintained here that all the various schemes for achieving a sense of ultimate unity, in the West as in the East, are both directly caused and profoundly conditioned by the original perception of duality, and that the dual structure remains the logical underpinning of any concept of the One. This is especially true in the linguistic medium of literature, in which the very words that boldly assert or humbly point toward the notion of transcendental unity are themselves inseparably derived from the logic of opposition in primary experience. What is of most importance to us here is that the various solutions that Western thinkers have seized upon in this great enterprise of the will—Platonism, Gnosticism, Scholasticism, Neo-Platonism, and more recently the historical dialectic—present significant contrasts to the logic of complementary bipolarity underlying the yin-yang dualism in the Chinese context.

The achievement of the allegorical mode of Western literature, then, lies in its ability to render one plane of existence intelligible in terms of another. This vision may perhaps be described as a unity in the sense that the single *intelligence* of author and reader (in imitation of God) comprehends the analogous patterns of both worlds. But it remains true that this intelligence functions only on the basis of the logical separateness of the two schemes. Turning back to our texts, let us consider some of the schemes of unity that are utilized in constructing encyclopedic mimeses of totality in Western literature. It is perhaps significant that none of the five poets considered here sees fit to content himself with a single scheme, but rather each moves from model to model depending on the nature of the particular duality confronting him at any given point.

Perhaps the simplest solution to the problem of cosmic duality is that of assigning all truth and value to one pole, and the absence of these qualities to the other, in some of the more clearly demarcated pairs of sensory opposites, such that good and evil emerge as contrasting areas of experience. Dante, Spenser, and Milton, for example, make extensive use of such antitheses as light and dark, night and day, or pleasance and

noxiousness in plotting their literary universes, as a few lines
will help us to recall:

Dolce color d'oriental zaffiro,
Che s'accoglieva nel sereno aspetto
Del mezzo puro insino al primo giro,
Alli occhi miei ricominciò diletto,
Tosto ch'io usci'fuor dell'aura morta
Che m'avea contristati li occhi 'l petto.
(Pur. i: 13–18)

Where griesly Night, with visage deadly sad,
That Phoebus chearefull face durst never vew,
And in a foule blacke pitchy mantle clad,
She findes forth comming from her darksome mew,
Where she all day did hide her hated hew.
(F.Q. i: v: 20)

As when from mountain tops the dusky clouds
Ascending, while the North wind sleeps, o'erspread
Heav'n's cheerful face, the louring Element
Scowls o'er the dark'n'd landscape Snow, or show'r;
If chance the radiant Sun with farewell sweet
Extend his ev'ning beam, the fields revive,
The birds their notes renew, and bleating herds
Attest their joy, that hill and valley rings.
(P.L. ii: 488–495)

Spenser, in particular, places special emphasis on his ability to
"discerne of colours blacke and white"[30] in arranging his
thickly populated canvas. Lewis has pointed out the importance
of contrasting images of disease and health, life and death, or
contrivance and spontaneity, in Spenser's poetic vision,[31] while
Dunbar has demonstrated the counterpoise of weight and light-
ness exploited by Dante.

The concept of unity comes into this antithetical arrangement with the application of the Boethian argument that the
forces of evil are devoid of any positive existence of their own:
"For I do not deny that those who are evil are *evil*; but I do

deny that they *are*, in the pure and simple sense of the term."[32] When the "fruit" of being is contrasted, in this manner, to the "chaff" of non-being, all positive existence may be seen as unitary by default. But once one has accepted the view that the dark and unpleasant aspects of life are evil and illusory, the converse soon follows that all illusion is necessarily evil. This may explain Spenser's recurrent association of the artificial or artful with the sterile and sinister, as opposed to the health and bounty of unperverted nature.[m] By the same token, we find within the dialectical opposition of truth and illusion a whole gallery of figures of markedly evil cast, whose malice is defined by their propensity to create phantom shapes and images. These arch-deceivers include Spenser's Archimago: "For by high mighty science he could take/As many formes and shapes in seeming wise,/As ever Proteus to himselfe could make,"[34] Proteus himself: "To dreadfull shapes he did him selfe trans-forme,"[35] Duessa: "For she could d'on so manie shapes in sight,/As ever could cameleon colours new;/ so could she forge all colours, save the trew,"[36] and the wayward Cupid: "Disguiz'd in thousand shapes, that none might him be-wray."[37] As a result the attribute of shifting formlessness be-comes in itself an icon of evil as in the case of Milton's Sin: "The other shape,/If shape it might be call'd that shape had none/Distinguishable in member, joint, or limb,/Or substance might be call'd that shadow seem'd,/For each seem'd either."[38]

Even more dangerous than the wiles of such masters of shapes, however, is the problem of self-deception, the accept-ance of a false or reflected "image" for true substance. This extremely important theme, presented in the Narcissus icon early in *The Romance of the Rose*, is frequently associated with the optics of reflection, either in artificial mirrors or natural water surfaces. For example, Jean de Meun's Nature warns that mirrors

[m]A. Bartlett Giamatti (*The Earthly Paradise and the Renaissance Epic*, Princeton, 1966), for obvious reasons, claims that: "through the Italians (and ultimately all the 'Platonic' philosophy in the air), Spenser learned to equate the good with the real, the evil with the illusory. . . ."[33]

> Si font fantosmes apparanz
> a ceus qui regardent par anz,
> font les neïs dehors parair
> touz vis, soit par aigue ou par air
> (R.R. 18151–18154)

while January's unbridled imagination in *The Merchant's Tale* is similarly described:

> Many fair shap and many a fair visage
> Ther passeth thurgh his herte nyght by nyght,
> As whoso tooke a mirour, polisshed bryght, . . .
> (M.T. 1580–1582)

Milton's Eve reveals this potential weakness immediately after her creation:

> As I bent down to look, just opposite,
> A Shape within the wat'ry gleam appear'd
> Bending to look on me, I started back,
> It started back, but pleas'd I soon return'd. . .
> (P.L. IV: 460–463)

and even Dante in Paradise is subject to the same unpurged inclination:

> Tali vid' io più facce a parlar pronte,
> Perch'io dentro all'error contrario corsi
> A quel ch'accese amor tra l'uomo e il fonte.
> (Par. III: 16–18)

It is in contrast to this kind of slippery multiplicity that the heroes of allegory move steadily towards a unitary goal. Guyon's pursuit of temperance, for example, consistently demands extreme moral choices rather than any formula of moderation. Even in cases involving morally neutral or theoretically multivalent figures (e.g. the Cupid on Busyrane's tapestry and the Cupid returned to the Garden of Adonis), we may not properly use the term "ambiguity" when the reader is provided with obtrusive iconographic signs that clearly define the decorum of the piece. As a result the seeming duplicity that marks out such figures as Duessa and January for our scorn must be interpreted not as actually ambiguous, but rather as placing them clearly at the wrong end of a scale of absolute value. Spenser leaves little room for doubt on this point in the vanishing of the House of Busyrane and the evaporation of the slushy Florimell when confronted with the truth.

Nor may we take the contradictory or heretical statements of allegorical figures (the Pardoner's sermon, La Vielle's advice, Genius' absolution, Satan's cosmogony, the Gyant's justice, etc.) as evidence of unresolved doubts on the part of the poets, since the words of a character are always "amplified" or "depraved" by circumstantial detail. This does not preclude the possibility, or even the probability, that those who are denied the crutch of decorum (the other characters in the fictional text) will misread their icons and consequently worship the false or neglect the true. Examples of this type crowd the mimetic level of allegory since they describe some of the most ubiquitous patterns of human experience.

A second means by which allegorical writers in the Western tradition imitate a philosophical solution to the problem of duality is the postulation of a hierarchy of degrees, whereby the aspects of experience that seem to be in conflict when viewed in isolation are integrated into a sequence such that all levels share in the perfection of the highest. This concept may be neatly encapsulated in such symbolic figures as golden chains, cosmic stairways, and mystical ladders, but what concerns us here is its evocation through general allegorical structure. This second view contrasts with the first scheme of unity described above, in that here there is no absolute difference of value or being, between the basest and the noblest of finite creation. At the very top of the ladder, however, the Principle of Continuity posited by Lovejoy as a necessary adjunct to the chain-of-being concept fails to function, since the relation between the top rung and the top rung but one is ontologically discontinuous.[n] Thus, while Dante's neatly structured progression of circles, pits, terraces, and spheres would

[n]It should be noted, in fairness, that Lovejoy acknowledges that the ontological reach of continuity was "little more than verbal."[39]

seem to suggest the idea of a continuous succession of degrees from level to level, in fact we are shown that the variously placed inhabitants of each division (most explicitly in the *Paradiso*) are with the exception of the very lowest and highest generally of equal ontological status. As a result, the upward passage of Dante the pilgrim is accomplished only by means of discontinuous hops, as the unconscious traveler is transported by a variety of vehicles and figurative "leaps":

> E così, figurando il paradiso,
> Convien saltar lo sacrato poema,
> Come chi trova suo cammin riciso.
>
> (Par. XXIII: 61–63)

This failure of the Principle of Continuity, however, need not reduce the chain of being to a cosmic antithesis between the Creator and the Created, so long as the lower order of the hierarchy is rightly ordered to its summit. In this sense, the mutable "order of nature"[40] presented throughout *The Faerie Queene* may be seen as theoretically "continuous" with the order of grace glimpsed at the end, while Dante's path down to the pit of Hell and up the Purgatorial Mount may be conceived as a straight line continuing on to the point where center and circumference meet. When the cosmic hierarchy is properly ordered in this way, grace may freely descend to the baser degrees, either actively interceding in time of distress (the "tre donne benedette" in Dante's *selva*, or Spenser's Prince Arthur), or passively providing the model for human transcendence: "*Gratia non tollit naturam sed perficit.*"[41] This formal relation of dominance and submission, without the ontological distinction of the cosmic scheme, is frequently projected into various sub-cosmic and microcosmic spheres, notably the kingdom, the marriage, and the individual constitution. Though the proper maintenance of hierarchical balance on one of these circumscribed levels cannot guarantee a corresponding amelioration of the cosmos, as Spenser's knights are often reminded, it can at least figure forth the possibility. The inversion or perversion of even the smallest hierarchical order, on the other hand, seems to add positive weight to the sin of Adam.

A significant feature of this second approach to the problem of duality may be seen in the fact that where the noxious extremes of experience were generalized and rejected as nonexistent in the antithetical view, here they are afforded a positive role in a universe which is conceived as totally good. Once evil is admitted to the universe, however, the problem of exactly where to place it becomes somewhat sticky. Both the Dantean and Miltonian Hells, for example, though carefully constructed as parodies rather than challenges to the divine will at the pinnacle of the hierarchy, have left room for the misattribution of dignity to the bottom of the heap. The point of the centrality of evil, however, whether represented in a spatial sense as in the Inferno or a dramatic one as in the Garden of Eden, is clear.° In both epics, the idea that evil is instrumental in the purposes of good on a cosmic level (Satan's inadvertent construction of the Purgatorial Mount and service as a ladder to the pilgrim in the *Commedia*, or his constant repetition of variations of the "Evil be thou my Good" refrain in *Paradise Lost*) is borne out on the human level in the *felix culpa* theme.

A third conceivable resolution of the dual nature of existence—the merging of opposites (*coincidentia oppositorum*) or the postulation of a *tertium quid*—may be passed over briefly. Such conceptions may be appropriate to mysticism, but their realization in the realm of postlapsarian literature is quite limited, as concrete images of absolute union are hard to come by in the world of experience. It is perhaps for this reason that we find such scant attention paid to the trinitarian concept in the great Christian allegories. Dante, to be sure, does face the issue at the height of the Empyrean, but his trinity is characteristically presented in a mystic flash from which he immediately backs off (through a string of "inexpressibility topoi") to the simile of the geometer. The vision at the end of the *Commedia* stands as a symbol of triunity, but not as a functional element in the

°The argument has been made that Milton's Hell is significantly *outside* of Creation, but the point is that, through the Fall, the new "world" joins Hell in a common federation of imperfection. Thus Satan's avowed aim: "League with you I seek" (IV: 375) is realized: ". . . and made one Realm/Hell and this World, one Realm, one Continent/of easy thoroughfare" (X: 391).

allegorical pilgrimage from the dark wood to the celestial rose. Spenser, similarly, pays homage to the trinity in the three brothers Priamond, Diamond, and Triamond "borne of one mother in one happie mold," and the triune circles of the dancing Graces (vi:x:12), as does Chaucer in the prayer that closes *Troilus and Criseyde*, and Jean de Meun in the three-faceted carbuncle (20525–96), but such instances are ornamental or, more exactly, add doctrinal rather than literary completeness to the works.

Examples of images of union in the Neo-Platonic sense are similarly rare and inconclusive in the five works. One may cite such examples as the reconciliation of Love and Hate in Spenser's Temple of Venus (iv:x:31–35), the bisexual image of Venus herself,[p] or the symbolic confluence of the Thames and Medway, but by the beginning of Book V we are back in the same world of polar contrasts and confronted with the *reductio ad absurdum* of the concept of merged opposites in the figure of the Gyant.

In considering the above possibilities by which allegory may arrange and deal with the two-level world-view upon which it is based, we may observe that in each case the resolution of duality carries a definite implication of movement, or at least a will to move, a motive. Moreover, this movement is invariably imparted with a pronounced sense of direction, from a state of relative imperfection, incompleteness, confusion, or downright evil towards a goal of perfect truth. The idea of a *terminus ad quem* is extremely important here, even if it can never be represented as having been attained, for without faith in the existence of a goal, all movement, even in one direction, may be seen as aimless wandering. As obvious as the point may seem, however, it must be noted that the mimesis of a process of becoming, or the impulse towards fulfillment of figure, is not an inevitable literary answer to the dual nature of existence, but rather a characteristic aesthetic feature of the Western literary tradition that, we shall see, stands in contrast to the

[p]More explicitly in the fleshly merger of Scudamour and Amoret in the original ending of the book.

approach manifested in the structure of the *Dream of the Red Chamber*.

The precise form in which such movement is embodied in allegorical fictions may be either externalized or internalized. In the former case the striving of imperfection for perfection is represented by a mimesis of action, typically a pilgrimage or quest: two journeys with clearly defined goals. In the latter case the characters and reader undertake a spiritual journey from ignorance to truth, from what Dante calls "the state of misery" to "the state of felicity"[42]: "The direction of this dual journey, once it gets underway, is the direction in which all signs point [from *here* to *there*]."[43] Usually, of course, an external and an internal progression are intricately interwoven on one or both levels of the allegorical vision. In *The Romance of the Rose*, for example, we have a parody of a quest that goes practically nowhere and gains a worthless object, while in Chaucer's *Canterbury Tales* the pilgrimage ends, for all practical purposes, in a tavern. But the reader who has finished the two works can scarcely deny that decisive steps have been taken in both towards the attainment of truth and "felicity." In the *Commedia*, on the other hand, the non-empirical nature of the literal journey keeps the spiritual pilgrimage before our eyes at every step of the way. Still, Dante is careful to focus attention on the forward momentum of the literal course through the recurrent use of travel metaphors, particularly those referring to sea voyage, while at the same time reinforcing the vertical dimensions of the spiritual journey with images of height and depth. In *The Faerie Queene*, Spenser utilizes the topical division into books and the romance technique of *entrelacement* to detour the inexorable forward motion of epic into a net of paths and byways that seem to have neither beginning nor end—hence the problems of the "ending" of the text. Yet within the framework of each book, and even, it is maintained, within the course of the "unfinished" work as we have it, the sense of meaningful movement in the direction of greater clarity of vision is inescapable. In other words, what Greene calls the "perpetual *becoming* of the characters" takes on a perceptible direction as the goal that is never actually reached comes gradually into sight. The narrative of *Paradise Lost* would seem perhaps to present an exception to the topos of end-oriented travel since the trajectories followed in the poem are journeys of exile, away from rather than towards the destination. The point is, however, that regardless of the direction actually traced by the characters within the text, a path is clearly staked out and its end-point defined. The driving sense of historical inevitability that pervades the work drives home the promise of a return in glory, even as Satan plummets and Adam prepares to enter the plain.

In general, what we are talking about when we speak of the movement from darkness and illusion to light and truth is the notion of *anagnorisis*,[q] whether subjective or objective. This structural element may take the form of an instantaneous disclosure, as in Spenser's "houses of recognition,"[44] or the recapitulation of Scipio's lesson at the end of *Troilus and Criseyde*, but in most cases what we find in allegory is a gradual, rather than an epiphanic, revelation of the truth. In *The Romance of the Rose*, the example, Amant remains blind to the to the truth to the very end, but as the iconographical evidence against him and his false teachers slowly locate him at the wrong end of the truth-spectrum, something of the nature of Truth is nevertheless uncovered. In the *Commedia* the two processes are yoked together as the multiple moments of sudden insight experienced by the pilgrim are set into an orderly scheme of gradual revelation. Typically, the more instantaneous *anagnorisis* is presented in some sort of an unveiling, or stripping away, of the *integumenta* that stand between perception and truth. Dante and Spenser, of course, make explicit and recurrent use of the unveiling motif both in revealing the true and the good (Una, Beatrice) and uncovering the ugly masquerading as beauty (Duessa, Siren). Dante, in fact, steps aside to call our attention explicitly to the veil of figure precisely at moments in which grace manifests itself in fallen nature

<hr/>

[q]Only Spenser, of the five poets considered here, stages a classic *anagnorisis* scene, mole and all (vi: xii: 7).

to protect the unredeemed pilgrim and ensure his progress towards the goal (Inf. IX: 63, Purg. VIII: 20). Milton provides an interesting inversion of the veil motif, whereby Adam and Eve are swathed in their own naked innocence: "no veil/Shee needed, Virtue-proof,"[45] until by covering their nakedness they succeed in stripping themselves of grace (for the time being). The Medieval onion-skin (*involucrum*) concept of truth and falsity is quite similar to the idea of *integumentum*, except that in the former case the process of getting at the truth involves a serial, rather than a one-shot, lifting of the barrier to vision.

Perhaps the clearest example of the gradual revelation of truth as a spiritual journey from finite image to infinite idea is the concept of figure and fulfillment so widely discussed in recent criticism of allegorical literature. What concerns us here is the fact that, in both the reading of Scripture and the composition of allegorical fiction, figuralism implies a clear temporal progression from a lesser to a greater degree of revelation. A. C. Charity, for example, places great emphasis on the sense of inexorable historicity implied in the use of figural typology as an allegorical device. Auerbach may state his personal preference in the argument that "figure surpasses fulfillment,"[46] but since literature can never actually present fulfillment, the *figurae* remain "ombriferi prefazii" that turn our eyes forward and impel us in the promised direction.

The point that figure is never actually fulfilled in allegory is extremely important and will require further elaboration here. The question emerges: since the invisibilia of the other world are by definition of an order that is simply not subject to the space-time coordinates of the world of experience, how can the language of this world presume to comprehend it in literary form? This being a logical impossibility, how can the poet express, without resorting to open-ended symbols, what he perceives to be the immanent reality of the other world? The answer, of course, lies in the acceptance of a partial solution. The poet may be unable to *grasp* ultimate reality and pin it down in earthbound language, but he can at least *approach*

ALLEGORY

the final vision or gain some understanding of its nature by means of various oblique devices of definition. This is the function of allegory as defined here: to illumine the nature of unseen truth by analogical projection from a pattern of symbols presented on the level of visible images and events. If it is perhaps objected here that Dante and Milton are dealing with the other world as explicit visibilia, we may point out that in both these cases what we see in Heaven is by no means the final vision, but rather its finite expression as filtered through the eyes of the poets and the veil of Scripture. Thus the end of Dante's pilgrimage is rendered in the terms of earthly geometry and optics, while Milton's Father and Son appear through the anthropomorphic attributes and deeds that have troubled so many critics. It is for this reason that the journeys and historical processes of allegory rarely come to a stated end, so that at the end of the *Commedia* we find Dante the poet back at the beginning desiring to write what he has just written, whereas the epic structure of Milton's encyclopedic vision shades off into an "untransmuted lump of futurity."[47] The same aesthetic impulse may also be seen at work in the sense of incompleteness, or at least unfinished business, that hovers over the end of each of the books of *The Faerie Queene*.

The actual manner in which allegory proceeds to approach the Other relies heavily on the principle of definition through negation or, more precisely, on the fine balance between similarity and disparity that we have seen to be the essence of the metaphorical relation on which allegory is based. The similarity of form involved in all comparisons may to a certain extent describe the nature of the invisible truth, as in Dante's triune point of light, but such words remain a mere dispensation to fallen intelligence that can understand only "By lik'ning spiritual to corporal forms."[48] As a result, poets, like theologians, must eventually turn to negative terms: "Immutable, Immortal, Infinite, . . . invisible, . . . inaccessible,"[50] to define the attributes of the Most High.

'Cf. Arthur O. Lovejoy, *The Great Chain of Being* (London, 1923): The attributes of God were "expressible only in negations of the attributes of this world."[49]

106

The various techniques of negative definition employed in allegory may be neatly summed up in the term "adumbration," in the painterly sense of evoking the illusion of light through outlines and shadings of dark.[5] On the most explicit level, the technique of adumbration involves the entire range of "inexpressibility topoi," as for example in Spenser:

> Her garment was so bright and wondrous sheene,
> That my fraile wit cannot devize to what
> It to compare, nor finde like stuffe to that
> (F.Q. vii: vii: 7)

But what concerns us more here is the practice of structural adumbration. Spenser offers a clear example of what we are talking about. In each book of *The Faerie Queene*, he approaches a definition of the particular virtue under consideration by presenting a series of confrontations between the persona of the virtue and its various opposites, or imperfect copies, so that by the end of twelve cantos we have a clearer idea at least of the specific reactions in which each virtue consists. "his *intermedled* adventures become the attributes of that essence he is trying to adumbrate."[51] But since elucidation by adumbration can achieve only an approximation of the true shape of virtue, we never see it in its perfect state. Thus Guyon cannot hide "the secrete signes of kindled lust" at the close of Book ii, and we find the courteous Calidore rudely disturbing the Graces late in Book vi, "The virtues are not fully attainable; their ground is Deity."[52]

In much the same way, Dante's attempts to define the Unmoved Mover in terms of perceivable attributes remain no more than a sign:

> Così parlar conviensi al vostro ingegno,
> Però che solo da sensato apprende
> Ciò che fa poscia d'intelletto degno.
> (Par. iv: 40–42)

---

[5]Cf. Spenser: "But never let th' ensample of the bad/Offend the good: for good, by paragone/Of evill, may more notably be rad,/As white seemes fayrer, macht with blacke attone." (F.Q. iii: ix: 2).

But to the pilgrim and readers who have passed through the darkness, stench, and parodic fixity of the underworld, the Purgatorial Mount and celestial spheres take on a significance otherwise inaccessible to them. Milton's Heaven and its model on Earth emerge with similar clarity after two books of sulphurous pools. Particularly striking in *Paradise Lost* is the contrast between the vivid description of Sin and Death in terms of likeness to the horrors of human existence and fantasy in Book II, and the far more telling *adumbration* of Sin and Death as the sudden and irrevocable deprivation of the innocence and immortality that hold sway from Book III to Book VIII. It is in such a sense of assertion through denial that such works as *The Romance of the Rose* and particularly Chaucer's tales, whose vision seems largely limited to the concrete details of the fallen world, may be seen as deeply religious affirmations of the existence of a true realm that both causes and renders intelligible its negative transformation.

One final method employed by allegorists to express the inexpressible is the use of numerological patterns to evoke, by analogy with mathematical principles, the sense of the incommensurability of the two realms of existence. We may note Dante's $9 (7 + 2) + 1$ structure in which the truths of each cantica are raised to a higher power of final significance, and the $3 + 1$ rhythm of pagan and Christian wisdom pointed out by Professor Hollander. In similar manner, the existing text of *The Faerie Queene* may be viewed as a finished (or at least terminated) volume of six inconclusive workaday books raised to a higher power of Sabbath grace in the parting vision of the seventh.

In order to demonstrate the assertion that the allegorical method considered up to this point is a particular, rather than a universal, occurrence of the mode, let us briefly review its counterpart in the Chinese literary tradition. As was mentioned at the start of this chapter, the Ch'ing novel *Dream of the Red Chamber* seems to be an allegorical composition in the sense that the text is structured in such a way as to elucidate a pattern of significance not directly presented. In proceeding to isolate that "other" pattern of meaning, however, we found that the analytical tools derived from the experience of allegory in Western literature have failed to yield a meaningful interpretation of the novel.

Perhaps the root of the problem may now be identified as the fact that the Chinese world-view[t] simply does not utilize the two-level cosmology that we have found at the heart of Western allegory. More accurately, the characteristic Chinese solution to the problem of duality is of another sort altogether. This solution, in brief (see Chapter III), consists in the conception of a given universe (of infinite proportions) within which all the conceivable opposites of sensory and intellectual experience are *contained*, such that the poles of duality are seen as complementary within the entire structure of totality. Such a world-view was referred to in an earlier chapter as a "spatial vision of totality" in the sense that existence is here characterized by a ceaseless process of antithetical alternation when viewed temporally, but that it manifests a sense of complementary balance in an all-embracing comprehension of space. Of particular importance here is the fact that the distinction between the sublunar and the metaphysical, the finite and the infinite, which we have seen as the basis of most Western solutions to the problem of duality, is held by the Chinese thinkers to be just one more of the many complementary pairs included within a single, total frame of reference. The point is not that the Chinese thinkers are more naturally practical or this-worldly than their Western counterparts, but rather that they do not regard the distinction between the physical and the metaphysical aspects of existence as of absolute ontological significance. They are either both real or they are both illusory, but in any event they are commensurable.

Since all reality, in the Chinese view, exists on one plane ("plane," as in Western thought, consisting of more than two dimensions), the other meaning to which allegory points is not to be sought vertically, in terms of correspondences between two separate phases of existence, but instead by increasing *breadth* of vision. Even more important, the trope by which individual symbols in a Chinese allegorical structure refer to the invisible configurations of truth must be identified not as the similarity-difference relation of metaphor, but if anything as the horizontal extension of synecdoche.ᵘ Each isolated element of the Chinese allegory, by virtue of the existential process of ebb and flow in which it is caught up, "stands for," or "partakes of," the sum total of all existence that remains invisible only in its extent, and not in its essence.

Because in this world-view truth is manifest in the ground of experience rather than removed or veiled by an ontological barrier, Chinese literature in general and such allegories as the *Dream of the Red Chamber* in particular are characterized by a distinct paucity of the kind of significant movement we have isolated in Western allegory. In actuality, of course, it is not the static absence of movement, but rather the infinite profusion and overlapping of patterns of alternation, that produces this impression of stillness. Since within this vision the given universe is seen as a self-contained world, inherently complete if not perfect, such that movement in any given direction has no particular significance, the journey or quest topos of such importance in Western allegory is relegated to a minor position in the Chinese tradition, a fact that perhaps goes a long way to explain the non-appearance of epic in that literature. Significantly, even in the examples of allegorical journeys that do occur,ᵛ the main emphasis is more on horizontal breadth than vertical depth of experience, and in *Hsi-yu Chi*, at any rate, the reader is clearly warned that the idea of a literal quest is wrong-headed from the very start.

In discussing the Chinese conception of a universe of ceaseless flux whose patterns of cyclical alternation add up to the

ᵘBurke's definition of synedoche as "representation" seems to describe quite well this Chinese "master trope," although he goes on to speak of it as if it were an "equation" of two terms.[53]

ᵛCf. *Hsi-yu Chi*, translated by Arthur Waley as *Monkey* (John Day, 1943), and *Ching-hua Yüan*, translated by Lin Tai-yi as *Flowers in the Mirror* (Berkeley, 1965).

total vision that comprises the object of encyclopedic allegory, we are easily tempted to cite a cluster of strikingly similar ideas in the Western tradition. Such passages as

> Pensa, lettor, s'io mi maravigliava,
> Quando vedea la cosa in sè star queta,
> E nell'idolo suo si trasmutava.
> (Purg. xxxi: 124–126)

and

> All be he subject to mortalitie,
> Yet is eterne in mutabilitie,
> And by succession made perpetuall,
> Transformed oft, and chaunged diverslie.
> (F.Q. iii: vi: 47)

within our allegorical texts would seem to indicate precisely the vision of permanence within change that has been singled out as characteristic of the Chinese tradition. It will be necessary, therefore, to pursue this question in greater detail, in order to locate the meaningful distinctions between the Chinese and the Western concepts of mutability. In the following discussion, it will be convenient to distinguish the same two general lines of reasoning described above in connection with the problem of duality: the antithetical approach implicit in the concept of Fortune, and the hierarchical one associated with the figure of Natura." In practice, of course, the two idea-clusters are often intricately interwoven, as in Spenser's Mutabilitie Cantos.

In the Medieval and Renaissance conception of Fortune, the entire system of observable mutability, along with its baggage of cyclical recurrence, is set off as something genuinely opposed to, or at least clearly distinguished from, the eternal World-Soul or Godhead by which the ideal of self-contained im-

---

"Cf. Northrop Frye, *Anatomy of Criticism* (Princeton, 1957): "To the extent that the encyclopaedic form concerns itself with the cycle of human life, an ambivalent female archetype appears in it, sometimes benevolent, sometimes sinister, but usually presiding over ... the cyclical movement."[54]

mutability is conceived, "the pillours of eternity, That is contrayr to Mutabilitie."[55] Whether the "regne of variaunce" subject to Fortune is conceived of as limited to the sublunar realm, or is extended to include the planetary spheres, as Spenser's Titanesse convincingly asserts, it is in both cases an imperfect dominion. We need not, however, go so far as to characterize the mutability of Fortune as evil in itself.[x] In the classical tradition inherited by the Latin Middle Ages, Fortuna is seen not as a demon, but as a quasi-goddess endowed with the authority to rule within her circumscribed dominion: ". . . fortune, That us governeth alle as in commune."[57] When viewed with neither intoxication nor rancor, Fortuna appears profoundly beautiful. Her iconographic blindness associates her more with the incomplete vision of the Synagogue, or the impartial sight of Justice, than with Satanic darkness. While Fortuna is strictly barred from the precincts of heaven:

> D'autre part ce rest chose expresse
> vos fetes Fortune deesse
> et jusques es cex la levez,
> ce que pas fere ne devez,
> qu'il n'est mie droiz ne reson
> qu'el ait en paradis meson:
> el n'est pas si bien eüreuse,
> ainz a meson trop perilleuse.
> (R.R. 5883–5890)

within her own sphere at least, she reigns supreme:

> Questa provede, giudica, e persegue
> Suo regno come il loro li altri dei.
> (Inf. vii: 86–87)

Since Fortune may potentially bring either prosperity or adversity upon her subjects, her dwelling is often represented iconographically by the combined presence in a single place of two trees, two rocks, two gates, or some such juxtaposed

[x]As Frye implies: ". . . a constant rotation within the order of nature is demonic in itself."[56]

112

duality. The ambiguous Isle of Fortune receives its fullest treatment in *The Romance of the Rose* (5891–6062), but it may also be detected in the grove of Fradubio and the "rocke" of Guyle in *The Faerie Queene*, or in the garden-gate in Chaucer's *Parlement of Foules*.

On the other hand, to the extent that all becoming and change in the world of finite forms moves steadily toward death, the workings of Fortune come to be viewed not as ambiguous, but exclusively in terms of the dark and threatening aspects of existence. Thus we find the extensive use of storm motifs in the allegorical texts, by which the elements of regular atmospheric change are "depraved" into "racking whirlwinds" and "blake wawes" which buffet rather than embrace the inhabitants of Fortune's realm.[z] Within the context of the allegorical sea-voyage, these elements appear in the form of hazardous rocks and treacherous whirlpools, as in Guyon's stormy passage to the Bower of Bliss. To those who are personally afflicted by such noxious influences, the Boethian argument that such phenomena are simply the manifestation of divine Providence in time is usually scant comfort, with the result that Fortune becomes the butt of bitter complaint in most of her appearances in allegory. Not only self-deluders such as Chaucer's Troilus: "For wel fynde I that Fortune is my fo" (I: 837), but even Spenser's grace-bearing Una: "And fye on Fortune, mine avowed foe" (I: viii: 43), and Prince Arthur himself: ". . . such happinesse/Heven doth to me envy, and Fortune favourlesse" (II: ix: 7), are prone to treat the embodiment of mutability as an adversary. These latter plaintiffs may perhaps be pardoned as simply venting spleen, so long as they do not accept Fortune as the true source of their trials. Those who do believe their own words, however, and "complain that Fate/Free Virtue should enthrall to Force or Chance,"[58] join the unconsoled Boethius in his dungeon of ignorance.

One iconographic representation of the Fortune concept of

---

[z] Cf. the use of the term *fortuna* or *ventura* as a literal storm, Howard R. Patch, *The Goddess Fortuna in Medieval Literature* (Cambridge, Mass., 1927), p. 39f., and Hollander, *Allegory*, p. 181.

113

particular interest to us here, insofar as it seems to coincide with the Chinese notion of cyclical recurrence, is the Wheel of Fortune emblem, the "ever-whirling wheele," also appearing in the form of a crystal ball, *ouroboros*-ring (F.Q. IV: x: 40) or other presentation of formal circularity. Theoretically, the wheel image may be interpreted as indicating the same sense of ceaseless alternation within a closed system that we have attributed here to the Chinese view of temporal process. It must be pointed out, therefore, that in actual literary practice Fortune functions not in a truly cyclical motion, but instead in a decidedly unilinear trajectory. That is, though the philosophical rationalization of terrestrial contingency admits both prosperity and adversity into the system of constant alternation, the mimesis of Fortune in literature concerns itself almost exclusively with the downward swing alone. Fortune's Wheel raises "fortunate" men such as Chaucer's Troilus to glory, only to dash them in the mud. Significantly, once man (or angel) has fallen due to shortsighted reliance on the gifts of Fortune at the top of the wheel, his humbling remains a lasting state. Although we find isolated references to the ability of Fortune to raise her subjects on the same wheel (F.Q. VI: viii: 46; T. & C. III: 1714), these are largely lip-service—generally from the lips of Fortune's servants—to a concept of circularity that is contrary to the aesthetic structure of allegory. As far as Fortune alone is concerned, the circle ends at the bottom of its revolution. Perhaps the clearest example of this fact may be found in Dante's "fortune canto" (Inf. VII), where those who placed their faith in the "ben che son commessi alla Fortuna" (l. 62) are damned to eternally trace the semi-circle they had accepted as the full picture. In the same way, the two crystal stones in the Narcissan fountain of *The Romance of the Rose* (the two rocks of Fortune's dwelling, in miniature) reflect at any given moment only half of the total garden:

> car torjors, quel que part qu'il soit,
> l'une moitié dou vergier voit;
> et c'il se torne, maintenant

> porra veoir le remenant
> (R.R. 1561–1564)

This is not to say, of course, that the Western literary universe makes no provision (providence) for an upswing as well. It is extremely important, however, that the missing section of the circle is supplied only through an act of an altogether separate order. The power that "upholdeth all that fall" is absolutely other than the circumscribed dominion of Fortune. It is wholly outside the circle of recurrence or, more precisely, it is an arc of the circle to which the swing of mutability can never reach. As a result, Fortune and Providence provide a clear antithesis of possibilities:

> Shal I clepe hyt hap other grace
> That broght me there? Nay, but Fortune
> (Duchess: 810–811)

> L'amico mio, e non della ventura
> (Inf. II: 61)

even though the latter's power is infinitely superior. Significantly, once the incomplete circle of Fortune is "perfected" by the motion of redemption the cycle comes to a definite end, so that what at first sight seemed to be a cyclical pattern must in fact be viewed as a series of unilinear movements with a precise direction and destination at every point. Dante, at any rate, seems to have such a formal structure in mind, when he analyzes his circular rose-symbol into two hemispheres, one pre-incarnational with its end-point in cosmic humiliation and the other approaching its redemptive end, which together form a single, non-repeating "cycle" of history. The circle motif is valuable, therefore, in expressing the sense of separation and return so basic to the Western literary experience, as long as the curvature of the lines is not permitted to obscure their essential unilinearity. But it should not be confused with the more truly "cyclical" repetitiveness, the ceaseless alternation, which was described in an earlier chapter as a unique feature of Chinese narrative.

Within the context of the preceding discussion of the circular
comprehension of experienced fall and promised rise, the literary categories "tragedy" and "comedy" take on a specific
dimension of meaning. We may note that in Christian allegory
of the type examined in this study the course of tragedy traces
a trajectory from the height of glory to the depth of despair:
ⅎ, while true "divine" comedy, wherever it starts, must end
with a final upward rise to (towards) a state of glory that will
never fall again: ⌐. Such, at least, is the view of tragedy and
comedy held by such lights of Western literature as Boethius:
"What else does the cry of tragedy bewail but the overthrow of
happy realms by the unexpected blow of Fortune?"[59] and
D. W. Robertson.[aa]

The true tragedy of Fortune, of course, lies not in the actual
onset of adversity, but rather in the spiritual blindness of those
who are bedazzled by her illusory gifts, most often taking the
form of a voluntary subjection to the "fikelnesse" and "brotel-
nesse" of Earthly love. The possibility of comic grace, on the
other hand comes to those who accept the unchallengeable rule
of Fortune as the temporal manifestation of Providence:

> Mes pren bon queur et si t'avance
> de recevoir en paciance
> tout quan que Fortune te done,
> soit bele ou lede, ou male ou bone.
> (R.R. 6821–6824)

> Tanto vogl'io che vi sia manifesto,
> Pur che mia coscienza non mi garra,
> Che alla Fortuna, come vuol, son presto.

> Non è nuova alli orecchi miei tal arra:
> Però giri Fortuna la sua rota
> Come le piace, e 'l villan la sua marra.
> (Inf. xv: 91–96)

Just as destruction is the necessary end of reliance on earthly

[aa]Cf. D. W. Robertson's article "Chaucerian Tragedy" in ELH, XIX
(1952), p. 1.

ALLEGORY

power, so salvation is the assured end-point of faith in divine love.

The apparent inevitability of these two end-points, however, leads to a knotty problem of interpretation. If the mighty must be cast down and the humble upraised, what is the significance of one individual's choice of allegiance? In other words, where is the free will of fiction in a literary universe of cosmic necessity? Each of our Western allegorical texts turns for a way out to the apt Boethian solution of conditional necessity[ab]: "Therefore, from the standpoint of divine knowledge these things are necessary because of the condition of their being known by God; but, considered only in themselves, they lose nothing of the absolute freedom of their own natures."[60] But to the extent that the encyclopedic poet's reduction of all existence into a single volume imitates the providential vision, no elements of his allegorical structure can, in fact, be "considered only in themselves." At best, therefore, the question remains an open one, depending for its balance on the degree to which the storyteller's impulse for dramatic development informs the poet's mimesis of divine authorship. Among our texts, the balance between the two is perhaps most finely precarious in *Paradise Lost*, where the knowledge of the end stated in the first line of the poem is so immanent that only the consummate skill of the poet keeps it at bay as the story gets told. Perhaps the essential ambiguity on this point in most allegorical fiction—which brings us back to the radical disjunction of vision within which we have seen the concept of Fortune to function—may be traced to the tension between the epic and romance elements in the Renaissance encyclopedic tradition. That is, the dimension of necessity implicit in the determinism of epic unity and the "free choice" that follows from romance contingency combine to set a literary stage in which human action is both predictable and significant at the same time.

A second somewhat different set of views on the problem of

[ab]E.g., R.R. 17237–17512, T.&C. iv: 1011–1078, Purg. xvi: 67–81, Par. xvii: 37–42, Par. xx: 130–138, P.L. v: 235–238, 524–534, ix: 349–352, x: 43–47, etc.

117

mutability in Western literature clusters about the concept of Nature. In some cases it is difficult to distinguish Natura from Fortuna, due to their common representation as what Frye calls "female archetypes" of recurrent change in the finite universe, but in fact the notion of Nature is ultimately based upon the logical method of hierarchical ordering, as opposed to the antithetical juxtaposition, of the physical and metaphysical realms. As a result, the multivalent processes of mutability at work in nature are here perceived as good and true, so long as they are "used" (in the Augustinian sense) or directed towards the *summum bonum* from which the plenitude of earthly bounty originally flows. Thus Nature becomes a Dame, whose beauty:

> Car Dex, li biaus outre mesure,
> quant il biauté mist en Nature,
> il an i fist une fontaine
> tourjorz courant et tourjorz plaine,
> de cui toute biauté desrive,
> mes nus n'an set ne fonz ne rive.
> (R.R. 16203–16208)

and majesty:

> Then forth issewed (great goddesse) great Dame Nature,
> With goodly port and gracious majesty,
> Being far greater and more tall of stature
> Then any of the gods or powers on hie
> (F.Q. vii: vii: 5)

are umbriferously analogous to those of the First Cause Himself. Because of these attributes, the larger concept of Nature is sometimes represented by the more specific figure of Venus in the hands of less meticulous allegorists than Dante and Spenser, who may fail to distinguish between the entire machine and its principal motor.[ac]

The figure of Natura, then, is an icon for the entire system of growth and decay by which the created universe continues to

[ac]Perhaps following the lead of Lucretius (Book i). Characters, of course, may also be prone to this misattribution, e.g. Scudamour (F.Q. iv: x: 47).

exist and sustain its inhabitants. It may perhaps be contained
in the Renaissance conception of "organism" described by
Poulet as a "network of interchanges and reciprocal influences which was animated, which was guided interiorly in its
cyclical development by a force everywhere the same and
perpetually diversified . . . ,"[61] but it certainly predates that
period. Thus Natura does not represent any single principle
or process, but rather the attribute of orderliness perceivable
within the sum total of all processes bounded by the coordinates of space and time. The lesser patterns of orderly mutability typically singled out to demonstrate her regime include
the operations of the "four contraries":

> Nature, the vicaire of the almyghty Lord,
> That hot, cold, hevy, lyght, moyst, and dreye
> Hath knyt by evene noumbres of acord.
> (P.F. 379–381)

the cycles of the months and seasons, as in Spenser's final
cantos, and all the bodily functions that follow the laws of
birth, maturation, death, and regeneration, particularly the
latter.

Two important features of Nature's system, therefore, are
inexhaustible fecundity and constant motion. These two concepts are often combined in the recurrent images of productive
labor that appear in each of our allegorical texts. Some of the
clearest examples of the ceaseless activity of nature in its proper
state have been pointed out by Hollander, in connection with
Dante's Matelda, and Hawkins, in his discussion of Spenser's
cycle of months. The hammers and other tools with which
Dame Nature herself takes charge of production are a further
elaboration of an idea that, though tempered with irony in
The Romance of the Rose and parodied in Spenser's Cave of
Mammon:[ad]

> · · · and all this worldes good,
> For which men swinck and sweat incessantly,

[ad]A similar parody may be seen in the House of Care (IV: v: 33–36).

Fro me do flow into an ample flood,
And in the hollow earth have their eternall brood.
(F.Q. II: vii: 8),

is reaffirmed in the stamping out of human forms in Spenser's
Garden of Adonis as well as in Dante's Paradise (XIII: 76–81).

With practically unlimited resources and such an enthusiastic
labor force, Nature, it would seem, functions as a totally self-
contained, "Self-sufficing Perfection,"[62] an Unmoved Mover
in her own right:

> This great grandmother of all creatures bred,
> Great Nature, ever young yet full of eld,
> Still mooving, yet unmoved from her sted,
> Unseene of any, yet of all beheld
> (F.Q. VII: vii: 13)

In each of our texts, however, we ultimately learn that the
organic system of Nature, for all its bounty and seeming self-
sufficiency, cannot stand alone. Her realm is ordered by a
"genius" far beyond the powers of human ingenuity, but it is
by definition incomplete, in that it encompasses less than the
totality of existence. The precise expression of this incompleteness takes many forms, ranging from Dame Nature's
ironic exhaustion in The Romance of the Rose or her empathetic
groan in Paradise Lost:

> Earth trembl'd from her entrails, as again
> In Pangs, and Nature gave a second groan,
> Sky lour'd and muttering Thunder, some sad drops
> Wept at completing of the mortal Sin
> Original;
> (P.L. IX: 1000–1004)

to the vague longing for rest that hangs over the otherwise
bountiful energy of Spenser's cantos. The unpleasant fact must
sooner or later emerge that Nature, unlike the Godhead, has
an external enemy: the threat of non-being, which stands to
her in the same relation of Timaean envy that sets Spenser's

Mutability against the gods and Milton's Lucifer against the Son. To the extent that it is this essentially optimistic, hierarchical view of phenomenal change with which we are dealing, we may have faith in Nature's continual victory over cosmic death through regeneration. Her advantage, however, is always precarious in the running battle whose pace is set by the adversary, "For who sees not that Time on all doth pray?" As a result, Nature must constantly look for aid to the top of the hierarchy that defines her existence. In simpler terms, the organic system of nature is limited to the sublunar, or otherwise demarcated, sphere of finite creation, and is logically subordinated to the First Cause. Nature both derives directly from God:

> Come natura lo suo corso prende
> Da divino intelletto e da sua arte;
> (Inf. xi: 99–100)

and is rightly expected to serve his Will:

> Nul autre droit je n'i reclaime,
> ainz le merci quant il tant m'aime
> Que si tres povre damoisele,
> an si grant meson et si bele,
> il, si grant sires, tant me prise
> qu'il m'a por chamberiere prise.
> Por chamberiere? certes vaire
> por connetable et por vicaire,[ae]
> don je ne fusse mie digne,
> for par sa volanté benigne.
> (R.R. 16745–16754)

It was stated that within this hierarchical view of existence, the finite level of nature is in some sense ordered, or linked, to the higher realm of truth and perfection. In order to emphasize the intercourse rather than the disparity between the two realms, however, a path of communication must be provided in the system. This element, of course, is the conception of

[ae]Cf. Chaucer: "Nature, the vicaire. . .," cited above.

Love as a flow between Self and Other on both the personal and the cosmic levels, which has played such a central role in the Western literary tradition that it is almost inconceivable to refer to the relations between the created universe and its source of being without treating the theme of divine and human love. Thus, the great chain of being appears in literature as the "faire cheyne of love." Using the analogy of the human sexual experience, the "self-transcendent fecundity" of Divine Providence is evinced by metaphors involving shining eyes, spontaneous warmth, and harmonious marriage. Of particular importance for us here is the power of love to attract a lover in the direction of his beloved, since the allegorization of the process may shadow forth the principal attribute of the Prime Mover, while at the same time establishing the direction of motion on which we have seen allegorical structure to be based. In the *Commedia* we find the clearest examples of the identification of love and movement. Not only does Love move the celestial spheres: "L'amor che move il sole e l'altre stelle," but it penetrates the darkest woods of Earth to set the pilgrim in motion toward his goal: "Amor mi mosse, che mi fa parlare" (Inf. II:72).[af] Dante's further association of love with light has no explicit basis in human love, but we need not resort to an elaborate discourse on the common origins of sun and sex symbolism, such as Dunbar provides, to see the inherent congeniality of the two concepts, particularly when they are both associated with warmth.

Like nearly everything in the Western allegorical universe, however, love is subject to right and wrong use. In his impatient fallen state, man is apt to abandon the proper source of Love and turn toward more immediate objects, the pursuit of which amounts to idolatry. Descriptions of this process, of course, occupy a major portion of the corpus of Western allegory. The point that concerns us most closely here, in our discussion of the self-contained system of Nature, is the fact that such attempts to replace charity with cupidity are generally reducible to cases of self-love. The theme of self-love takes many forms

[af]The "mi" is Beatrice, who in turn moves the pilgrim.

in our allegorical texts, from the simple misuse of sexual pleasure: "Moore for delit than world to multiplye" (*Nun's Priest's Tale*: 3345), or the explicit worship of a self-image, as in the Narcissus and Pygmalion pieces in *The Romance of the Rose*, to the tragic flaw of vanity:

> Ne me to love, a wonder it is nought;
> For wel woot I myself, so God me spede,
> Al wolde I that noon wiste of this thought,
> I am oon the faireste, out of drede,
> And goodlieste, whoso taketh hede,
> And so men seyn, in al the town of Troie.
> What wonder is though he of me have joye?
> (T. & C. II: 743–749)

In Spenser, finally, the implications of self-love are pushed to their ultimate conclusion and clearly labelled as sterile "peepes" and wanton "toyes": "Such love is hate and such desire is shame" (III: i: 50).

Perhaps still more sinister than idolatry of the self is its outward manifestation in pride, "for pride and love may ill agree."[63] The theme of arrogant self-sufficiency is extremely prominent in Christian allegory as a negative transformation of the conception of love as self-transcendence. In addition to its most explicit treatment by Spenser (Braggadocchio, Orgoglio, Disdain, the House of Pride) and Dante (the Terrace of Pride), the haughtiness of assumed self-sufficiency rises before us in the guise of Saracens, Persians, and other Eastern potentates, notably Nimrod, whose brazen tower is rebuilt in various forms in each of our texts (pandemonium, the Palace of Lucifer, the Castle of Jealousy, the Temples of Venus). The same motif is also at work in the parade of giants and other overblown monsters that lumber through Milton's Hell and Spenser's fairyland, with perhaps the most audacious appearance in the Titanesse of the Mutabilitie Cantos.[ag] The true horror of the giants, however, is not simply their fearful size

[ag]The words "selfe" and "bold" occur with incantational repetitiveness in the first Mutabilitie Canto ("bold" six times in ten stanzas, 21–30).

and power in the service of evil, but rather the vaunt of over-weening self-sufficiency with which they challenge the hierarchical dependence of the natural universe on its Maker. The upshot of such Titanic self-affirmation is blasphemy, incest (Lucifer and Sin, the parents of Argante and Ollyphant), and tyranny, all of which unite in the single self of Milton's Fiend. Possibly the most heinous of all allegorical representations of outrageous self-reliance is realized in Satan's denial of the very creation of the universe:

> We know no time when we were not as now;
> Know none before us, self-begot, self-rais'd
> By our own quick'ning power, when fatal course
> Had circl'd his full Orb, the birth mature
> Of this our native Heav'n, Ethereal Sons.
>   (P.L. v: 859–863)

We have attempted here to demonstrate that the concept of a self-contained natural universe in the Western literary tradition differs radically from its Chinese counterpart in that this system, in its entirety, is inextricably imbedded in a dual ontological structure within which it constitutes the lesser phase of being; whereas in the Chinese scheme the realm of flux is seen as *including* rather than *excluded from* the ultimate truth. It is interesting, therefore, that the figure of Dame Nature in the Western tradition seems in many respects to be identical to the Chinese "goddess" Nü-kua described in Chapter II. Both figures are mythologized as overtaxed creatrices of transitory natural forms, both are associated with the principle of orderly cohesion of the elements of phenomenological change, and both serve as initiatory guides into the mysteries of human union and regeneration.

Perhaps the most obvious difference between the realms subject to these two "goddesses" is the manner in which the human sexual relation is built into their respective systems. The concept of love as the energy of cosmic attraction or the out-pouring of divine bounty that breathes life-force into the finite universe and binds it to the source of Being, of course, has no meaning to the unilevel Chinese system. Consequently the abstract notion of love is peripheral at best in Chinese philosophical thought, replaced instead by the concepts of harmonious union and finely ordered kinship relations. If marriage is the "solution to the problem of love"[64] in the Western tradition, the image of "wedded Love" in Chinese literature evokes far sooner an idea of stationary symmetry than one of dynamic movement or energy informing matter.

It would be possible to conclude from this and the preceding discussion that the Chinese world-view is more practical and the Western more idealistic, or that they correspond roughly to the "this-worldly" and "other-worldly" outlooks described by Lovejoy. It is hoped, however, that the preceding pages have demonstrated that the Chinese literary tradition is equally concerned with an unseen dimension of meaning beyond the surface configurations of its texts, while conversely the Western striving towards absolute Truth remains grounded in the surface details which support the metaphorical projection. The significant difference between the two traditions seems to lie in the precise relationship that holds between sense and *sententia*. We have seen how the Western literary vision in general, and allegory in particular, moves "upward" by the logical relations of similarity and difference yoked together in metaphor to approach a ground of eternal Being that lies by definition beyond the temporal process of becoming. The Chinese allegorist, on the other hand, looks *outward* towards a total vision that remains inaccessible only due to the vastness of space. He strives for *extension* where his Western counterpart seeks elevation through *intension*. The term "spatial" to describe the Chinese view may perhaps be misleading, in that it seems to overlap with the Boethian idea of the simultaneous present-ness of providential vision: ". . . And such a condition should be seen, according to Boethius, under the category of spatial form rather than that of temporal process or extension: not *praevidentia*, but *providentia*—the prospect, as it were, from a mountaintop."[65] Yet it must be repeated that such a total vision, in the Western tradition, is reserved for God alone, while fallen man may strive to *approach* this vision of simultaneity only through the *process* of temporal and historical revelation. Even when truth is expressed "spatially," as in Spenser's pageants or Dante's flashes of insight in moments extracted from time, the whole thrust of allegorical structure consists in *linking* such isolated moments of intelligibility into a causal progression that is in the final analysis temporal in nature.

CHAPTER VI

WESTERN ALLEGORICAL
GARDENS

THE following three chapters will consist of a direct examination of one specific *topos*: the garden or earthly paradise, as an example of the structure and functioning of allegory in the Chinese and Western traditions. We must again apologize for the attempt to reduce the monumental encyclopedic works that form the object of this study to a single point of comparison. It will, however, be maintained that the treatment of the garden motif, in each case, serves as a nexus for the entire problem of the aesthetic structure of encyclopedic allegory, and that the characteristic solutions to the problem in the Western literary gardens present a clear contrast to those taken in the garden of *Dream of the Red Chamber*.[a]

In both the Chinese and the Western literary traditions, the presence of a delimited landscape of earthly delights serves as an attempt to grasp in concrete terms the "other" dimension of significance by which we have defined allegory. It may be described as a telescoping of the encyclopedically conceived universe down to proportions that are commensurable with the evocative powers of the poet and his tradition, and to the demand for mimetic credibility on the part of his audience. In view of the distinction drawn in the preceding chapter between the "horizontal" and "vertical" perspectives of Chinese and Western allegory, it is perhaps not accidental that the concourse between the Western gardens and the remainder of existence is often seen in terms of ascension (Dante) or

---

[a] It may be noted that the association of the earthly paradise with a dream-vision in Western literature (the *Romance of the Rose, Parlement of Foules*, and perhaps the *Commedia*) is borne out in the Chinese text.

descent and fall (Milton), as opposed to the horizontal excursions that define the location of the Ta-kuan Yüan garden with respect to the universe beyond its walls. This ontological thrust, as described by Eliade: "the irruption of the sacred does not only project a fixed point into the formless fluidity of profane space, a center into chaos; it also effects a break in the plane, that is, it opens communication between the cosmic planes (between earth and heaven) and makes possible ontological passage from one mode of being to another,"[1b] contrasts sharply with the Chinese garden projection, although in both cases it is the intersection of finite creation and infinitude which is at issue.

Let us not, however, neglect our own gardens. Since a number of studies exist in which the common features of the Christian *locus amoenus* are traced back from the bowers of Tasso and Camoens to their sources in scriptural paradise and classical pastoral,[c] we will concern ourselves here with the precise manner in which the five poets use their gardens to establish, and attempt to "unify," the dual ontological structure of allegory. We shall see that the various examples in our texts may, at the risk of oversimplification, be categorized according to the same two general patterns of resolving duality discussed above: the antithetical view in which the disparity between the true earthly paradise and its negative transformations is stressed; and the hierarchical view, which uses the circumscribed garden to figure forth, by analogy of form, the celestial paradise to which it is ordered as a lesser to a greater truth. Of course, the two possibilities are in fact two sides of the same coin (much as we have seen the relations of similarity

[b]In his bid for universality Eliade cites the Chinese Altar of Heaven as an example of just such a "center of the world," but he fails to distinguish its function as a centripetal nucleus, rather than a point of passage.

[c]See Ernst Robert Curtius, *European Literature and the Latin Middle Ages* (New York, 1953); Joseph Ellis Duncan, *Milton's Earthly Paradise* (Minneapolis, 1972); Harry Levin, *The Myth of the Golden Age in the Renaissance* (Bloomington, Indiana, 1969); and A. Bartlett Giamatti, *The Earthly Paradise and the Renaissance Epic* (Princeton, 1966) in bibliography.

and difference combine in the trope of metaphor on which the allegorical projection of truth is based). Thus it may be argued that both the true and the false gardens function to affirm, by positive or negative statement, the attributes of the celestial paradise, while conversely the similarity between the hierarchically ordered earthly garden and its heavenly Idea serves primarily to reinforce the ontological disjunction between them. Yet the differentiation will be retained here on the grounds that our actual texts provide us with two distinct types of literary gardens in practice. Without making too much of the terms themselves, we will find it convenient to refer to the two types as "tropological" and "anagogical" respectively, in the sense that the space artificially roped off in each garden serves either as a setting for significant human action in the former case, or as a structural model of truth in the latter.

Before proceeding, we will find it necessary to review briefly some of the major motifs in the classical and scriptural tradition inherited by the Christian poets, so that we will be able to distinguish the allegorically significant elements from those which are simply retained as a "poetical requisite."[2] All of the studies mentioned above agree that nearly every specific feature of the *locus amoenus* was available in at least some corner of the pagan heritage. Such features include geographical remoteness enforced by a water barrier, a benign profusion of trees, flowers, birds, and animals, often presented in the form of a "catalogue,"[3] fertile well-watered soil producing abundant fruit and grain with a minimum of labor, and a pleasant climate fanned by warm (West) breezes. As a setting for earthly love, the pastoral landscape might boast intoxicating fragrances and colors, soft grassy banks, cool refreshing shade, and the leisure and privacy with which to enjoy them. Interestingly enough, nearly all of these amenable motifs may be found in one locus clustering about the Garden of Alkinoos in the *Odyssey* (Books VI and VII), although they most likely reached the Middle Ages by diverse routes (notably Virgil's pastoral poems).

With the development of the Christian scriptural and

exegetical tradition and its geographic shift to the more continental climate and topography of Western Europe, certain changes in emphasis seem to emerge in the handling of the garden *topos*. One of the most marked changes is the importance now placed upon the enclosed nature of the garden, with the particular ramifications in terms of vertical orientation described above. This is not to say that pagans had never used the wall image as a frame to set off a delightful scene, but rather to point out the extremely important role of the "garden inclosed" of the Song of Songs in the Christian exegetical tradition, as it came to provide both the method for the proper use of sensual beauty and earthly love, and a specific list of images: turtledoves, towers of ivory, etc., with which to evoke them. As a result, the very mention of a walled garden in Christian literature immediately implies a fully realized standard against which to measure its right or wrong use in a given occurrence. The enclosure may take the form of a wall of fire, as in Dante's Earthly Paradise and Milton's postlapsarian Eden,[d] a castle rampart, or even a dry ditch in Chaucer's *Nun's Priest's Tale*, but in each case it provides an essentially moral focus on the actions of those within (the primary feature of the garden of Genesis).

A second significant modification in the Christian adaptation of the pagan garden *topos* may be noted in the increased use of a mountain location in place of the insular motif, particularly in such hierarchically conceived gardens as Dante's Earthly Paradise, Spenser's Garden of Adonis and Arlo Hill, and Milton's prelapsarian Eden.[e] This may be explained partly by the geographical shift of the tradition to land-based societies, but it may be better understood in terms of the vertical redirection of vision discussed earlier. In the same sense, we must interpret the preference for bright sunlight over protective

[d]Cf. Eliade's description of the "wall of fire" in shamanistic ritual.[4]
[e]The Greeks, of course, had their delightful mountains, an association not missed by Dante in framing his purgatorial garden (XXXI: 141), but the doctrinal necessity of the mountaintop in Christian paradises seems nevertheless clear. It may be noted that the garden of Genesis is not specifically elevated, while a "mountain of spices" appears in the Canticles.

shade, or the substitution of fountains and wells for flowing streams, in terms of specifically Christian symbolism, rather than the influence of a cooler and wetter climatic orientation. As we shall see shortly, the accumulation of images with explicitly Christian associations results in the establishment of a total *paysage moralisée* against which characters praise or damn themselves by their own actions.

This is not to say, of course, that the obviously pagan elements were subsequently dropped from the tradition. Nor can we agree with Lewis that the Christian transmitters of classical garden motifs were simply acting "under the pretext of allegory"[5] to justify dealing with sensually pleasing images. Instead, the allegorical poets under consideration here seem to make a careful selection of pagan motifs in accordance with the demands of Christian art. That is, those elements which do not conflict with Christian symbolism are freely retained, while those with clearly pre-Christian associations are reserved to identify the false, or at least the incomplete, versions of earthly delight. For example, the island sanctuaries of Spenser's Phaedria and his Venus of Book IV label themselves by their very pleasance as paradises of an illusory or incomplete nature, respectively. Similarly, the catalogues of trees in Chaucer's *Parlement of Foules*, Milton's unfallen Eden, and Spenser's wandering woods (I:i:8–9) seem in themselves to add a sinister hint of paganism to the landscapes. On the other hand, the fragrances in Dante's Valley of Princes or the mild wind in his Earthly Paradise are not out of place since they do not interfere with Christian symbolism.

Turning now to what we have termed the tropological gardens, let us consider some of the ways in which the original neutrality of the natural setting is turned into a dramatic stage for moral action. It must be repeated at the outset that all iconographically "false" gardens may be taken as negative transformations of the true, while all "true" examples are by their very incompleteness illusory copies of the Idea of paradise. The point, however, is not that such gardens are morally ambiguous, since the choice of how to "use" them, *in bono* or *in malo,* presents a clear standard of values at any given moment. More precisely, we may state that the very existence of ambiguity in our minds and the minds of the characters of an allegorical fiction is a blatant symptom, in such gardens, of wrong use. By "use," of course, we refer to a mental process of recognition or spiritual re-direction, in the Augustinian sense, that either precedes or forestalls the *quid agas* step.

As soon as we follow an allegorical figure into a tropological garden, circumstantial evidence begins to mount up to indicate the manner in which the sensory objects presented are likely to be used. Generally, such evidence is damning. Theoretically, of course, iconographic details, or even full-blown icons, should not be taken as absolute proof of a tropological fall as long as the possibility of repentance or conversion remains open; but in practice such a turn-about is well nigh impossible, particularly insofar as the poet is concerned with an accurate mimesis of fallen man. If anything, any reversal usually proceeds in the opposite direction, as we shall see in Chaucer's *Parlement of Foules,* Spenser's Temple of Venus, and Milton's Eden, from the potential or actual "enjoyment" of created beauty to something less than this.

We have already seen that the presence of an enclosing wall, in itself, may serve more to evoke the proper pleasure of the canticular vision than to isolate the self-contained ego of those within. Even before entering the ground of delight, however, we may be alerted to the possibility of misreading the Song of Solomon, like Chaucer's January, as a ribald verse of "old lewed wordes." The Amant of *The Romance of the Rose,* for example, has already begun to cast doubts by his own self-description (98–102) and his unmistakably Narcissan pose (118–121), before he even reaches the Garden of Deduit. By the time he actually enters the grounds themselves, by his own admission through the wicket of accidia, we have seen him pass directly by an unequivocal lesson in the nature of earthly love only to conclude:

car tel joie ne tel deduit

132

ne vit mes hom, si com je cuit
(473–474)

As soon as the door is safely shut behind us, the tropological garden presents us with a host of iconographical imagery that, though potentially usable in praise of the true Maker of the garden, is turned under the weight of Adam's sin and centuries of Christian convention in an opposite direction. Thus, for example, the May morning of *The Romance of the Rose*, taken up with relish by Chaucer and bequeathed to Spenser

> Then came faire May, the fayrest mayd on ground,
> Deckt all with dainties of her seasons pryde,
> (F.Q. vii: vii: 34)

turns our attention from the springtime of Christian renewal to the fleeting pleasures of a "mayd on ground." Similarly, the fruit-laden trees may soon reveal their Saracen origins (R.R. 590), while their haughty boughs, ignorant of their incarnational implications, are used for unnatural production (R.R. 1328–1329), cuckoldry (the "pyrie" in the *Merchant's Tale*), and ultimately idolatry:

> So saying, from the Tree her step she turn'd,
> But first low Reverence done, as to the power
> That dwelt within, whose presence had infus'd
> Into the plant sciential sap . . .
> (P.L. ix: 834–837)

Of the same order are the furry creatures, whose significance is clear enough without the added touch of Anglo-French paronomasia, the garlands of flowers hung often enough on Priapus' staff to render the association conventional, and the merry caroling and "quaint" dancing that introduce the rites of the servants of earthly love:

> Les queroles ja remenoient,
> car tuit li plusor s'en aloient
> o lor amies ombroier
> soz ces arbres por donoier.

133

Dex! com menoient bone vie!
(R.R. 1289–1293)

Just in case the *in malo* drift of such iconographical details may still escape the reader, the allegorists go on to present full iconic figures: Narcissus and Pygmalion, Oiseuse and Acrasia, Phaedria and Priapus, whose very iconicity makes them objects of idolatry for the unwary.

The actual configurations of the abuse of worldly goods take many different forms in the allegorical texts. At the start of *The Romance of the Rose*, for example, the misuse seems pardonable as Amant, like many of his followers in the tradition, finds himself alone and without a guide (504–505) in a maze of uncertain paths, so that he sees the soft grass only as a place to "couchier come sus une coute" (1393), and treats the rosebud as a desired possession (1651–1652). By the end of the poem, however, Amant is guilty of a form of idolatry perhaps even graver than that of Narcissus and Pygmalion, since he has sworn fealty to the God of Love,[f] enlisted the aid of a venereal army, and perverted the ivory-pillar imagery of the Canticles into an altar of an altogether different sort. It is perhaps possible to view the final act of "love" as a means of achieving anagogic bliss, as Genius suggests and Gunn accepts, but with any degree of unprejudiced reading the assault on the rose-maiden (even granting her compliance) emerges as nothing more or less than a rape, and a particularly ugly and violent one at that.[g]

In Chaucer, the abuse of Venus' legitimate role typically takes a more domestic turn. Without pausing to review the "upsidoun" justification of improper enjoyment by such figures as the Wife of Bath, we may simply note the ways in which Chaucer ties the theme of "wo that is in mariage" to his tropological gardens. The inversion of hierarchical order that sees a wife as "parfit felicitee" (M.T. 1642), as a prize for martial or forensic combat (*Parlement, Knight's Tale*), or even

[f] Cf. Pandarus: "Immortal God . . . Cupid I mene" (*Troilus and Criseyde* III: 185–186).
[g] Perhaps Jean de Meun is taking up a hint in the unsavory love of Deduit and Leesce in the opening section (832–833).

as a valued lost possession (*Book of the Duchess*), is also apt to accept an enclosed garden of earthly delights as a full-fledged paradise on a par with those of Scripture.[h] In such a retreat, the leafy bower turns from a shrine into a boudoir, and the wall of enclosure, as in January's garden, is used as a shield of privacy, a means of hiding from the sight of God to engage in "disport."

This emphasis on idle, and thus sterile, play in the garden of delights finds its clearest expression in the patently false paradises of Spenser. Here the desire for sexual play without its proper goal in fruitful multiplication is reduced to its barren absurdity in the immobilized embraces of Phaedria, Acrasia, and the Venus of Castle Joyeous, a subtle parody of the regenerative activity of Nature's realm.

In order for such iconographically abused gardens to retain their tropological significance, however, the possibility of correcting their infelicitous condition must remain a real alternative. We have seen that the actual representation of moral *action* to restore the proper hierarchy of values is rarely emphasized in encyclopedic allegory. Even Guyon's final destruction of Acrasia's bower must be interpreted as an act of external grace, through the medium of the palmer, rather than as a moral triumph of the Knight of Temperance who remains weak-kneed to the very end.[i] Instead, the possibility of a successful struggle of the true against the false perception of the beauty of creation shifts its locus to the human mind itself. Perhaps the most important example of such a victory in the Christian tradition may be found in the psychomachia and ultimate conversion that occurs in Augustine's own private garden.[6] The "conversion"[j] of Dante the pilgrim in the garden at the summit of his purgatorial body seems to echo the earlier

[h]Cf. "je cuidai estre/por voir em paradis terrestre" (R.R. 633); "His fresshe May, his paradys" (M.T. 1822); "Or Eden selfe, if ought with Eden mote compayre" (F.Q. ii: xii: 52), etc.

[i]See Harry Berger, Jr.'s discussion of the "faint" in *The Allegorical Temper* (New Haven, 1957).

[j]Cf. Charles S. Singleton, *Dante Studies 2: Journey to Beatrice* (Cambridge, Mass., 1958), *passim*, and A. C. Charity, *Events and Their Afterlife* (Cambridge, Mass., 1966), Chapter 12.

work, as do the parodic garden-conversions of Chaucer's Troilus, or the Amant of *The Romance of the Rose*, to a faith of more immediate rewards. In connection with our earlier discussion of cosmic redemption as the intersection of grace in the otherwise incomplete cycle of Fortune's Wheel, the Christian tendency to associate tropological victory with the contemplative faculties in the garden of the soul is quite significant. It is in this sense that Dante's *active* pilgrimage (his moral journey), which ends with his conversion in the now-empty Garden of Eden, must continue on as a *contemplative* one until Beatrice finally "'mparadisa la mia mente," (Par. xxviii:3)[k] and delivers the pilgrim into the meditative hands of Bernard to be ushered into the presence of the highest figure of the *Commedia*. In the same way, Spenser's glimpse of the Sabaoths sight of paradisial rest occurs in the all-embracing mind, his own, which has served as the locus of six long books of psychomachia, while Milton makes it explicit that the paradise of faith and hope "within thee" has replaced the spatial Garden of Eden as the combined setting and reward of tropological victory.

This important shift in the locus of the true paradise does not, of course, preclude the possibility of its representation in positive imagery, as in the "biau parc" described by the Genius of *The Romance of the Rose*. Although Genius' iconographic decorum and the conclusions he draws from his own sermon clearly place him "smack in the middle of Deduit's garden,"[7] his description stands as a major attempt to realize the Idea of paradise in earthly figures. It is important to remember, moreover, that this case of positive evocation of the true paradise occurs in the earliest text of our study, and that even here it is set in a frame that detracts from its force as a tropological alternative (although not from its anagogical truth).[1] Interestingly enough, Genius' choice of images corresponds quite

[k]Milton's Satan, significantly, sees only that the primal parents are "Imparadis't in one another's arms" (P.L. iv: 506).

[1]Genius himself notes that his park differs, in two senses, from that of Adam (20565).

neatly to the examples cited by Frye to illustrate his concept of "apocalytic imagery."

Before turning now to the second category of Western allegorical gardens, we must consider in greater detail several tropological examples that seem to border on what we have styled the anagogical type. In the following discussion we should bear in mind that the original distinction drawn was between those gardens in which truth is set against falsity as a setting for a dramatic moral choice, and those in which earthly imperfection is ordered to celestial perfection through a series of hierarchical degrees that obviates the need for a tropological climax. It was seen that the two views are in fact obverse sides of a single problem of duality, but that their literary presentations fall into two distinct classes.

In Chaucer's *Parlement of Foules*, the difficulty presented by an initial situation of ambiguity is quickly resolved as iconographic details of falsity gain control of the piece. Even before entering the precincts of the garden itself, the reader finds that the inscriptions on the gate begin to provide clues by the fact that the choice between good and evil is phrased in parody of Dante's Hell-gate, "Thorgh me men gon . . . ," and even the "blysful place" is described in dangerously ambiguous terms: "lusty May," "good aventure," "Al open am I." Faced with this situation, the dreamer immediately confesses to a state of moral quandary:

> That oon me hette, that other dide me colde:
> No wit hadde I, for errour, for to chese,
> To entre or flen, or me to save or lese. (145–147)

such as we have already seen to be symptomatic of tropological misuse. He is quickly reassured that

> For this writyng nys nothyng ment bi the,
> Ne by non, but he Loves servaunt be: (158–159)

but upon meeting the figure of Cupid he immediately acknowledges him as "oure lord" (212). By this time, the catalogue of trees, the sweet song of birds, the scampering of "litel conyes" and other "bestes smale," and the rustling of leaves take on their clear iconographical significance, so that the gay dance of "dishevele" women (235) about the "temple of bras," the hot winds of Jelosye, the garlands with which Priapus is festooned, and Venus herself, "untressed" on a "bed of gold" in a "prive corner," present no further ambiguity. In the second section of the poem, however, Chaucer reverses his field to describe Dame Nature in hierarchical terms. Noting her surpassing beauty

> a queene
> That as of lyght the somer sonne shene
> Passeth the sterre, right so over mesure
> She fayrer was than any creature.   (298–301)

he sets Nature above the war of opposites encountered in the first section, as a "noble goddesse," "the vicaire of the almyghty Lord." Thus when he finally returns to the antithetical mode towards the end of the poem, allowing the Dame to assent to the formel egle's unreasonable request, it is with a lighter and surer sense of Nature's proper limitations, and he is ready now to offer a hymn to St. Valentine in praise of the true spring.

A similar problem of interpretation is encountered in Spenser's Temple of Venus episode. Like "Dan Geffrey" before him, Spenser moves in and out of the two approaches to the problem of sensual beauty in order to establish the two possible "uses" of Venus' gifts (although in both cases the opposition never comes down to an actual contest). The piece begins with images highly reminiscent of the Garden of Deduit in *The Romance of the Rose*: the hero Scudamour (or, Amant in search of his shield) appears outside a castle wall guarded by such vaguely familiar defenders as Doubt, Delay, and Danger, whose combined forces of deterrence are insufficient to prevent his entry. Once within the garden, the lover observes a scene that might well have come from the pen of Guillaume:

> And all without were walkes and alleyes dight
> With divers trees, enrang'd in even rankes;

138

WESTERN ALLEGORICAL GARDENS

And here and there were pleasant arbors pight,
And shadie seats, and sundry flowring bankes,
To sit and rest the walkers wearie shankes;
(IV: x: 25),

all of which confirms his opinion that he has reached "a second paradise." At this point, however, Scudamour's attention turns to "another sort" (26) of lovers, not subject to Cupid's rule, whose "bands of friendship" introduce the famous reconciliation of Love and Hate by Concord. But once again, Spenser here does an about-face and proceeds to depict Venus' "inmost temple" in the same language Chaucer had used for the conventional associations of idolatry: "marble pillors," "girlands gay," "fresh as May," "brasen caudrons," and the like. The inevitable conclusion of the imperfection or incompleteness of Venus herself, with her hermaphroditic, snakering, crystal ball, assumption of self-sufficiency: "She syre and mother is her selfe alone,/Begets and eke conceives, ne needeth other none" (41), is subsequently reinforced by the hosts of complaining lovers whose sadness seems to stem from their reliance on the circumscribed goddess alone: "So all the world by thee at first was made" (47). The point here is not that Spenser is unsure of the proper relation of permanence and mutability in the garden of this world, as Berger seems to suggest,[m] but simply that he recognizes the existence of two clear alternatives which define the coordinates of morality. While good and evil remain in constant antithesis until

time shall come that all shall changed bee,
And from thenceforth none no more change shall see,
(VII: vii: 59),

[m]Cf. Harry Berger, Jr., "The Mutabilitie Cantoes: Archaism and Evolution in Retrospect," in *Spenser: A Collection of Critical Essays* (Englewood-Cliffs, New Jersey, 1968), p. 173: "Having oscillated between the elemental divisions of pagan pessimism and the organic harmony of medieval optimism, he attains to a more complicated and dynamic equilibrium at the end, still looking backward, still thrusting forward, still revolving doubts."

139

it is the role of the virtuous man to exercise his free choice and use the delights of Venus' garden as the fulfillment of chaste Love:

> Blessed be the man that well can use his blis:
> Whose ever be the shield, faire Amoret be his.
>
> (IV: X: 8)

The nature of the Garden of Eden in *Paradise Lost* is still further complicated by the intricacy with which Milton has interwoven elements of Heaven and Hell to produce an earthly garden that is both fully true and fraught with falsity at the same time. As we have noted above, we may not properly speak of Milton's epic as an allegorical text, but the fact remains that he does draw upon and even deepen the Renaissance tradition of allegorical gardens in framing his own example of the *topos*. Given the primary concern with encyclopedic structure in Milton's poem, it is interesting that he spends far more time in developing the dramatic possibilities of the antithesis between truth and falsity than in defining the functions of his paradise within the cosmic hierarchy he no doubt envisions. On the "true" side, Milton describes the prelapsarian existence of Adam and Eve as an endless ritual of gratitude to their unseen Maker. Significantly, their paradise is not roofed over by its thick vegetation, but is open:

> a woody Theatre
> Of stateliest view. Yet higher than their tops
> The verdurous wall of Paradise up-sprung:
> Which to our general Sire gave prospect large
> Into his nether Empire neighbouring round.
>
> (IV:141–145)

The fertile hill, sweet fragrances, abundant fruit, soft breezes, and bird-song that identify their territory as a conventional paradise all seem to be properly "used" to glorify the source of this bounty. The primeval pair are busy all day in fulfillment of the commandment to keep their garden, and busy at night in fulfillment of the command to be fruitful. Their joyful

140

service to the "celestial messenger" Raphael[n] reflects their proper hierarchical relation to the Almighty, while Eve's willing subordination to her husband's government: "O thou for whom/And from whom I was form'd flesh of they flesh,/ And without whom am to no end, my Guide/And Head," (IV: 440–443), defines the perfection of their "wedded Love."

At the same time, however, Milton intermeddles his vision of tropological perfection with insinuations of imperfection that gradually coalesce to turn the blank prophecy of the first four lines of the poem into a clear alternative by the time a choice must be made. Until the final moment, of course, all these "fair defects" remain as innocent as the couple's "naked majesty," although nevertheless damnable from the fallen perspective for which they bear the original blame. Since these various flaws in the innocent texture of Milton's Eden have been treated at length by many critics, it will suffice here to note that such images as "vegetable gold," Adam's "blissful bower," the thornless rose (IV: 256), Eve's "dishevell'd . . . wanton ringlets," and many more harken back to the proud illusion of self-sufficiency and the sort of self-love that demands the uxorious capitulation of the reason to the senses, such as we see in so many false allegorical gardens. The point, again, is not that Milton's Garden of Eden is an unequivocally false one, but rather that it remains problematical, one in which the issue of cosmic obedience devolves upon the choice between submissive enjoyment or self-centered abuse of worldly goods.

The remaining two literary gardens encountered within the scope of this study—Dante's Earthly Paradise and Spenser's Garden of Adonis—have been isolated on the basis of their greater concern with the cosmic order of things than with the significance of man's actions within this system. In both cases, the garden itself may be interpreted as a synecdoche for the entirety of finite creation—as opposed to Milton's Eden, which

[n] It may be noted that even in this impeccable scene the reception of the celestial messenger by the faithful couple, by figuring a similar visit by annunciators of blessing and doom to Abraham (Gen. xviii), implies a forecast of dire events. See Thomas Greene, *The Descent from Heaven* (New Haven, 1963).

is explicitly less than the sum of terrestrial existence, "all the Earth,/Not this Rock only," (XI: 336)—although the two poets necessarily go on to subordinate that spatial vastness to a higher totality of truth. In plotting the vertical relations between the finite realm and the infinite Ideas above it, both poets have extensive recourse to vegetable, or "horticultural"[9] imagery to trace the upward reach of growth and the providential descent of solar energy that define the links in the hierarchy of worlds.

In treating Dante's Earthly Paradise in anagogic rather than in tropological terms, we do not intend to overlook the significance of the pilgrim's return to Eden as a stage in his moral journey from sin to redemption that has already been discussed above. Nor may we minimize the intensely dramatic nature of his encounter with Beatrice, his traumatic confession, and his conversion to the order of grace. We must, however, realize that Dante is simply not working within the coordinates of truth and falsity, with their respective iconographical pointers, which we have seen to function in what we have termed the tropological gardens. This fact becomes even clearer when we note that Dante's Earthly Paradise is both prelapsarian and postlapsarian at the same time, with no tension between the two dimensions. The contrast with Milton's Eden is particularly sharp, in that Dante conspicuously avoids a dramatic presentation of the tropological Fall itself, since his entire Commedia—indeed any Christian comedy, as we have seen— must by definition take place after the Fall is an established fact. It is therefore a significant detail that the Purgatorial garden has survived both the fall and the expulsion of its keepers, while Milton's paradise is necessarily "lost," since the position of Dante's Earthly Paradise in the postlapsarian hierarchy of existence is not affected by its abuse in the hands of man.

The significance of the *divina foresta*, then, consists in its central location along the route from the *selva oscura* to the

[9]Cf. C. S. Lewis, *Studies in Medieval and Renaissance Literature* (Cambridge, England, 1966), p. 90ff.

celestial rose.[p] Its position within the vertical layout of the Dantean universe is unique in that it sits at the summit of creation, hard by the lower limits of the celestial spheres. Within such a framework, of course, the mountain location is mandatory, although such elements as the song of birds, grassy banks, and colorful flowers may be seen as traditional ornamentation. The mountain rises by definition above the spheres of earthly change (xxviii: 97–102), but in its intermediate position it serves both as a path from the sea to the sky, and as a mediation between infinite providence and its time-bound beneficiaries (xxviii: 103–114). This role of Dante's terrestrial paradise in translating divine love into earthly fruitfulness requires that it bear a double nature: it must be commensurate with both Heaven and Earth. It is in this sense that the pilgrim's baptism, the second coming of Beatrice, and the mystery of the Griffin—all of which figure forth the miracle of the incarnation—coincide precisely at this confluence of realms in Dante's hierarchically conceived garden. And it is necessarily at this point that the circumscribed perfection of finite creation—the natural virtues identified by Singleton in the four stars, rivers, and nymphs visible in the garden—are joined by their three noble cousins in celebration of the hierarchy that reveals grace in nature. Within this ordering of the natural to the supernatural degrees of knowledge and love, the role of Matelda becomes clear. From Dante's (and our own) perspective of fallen seasonality she is likened to Proserpina (xxviii:49–51), but she remains, like Leah, an immutable figure of the active attainment of happiness, the permanent Genius of the garden of innocent delight that forms an indispensable link in the great chain of being. Even more important, she assists in the pilgrim's "continuous" passage by preparing him for his spiritual marriage to Beatrice and his next step up the ladder.

Lest the reader be tempted to leave the advancing pilgrim

[p] A route marked out by no less than 22 transformations of the vegetative metaphor, including occurrences in Inf. i, iv, xiii, xiv, xxxiii, Purg. ii, iii, vii, viii, xx, xxii, xxiii, xxiv, xxviii–xxxiii, and Par. ix, xv, xvii, xviii, xix, xxiii, xxvi, and xxx–xxxiii.

with his trans-substantial metaphors and stay behind to enjoy the more tangible delights of Matelda's garden, Dante feels constrained to call special attention to its incompleteness, its lower position in the hierarchy of being. To rejoin Matelda in the garden of innocence

> Qui fu innocente l'umana radice;
> Qui primavera sempre ed ogni frutto;
> Nettare è questo di che ciascun dice.
> (XXVIII:142–144)

would be to attain lost paradise, but to the pilgrim born after the Fall Matelda stands on the far side of an ontological river-barrier that appears as impassable as the Hellespont as long as his goal is natural happiness alone, but then turns out to be as quiet as the Jordan when crossed with the aid of grace. Thus the Earthly Paradise, for all its importance in the hierarchical scheme of things, remains an "empty" dream now that Eve has impatiently removed her veil (XXIX: 27) and Adam's tree is despoiled (XXXII: 38). Perhaps the most forceful image of the circumscribed role of the Earthly Paradise in the postlapsarian hierarchy may be seen in the thunderclap that resounds at the end of Canto XXIX, in sharp contradiction to the storm-free climate of the *locus amoenus* tradition.

The Garden of Adonis in *The Faerie Queene* may similarly be viewed as an important stage in Spenser's own spiritual journey from the wandering wood to the Sabaoths sight, a journey that also takes the reader through a long chain of positive and negative transformations of the earthly paradise tradition.[q] But its position within the hierarchy of existence may perhaps be better understood as a concretization of the entire system of Natura in the finite world. Thus, while the enclosing wall (III: vi: 31), "continuall spring," "laughing blossoms," and "joyous birdes" clearly place the piece within

[q]No less than 21 uses of earthly paradise motifs (Book I: i: 7, ii: 28, vii: 4, IV:viii: 54, x: 23; VI: iii: 23, v: 34, ix: 8, x: 4; and VII: vii, etc.), plus numerous negative transformations in the form of caves, gloomy glens, etc.

the tradition described here, this garden, like the concept of Natura in general, is painfully circumscribed by the presence of cyclical Time, an alien element in the conventional paradise *topos*. It would perhaps accord well with the notion of hierarchy to think of the Garden of Adonis as actually a series of gardens ranging from a treadmill race against Time and Death to a timeless moment of pleasure, as Berger and Cheney suggest, but such an interpretation seems to be based on a misreading of the lines:

> But were it not, that Time their troubler is,
> All that in this delightfull gardin growes
> Should happy bee, and have immortall blis   (41)

That is, the ravages of time do not leave off halfway through the garden but rather serve as the ground of the entire construction, necessitating its ceaseless activity. Even when Spenser describes Adonis as "eterne in mutabilitie" the stress must be placed on the final word, since the poet has already noted that he is "subject to mortalitie"—as opposed to He who is "eterne" in immutability. If anything, then, the motionless pose of the final scene recalls the strikingly similar posture of Venus and Adonis in the tapestry in Castle Joyeous (and thus those of Phaedria and Acrasia as well), thus further delimiting their garden to the imperfect, dependent sector of the chain of being. Moreover, as a final touch, Spenser tethers an unmistakable symbol of Adonis' mortality under his own bed, to prevent the wrong identification of a moment extracted from time with the timeless present that only dwells further up the hierarchy. Given this essential location of the Garden of Adonis within the larger picture, the dominant position of Venus over her mate at the top of the mount need not cause us to cry "upsidoun" or send us scurrying to Lucretius and the Neo-Platonists for models. As long as the realm of Nature is kept subordinate to the higher orders of existence, it is altogether proper that the lower level, taken as a whole, be placed under the vicarage of a "female archetype."

CHAPTER VII

THE CHINESE LITERARY GARDEN

HAVING traced the earthly paradise *topos* through several Western works with a view toward demonstrating the nature of allegory in that tradition, let us return now to the garden of delights within which the major portion of the narrative of the *Dream of the Red Chamber* unfolds. It has already been suggested that the allegorical "meaning" of the Ta-kuan Yüan—the extended structure of significance beyond the surface of the text—is not to be sought, as in the works considered in the preceding chapter, in terms of metaphorical correspondences between figure and truth, but rather by way of horizontal extension through the trope of synecdoche. That is, while the enclosed space of all literary gardens clearly "stands for" the sum total of finite creation, here the implied projection from a limited field of perception to some more total form of vision takes the form of synchronic spatialization, as opposed to the diachronic process of revelation seen to be the ground of Western allegory. Since the Chinese literary garden does not function in terms of dialectical progression, neither the concept of tropological choice between true and false versions of paradise nor that of anagogic ordering of finite creation to the *summum bonum* will be relevant to the following discussion. Instead, our attention will focus on the precise manner in which the structural patterns presented within the limited confines of the Ta-kuan Yüan garden evoke a vision of far broader dimensions.

Before we proceed to investigate the nature of this spatial vision of totality it will be necessary to locate the aesthetic features of the Ta-kuan Yüan within the Chinese tradition of literary gardens. In doing so, we must bear in mind that we are dealing here with the specific problem of the garden as an arbitrarily delimited space under more or less strict aesthetic control, and not with the broader conception of natural landscape. Although the artistic presentation of unbounded landscape on the one hand and the enclosed garden on the other often tend to overlap,[a] notably in the "nature poetry" of the Six Dynasties and T'ang periods, by the latter half of the empire the enclosed garden has become a specific *topos* with its own conventional "furniture" and philosophical issues. This standardization may perhaps be explained as due to the formalization of the conventions of garden architecture during this period, but it could with equal justice be claimed that the characteristic configurations of the actual gardens of China owe a great deal to the literary tradition under consideration here. In any event, the term "literary garden" will be used below to refer to both written descriptions of existing gardens and examples of self-conscious garden compositions based upon conceptions drawn from literature.

Most of the occurrences of the garden idea in early Chinese literature seem to speak of a *locus amoenus*, a paradise of earthly pleasures much as we have seen it in the Western tradition. Already in the *I Ching* we are reminded of "grace in hills and gardens" 賁于丘園,[1b] while the "Ho Ming" ode of the *Shih Ching* sings of the graces of a similar scene: "delight in the garden" 樂彼之園.[2] But it is only in the Chan-kuo period that we begin to see a more fully realized treatment of the specific delights involved. In the *Ch'u Tz'u*, for example, we visit a garden called Hsüan P'u 縣圃 in the course of the "Li-

[a]This is of course true in Western literature as well, particularly in the classical period: cf. Alkinoos' "garden," Virgil's pastoral retreats, etc. But in the Middle Ages and the Renaissance, at any rate, the concept of an enclosed garden was certainly specific enough.

[b]Yüan Mei 袁枚 (*Sui-yüan Ch'üan-chi* 隨園全集, Hong Kong, n.d., p. 83) cites this line and its interpretation by the exegete Wang Pi 王弼 to justify his insatiable puttering in his own garden.

sao" journey[3] and a "jasper garden" (*yao chih p'u* 瑤之圃)[c] in the "Nine Declarations" section.[4] The actual association between these citations of place names and the notion of fulfilled desire is made in the two "summons" poems, in which the delights of this world are enumerated in order to entice the departed soul to return to its terrestrial abode:

坐堂伏檻臨曲池些……蘭薄戶樹瓊木籬些
騰駕步遊獵春囿只……孔雀盈園畜鸞皇只

Seated in the hall, leaning on its balustrade, you look
down on a winding pool . . .
An orchid carpet covers the ground; the hedge is of
flowering hibiscus.
Here you may gallop or amble at leisure, or hunt in the
spring-quickened park.
Peacocks fill the gardens; phoenixes too are kept there.[5]

The motif of some sort of a "sacred" garden (帝之囿時),[6][d] appears later[e] in the *Shan-hai Ching* while in *Mu-t'ien-tzu Chuan* the Emperor Mu of Chou is represented as visiting the Hsüan P'u garden during his legendary journey:

清水出泉溫和無風，飛鳥百獸之所飲食，先王所謂縣圃.

"Clear water came forth from springs, it was warm and pleasant with no wind. This was where flying birds and numerous creatures took their food and drink. This was what former kings had called 'Hsüan P'u.' "[7]

Interestingly enough, we see in this passage all of the characteristics—warm climate, sparkling streams, no wind, teeming

[c]This and the preceding garden are identified by the Ch'ing commentator Chiang Chi 蔣驥 (Shan-tai Ko 山帶閣) with the legendary K'un Lun mountains. Cf. the jasper pool *yao-ch'ih* 瑤池 traditionally associated with the abode of Hsi Wang Mu on K'un Lun.

[d]In a note on this passage, the Ch'ing subcommentator Ho I-hsing 郝懿行 explains the character 時 as a substitute for 埘, indicating the idea of divine precincts.

[e]Cheng Te-k'un 鄭德坤 (*Shan-hai Ching chi ch'i Shen-hua* 山海經及其神話, n.p., n.d.) concludes that the "Shan Ching" 山經 sections of the text, in which this passage appears, date from the Chan-kuo period (p. 7).

animals—that we have enumerated as necessary details of the Western *locus amoenus*.

In the Han and Six Dynasties periods the variety of phenomena within the garden landscape provides a fine subject for the exuberant description of the *fu* genre. Most well known, of course, is the imperial hunting park presented by Ssu-ma Hsiang-ju in the "Shang-lin Fu," in terms that strain both the imagination and the lexicon in an effort to convey the vastness of the resources at the disposal of the Han Emperor. Although the sheer breadth of territory and the endless catalogues of rare objects heaped within this park place it in a class beyond that of the Ta-kuan Yüan (a class including the A-fang Kung [阿房宮] palace of Ch'in Shih-huang-ti,[f] the Ken Yüeh [艮嶽] pleasure grounds of Sung Hui-tsung, and the Yüan Ming Yüan [圓明園] and other gardens of the Ch'ien-lung Emperor which bedazzled his European visitors and set off decades of garden polemics in the West), we shall see below that the formal categories of description into which Ssu-ma Hsiang-ju pours his effusive language provide a model for later garden descriptions on a smaller scale.

At the other end of this scale of magnificence, we may note the appearance during this same period of the *topos* of rural retreat as a counter-balance to the excesses of the imperial parks. While it is the stated intention of this study to refrain from considering unbounded scenery within the context of the garden idea, it must be recognized that the rural motifs and landscape descriptions of such Six Dynasties poets as T'ao Yüan-ming and Hsieh Ling-yün remain the *locus classicus* for much of later Chinese garden literature.[g] By the same token, Wang Hsi-chih's famed description of an outing at Lan T'ing pavilion at Shao-hsing, Chekiang Province, although not strictly speaking an enclosed landscape, will also serve as a major document in the history of Chinese garden aesthetics.

[f]Ssu-ma Ch'ien locates the A-fang Palace in the Shang-lin Park (*Shih Chi*, 6/18b).

[g]T'ao Yüan-ming's recurrent use of the term *t'ien-yüan* 田園 seems to refer to an agricultural plot rather than an actual garden in our sense, but in certain places he does appear to be speaking of the latter.

The remainder of the literary gardens considered in this study will fall somewhere along a continuum between the royal pleasure grounds and the hut of the recluse, and already in this early period we find examples of widely varying positions within this spectrum. Yü Hsin's "Hsiao Yüan Fu" 小園賦, for example, draws heavily on the recluse ideal within an explicit garden setting:

余有數畝敝廬，寂寞人外⋯⋯
三春負鋤相識.

I have a few acres, a shabby hut,
Lonely and still, beyond the world of men . . .
Late spring I shoulder my hoe along with friends.[8]

while P'an Yüeh ("Hsien-chü Fü") describes his more prosperous garden reminiscent of Alkinoos' *locus amoenus* in Book VII of the *Odyssey*:

於是覽止足之分，庶浮雲之志，築室種樹，逍遙自得. 池沼足以
漁釣，春稅以代耕.

"And so I have turned my eyes toward that life that knows what is enough, that knows where to stop; my desire is now to be like the drifting clouds. I have built rooms and planted trees where I may wander at will in perfect contentment. I possess ponds sufficient for all the fishing I will ever do, and the revenue from my grain-husking operations takes the place of farmlands."[9]

The most opulent of the private gardens of the period, however, is that of Shih Ch'ung 石崇 of the Eastern Chin. After amassing a personal fortune through merchant shipping and other pursuits, this stock figure of the upstart rich devoted his newly acquired wealth to the construction of the sumptuous Chin-ku Garden 金谷園 a few miles outside of Loyang, as described in the official Chin history:

如此財產豐積，屋宇宏麗，後房百數⋯⋯絲竹盡當時之選，庖膳
窮水陸之珍.

"In this way he amassed lavish amounts of wealth and

property, his dwellings were vast and exquisite, with hundreds of outbuildings . . . As for the music of strings and pipes, he exhausted the selection of the time, for culinary feats he plumbed the delicacies of land and sea."[10]

Interestingly enough, Shih Ch'ung sees fit to describe his own garden, later a byword for conspicuous consumption, as a "retreat cottage" (*pieh-lu* 別廬), drawing in feigned modesty upon the recluse tradition.[11]

Although we have seen that the Chinese garden tradition offers a broad range of earthly pleasures, it has been observed during the course of this study that the idea of the garden as an outdoor setting for love is rarely emphasized. The close association of the grassy banks and leafy bowers of the Western paradise *topos* with sexual love, in all its terrestrial and divine transformations, does not seem to apply in Chinese literature, where sublunar embraces are generally relegated to the inner chambers. Nevertheless, we should not overlook, in passing, several important examples in which the Chinese tradition does move from an ideal of sensory fulfillment to a more sensual one within the garden setting. It is noteworthy that a good deal of the erotic imagery in Chinese literature finds its *locus classicus* in the *fu* tradition, and specifically in such works as Sung Yü's "Kao-t'ang Fu" and "Shen-nü Fu," and Ts'ao Chih's "Lo-shen Fu."[h] Although these works do not represent gardens as such, they do provide mountaintop (specifically Wu-shan 巫山) and riverbank settings for love to which later authors often turn in handling garden themes. Perhaps the clearest examples of this type are to be found in the later dramas *Hsi-hsiang Chi* and *Mu-tan T'ing*, where such expressions as 雲歛巫山 "clouds envelop Wu Peak,"[12] 雲雨會巫峽 "We meet like clouds and rain by the Wu Gorges,"[13] 夢中巫峽 "The Wu Gorges (visited) in dream,"[14] etc. link specific garden encounters with these major sources of erotic convention.[i]

[h]The name "Sung Yü" should alert us to the connection between *fu*-eroticism and *sao*-passion.

[i]In the frank descriptions of garden love-play in *Chin P'ing-mei*, *Sui Yang-ti Yen-shih*, and other later novels, we can note the recurrence of the same conventional allusions.

While it was stated at the outset that the idea of a tropological cal choice between the true garden of divine love and the false garden of earthly delights is foreign to the Chinese literary tradition, nevertheless the moral implications of such concentrated scenes of fulfilled desire as the garden motif provides did not escape the early Chinese thinkers. Among philosophers of widely-varying schools the garden concept is consistently used to convey the idea of extravagance, ostentation, or unwisely deployed resources. Mencius, for example, condemns the proliferation of garden construction in pre-Chou times as evidence of the universal decay which called forth the mandatory overthrow of the Shang:

> 堯舜既没聖人之道衰，暴君代作，壞宮室以為汙池，民無所安息，棄田以為園囿，使民不得衣食. 邪説暴行又作，園囿汙池沛澤多而禽獸至，及紂之身天下又大亂.

"After the death of Yao and Shun, the way of the sages declined, and tyrants arose one after another. They pulled down houses in order to make ponds, and the people had nowhere to rest. They turned fields into parks, depriving the people of their livelihood. Moreover, heresies and violence arose. With the multiplication of parks, ponds and lakes, arrived birds and beasts. By the time of the tyrant Tchou, the Empire was again in great disorder."[15]

In an earlier passage, he further distinguishes between a minimum of disruption in the open lands of King Wen's park of 70 square li and the major pitfall created by King Hsüan of Ch'i's smaller preserve.[j] Hsün Tzu also speaks of gardens in his "Wang Pa" 王霸 Chapter as an example of harm to the state through short-sighted investment of wealth:

> 其於聲色臺謝園囿也，愈厭而好新，是傷國.

"As for delights of the ear and eye, towers and pavilions,

[j]An association no doubt noted by Ssu-ma Kuang when he chose the expression *tu-leh* 獨樂 from the immediately preceding passage in Mencius for the name of his own garden (*Ssu-ma Wen-kung Wen-chi* 司馬溫公文集, Taipei, 1967, p. 305).

gardens and parks, when one is insatiable in his desire for novelty, this will bring harm to the state."[16]

This same view of the dangers inherent in expensive pleasure grounds is also voiced by Ssu-ma Hsiang-ju at the beginning of the "Shang-lin Fu," and ultimately affirmed by the Emperor as well when the poet's enumeration of rhymeprose delights becomes too much even for him to bear:

天子芒然而思, 似若有亡, 曰嗟乎此大奢侈.

". . . the Son of Heaven becomes lost in contemplation, like one whose spirit has wandered, and he cries, 'Alas! What is this but a wasteful extravagance?'"[17]

Even in later times when smaller gardens became more common in China, the problems of extravagance and ostentation remained necessary associations of the garden idea, as the following passage from *Lo-yang Ch'ieh-lan Chi* attests:

於是帝族王侯外戚公主擅山海之富, 居川澤之饒, 爭植園宅, 互相誇競……家家而築花林曲池, 園園而有桃李夏緑, 竹柏冬青……

"At this time the Imperial family, princes and marquises, relatives by marriage, and princesses all arrogated to themselves the riches of mountain and sea, occupying the choicest land by rivers and lakes and competing to plant gardens and (build) dwellings which vied with one another in extravagance . . . every house designed its groves of flowering trees and winding ponds, every garden had peach and plum trees for the bright green of summer and bamboo and cypress for the deep green of winter."[18k]

As a further moral dimension, we should also not fail to mention the garden concepts embodied within the tradition of Confucian exegesis. In the commentaries on the *Shih Ching*, for example, we find such serious issues as the restraint of

---

[k] Cf. Kuei Yu-kuang 歸有光, "Ts'ang-lang T'ing Chi" 滄浪亭記: 乘時奢僭宮舘苑囿, 極一時之盛 ("In no time at all they spent lavish sums on palaces, estates, parks, and gardens, exhausting the resources of the age").

license through filial self-discipline (on the poem "Chiang Chung-tzu" 將仲子), the improper use of ministers by the state (on the poem "Yüan Yu T'ao" 園有桃), and the interplay of virtue and vice in human relations (on the poem "Ho Ming" 鶴鳴),[19] brought in to interpret the garden imagery of the Confucian Odes. In addition, we must bear in mind the ethical values of moral strength and incorruptibility traditionally attributed to such garden plants as the pine, the bamboo, and the plum, although as we shall see the important philosophical implications of the Chinese garden are not in the area of ethics. By the T'ang period, in any event, we begin to see the type of highly self-conscious landscape art to which most discussions of the Chinese garden refer and to which the Ta-kuan Yüan clearly belongs. In the following pages, therefore, we will draw freely on examples from T'ang through Ch'ing, both actual and fictional, to provide a composite picture of the fully developed literary garden tradition.

Since a number of works exist in which the characteristic features of the Chinese garden as an architectural phenomenon are described in detail,[1] let us simply review some of the more important among them. The first question to be considered of course, is the location of the site selected for garden construction. A Ming treatise on gardening, *Yüan Yeh* 園冶, lists six possible garden sites: in the mountains, in cities, in rural villages, on suburban plots, adjacent to homes, and in waterfront locations. But since the very impulse towards the garden ideal arises most naturally out of the dust and anxiety of city life, the second, fourth, and fifth of these choices seem to have been favored by China's garden designers.[m] Thus Yü Hsin's garden (in his "Hsiao-yüan Fü") is described as near the city: "Like P'an Yüeh, I face the city, Savoring delights of

[1]See bibliography: Oswald Siren, *China and the Gardens of Europe* (New York, 1950); Henry Inn, *Chinese Houses and Gardens* (Honolulu, 1940); T'ung Chün, *Chiang-nan Yüan-lin-Chih* 江南園林志 (Peking, 1963); Wango H. C. Weng, *Gardens in Chinese Art* (New York, 1968).

[m]Accordingly, many traditional garden surveys are organized according to cities: e.g. *Lo-yang Ming-yüan Chi* 洛陽名園記, *Yu Chin-ling Chu-yüan Chi* 遊全陵諸園記, *Wu-hsing Yüan-lin Chi* 吳興園林記.

an idle life" 潘岳面城且適閒居之樂,[20] and even T'ao Yüan-
ming reveals that his retreat is not so far removed from urban
society: "I built my cottage within range of other people"
結廬在人境.[21] Even when gardens are clearly located outside
of the city, as is Po Chü-i's Ts'ao-t'ang 草堂 in the area of
Mount Lu 廬山 in Kiangsi Province, they are often associated
with human habitation in the form of temple complexes. In all
cases the guiding principle is separation from city commotion,[n]
but if such an end can be achieved by structural ingenuity it
need not be applied in a geographical sense, as the author
of Yüan Yeh concludes: 能為鬧處尋幽, 胡舍近方圖遠? ("If one
can seek out remoteness within a noisy place, why should he
abandon a nearby site in his desire for distance?").[22] The
famous aesthete Li Yü concurs that the true art of gardening
lies in transforming city acreage rather than abandoning it:
然能變城市為山林 ("But one can change the city into a mountain forest").[23] An extreme case of isolation is envisioned in
the garden granted by imperial favor to Chuang Shao-kuang
in Chapter 35 of Ju-lin Wai-shih. Located on an island in the
middle of Hsüan-wu Lake (玄武湖) near Nanking, this garden
can be reached only by a boat which, when beached, leaves no
other means of access.[o] A less extreme situation is described by
Su Tung-p'o in his account of the garden of a certain Chang
family outside K'ai-feng (in the essay 靈壁張氏園亭記) that is
located far enough from the city to allow the illusion of recluse
life, but near enough that the master's sons and grandsons may
participate in official life all day and return to the family compound at night—an ideal quite familiar to us today. A further
consideration in choosing a garden site is whether to prepare a
new lot or rebuild a pre-existing garden. The Yüan Yeh treatise

[n]Cf. Hsieh Ling-yün, Hsieh Ling-yün Shih-hsüan 謝靈運詩選 (Shanghai,
1957), p. 67: 中園屏氛雜 ("Within the garden all commotion is blocked
off"), and Tu Fu, Tu Shih Ch'ien-chu 杜詩錢注 (Taipei, 1969), p. 314: 終
防市井喧 ("Warding off permanently the noise of the marketplace").

[o]Professor F. W. Mote has informed me that this island was used as a
well-guarded storehouse for important official documents in Ming and
Ch'ing times, so that the author's choice of the location for an idyllic
retreat may bear a certain degree of irony.

states its preference for the latter course, a choice followed by the masters of the Ta-kuan Yüan.

By very definition it is the fact of enclosure that distinguishes a garden from any other natural landscape. The enclosing walls of Chinese gardens take many forms, from simple whitewashed plaster (*fen-ch'iang* 粉牆) to simulated ramparts (*fei-tieh* 飛堞),[p] but they are generally distinguished by the feature of following the rise and fall of the land, thus producing a dragon-like effect. It has been pointed out that the bare whiteness of the common plaster walls is intended to serve as a background for the viewing of flowers or the play of shadows, much like the paper beneath an ink drawing. Wherever there is a wall (even around a prison) there must also be a gate, and the gates in Chinese garden walls often bear an unusual degree of artistic ingenuity in their varying aperture shapes and structural details. Even more important, the doors and windows, or even the railings for that matter,[q] are carefully placed in order to serve as frames for the view beyond, in accordance with shifting angles of vision. With this fact in mind, the first step into the Chinese garden is often the decisive one, as the author of the *Yüan Yeh* indicates: 涉門成趣 ("Upon passing through the gate the tone is set").[24]

With regard to the garden buildings and their unique structural features—lattice-work, roof tiles, carved beams, etc.—the reader is referred to more specialized studies on the subject. It is a commonplace of such works that signs of human habitation are an indispensable element of the garden composition, much as the scholar's pavilion, mountain hut, or fisherman's boat renders complete a Chinese landscape painting. It should be noted, however, that—the Ta-kuan Yüan notwithstanding—the structures in Chinese gardens are

[p]In the gardens of Prince Kung in nineteenth-century Peking there was even a replica of the Great Wall, referred to jokingly as the "Half-mile Great Wall" (*pan-li ch'ang-ch'eng* 半里長城); see H. S. Ch'en and G. N. Kates, "Prince Kung's Palace and its Adjoining Garden in Peking" (*Monumenta Serica*, v, 1940), p. 60.
[q]Cf. *Yüan Yeh* 園冶: 欄杆信畫因境而成 ("The railings and balustrades are left to mark out lines, taking shape in accordance with the scene").

generally designed for temporary use and not for permanent residence. In fact, the twentieth-century scholar T'ung Chün goes as far as to suggest that the most sophisticated of garden artists would rarely even visit their four-dimensional master-pieces.[25r] If anything, the inhabitant would select one of the garden buildings as a permanent residence and use the other structures for such specific purposes as studying, drinking, or composing poetry. In the case of a back garden attached to a main building, such as we see in *Hsi-hsiang Chi*, there is no question of living in the garden. In any event, a major principle *in the execution of garden architecture lies in selecting the proper structure for the proper site both from the compositional and the practical points of view.* Fine examples of architectural adaptation to the physical nature of the site include the Wang family garden outside Chungking described in *Fu-sheng Liu-chi*:

既限於地，頗難位置. 而觀其結搆作重臺疊舘之法.

"... there was quite a bit of difficulty in laying it out due to the limited space, and so one could observe the ingenious structural device of constructing overhanging terraces and multiple-storied halls."[26]

as well as the simple hut which Ssu-ma Kuang contrived in his Tu-leh Yüan outside Loyang by tying together the tops of a circle of bamboos, thus forming a structure of sorts. Under the heading of structures, we may also mention the winding pathways, varied forms of bridges, and covered promenades, etc., which, according to Siren, provide the third dimension of the garden composition.[27]

The most indispensable element of a garden, of course, is its greenery (with certain well-known exceptions), and the Chinese garden is noted for its variety of plant life. As a result full descriptions are often reminiscent of the catalogues of the *sao* and *fu* traditions (and indeed, Pao-yü makes this association in

---

[r]Cf. Yüan Mei's quote of a certain Nu T'an-li 偃檀利: 作者不居, 居者 不作 ("He who designs it does not occupy it, he who occupies it does not design it"). *Ibid.*, p. 81.

his first visit to the Ta-kuan Yüan). Sometimes it seems that it is the garden that has been conceived as a setting for prized flowers, rather than vice versa. It should be noted, in this regard, that while great emphasis is placed on the patient cultivation of spontaneous growth, as suggested in Liu Tsung-yüan's famous essay "Camel Kuo, the Gardener": 能順木之天以致其性焉爾 "What I *can* do is comply with the nature of the tree so that it takes the way of its kind . . ."[28] traditional Chinese gardens were often equipped with hothouses, trellises, potted shrubs, and the like. In addition, in keeping with the semantic breadth of the term *yüan* 園, the garden-as-park might also include vegetable or herb-gardens within their walls.[s] One interesting point about the flora of the Chinese garden is the apparent absence of the grassy fields or tended lawns so necessary to the European garden landscape. While this fact is often cited as evidence of the greater "artificiality" of Western gardens—an issue we will return to shortly—it may perhaps be better explained as reflecting the fact that the image of the meadow, with all its pastoral implications, never gained a hold on the Chinese imagination as it did in the West. Where the bright, flowery lawns of the European garden set it off from the dark forests (*selva oscura*, gloomy glens) beyond its walls, a flat expanse of grass would be more reminiscent of barbarian steppes in the Chinese context. In any event, the idea of stretching out on turf couches shepherd-style rarely emerges in Chinese literary gardens, a point no doubt related to the de-emphasis of outdoor love-play in the Chinese tradition.[t]

Another essential consideration in the planning of a garden is the provision of an adequate water supply in order to ensure the continued growth of plant life, and literary descriptions of

[s]As in Ssu-ma Kuang's Tu-leh Yüan.
[t]When visitors to the Chinese literary garden do sit down to enjoy a scene, it is generally on mats, as in Li Po's essay "Ch'un-yeh Yen Tsung-ti T'ao-li-yüan Hsü" 春夜宴從弟桃李園序: 開瓊筵以坐花 (". . . unroll ornamented mats and sit among the flowers"). Cf. *Fu-sheng Liu-chi* 浮生六記, p. 114: 擇柳陰下團坐 (". . . we chose a spot under the shade of the willows and sat together on the ground").

Chinese gardens often dwell at length on the configurations of their streams and ponds. Ssu-ma Kuang, for example, devotes a major portion of his short essay on his Tu-leh Yüan garden to a description of its water courses. More than simply as a practical necessity, the meandering streams and lotus-studded sheets of the Chinese garden serve to instill a sense of life-force flowing through the veins of the land-organism. They act as a "sounding board,"[29] or perhaps more precisely a mirror, of the subtle and obvious changes constantly taking place in the garden.

Finally, this review of physical features would not be complete without mention of the rocks which have come to be the identifying characteristic of the Chinese garden landscape. It should be immediately pointed out that the passion for strange rockery, and in particular for the famous *t'ai-hu* stones 太湖石, is a relatively late phenomenon, seemingly traceable to the Sung period. It will be recalled that it was in this period that the Emperor Hui-tsung's demand for prize rock specimens, through the offices of the infamous minister Chu Mien 朱勔 (and the Hua-shih Kang 花石綱), reached proportions grave enough to precipitate rebellion. Part of this fascination for the unusually shaped rocks—often set up as centerpieces, at curious angles, or even on pedestals—may be attributed to pure caprice ("playful ornamentation"[30]). But their selection and positioning were certainly a serious occupation of Chinese garden masters, as Li Yü describes:

且磊石成山另是一種學問，別是一番智巧

"Now to pile together many rocks to form a mountain is a type of learning in its own right, it is an altogether different kind of ingenuity."[31]

Similarly, the *Yüan Yeh* also notes the expressive capacity of inanimate rockery: 寸石生情 ("the smallest stone gives rise to feeling").[32] Much of the interest in *t'ai-hu* stones may be related to the above-mentioned respect for the deceptive power of water, as the strange shapes and swiss-cheese effect were produced by uneven underwater erosion of the variously textured stone.ᵘ It is interesting that these prominent garden features often seem to be singled out in fiction and drama as a location for amorous assignations and other mischief (e.g. *Hsi-hsiang Chi*, p. 124: 一箇潛身在曲檻邊, 一箇背立在湖山下 ("One hides herself by the winding balustrade, the other stands with his back to a *t'ai-hu* 'peak'"); *Mu-tan T'ing*, p. 47: 轉過這芍藥欄前, 緊靠着湖山石邊 ("Circling the peony-decked railing, keeping close to the *t'ai-hu* stone"). Whether this is due simply to the fact that the large rocks offer a convenient hiding place, or to their assumed resemblance to the mountains of the immortals (or perhaps to Wu-shan 巫山, whose associations we have traced to Sung Yü's "Kao-t'ang Fu"), the implication is clear in the dramas cited above and, we shall see, in the *Dream of the Red Chamber* as well.

At this point it will be necessary to confront an issue that should never have been raised, but that unfortunately turns up in many comparative studies. This is the question of the relative "naturalness" of gardens in various cultures. We are often reminded of the straight alleys, manicured lawns, marble-block structures, and such features as mazes, parterres, geometric fountains, and particularly topiary hedgework as examples of the artificiality of the Western garden. In the Chinese garden, by way of contrast, the meandering paths, half-hidden buildings, and general distaste for symmetry or geometric patterns are cited as evidence of faithfulness to nature. The question, however, cannot be reduced to a simple distinction between controlling natural forms and "harmonizing" with them. We have already seen that Chinese gardens insist on a human presence within the landscape, and are quite willing to make use of hothouses, parterres, and even the careful training of plants to produce desired shapes and sizesᵛ (though stopping

ᵘAs a result, clever forgers often "produced" *t'ai-hu* stones for the market.
ᵛThe ubiquitous inscriptions and engravings of literary names for favorite spots must also sharply qualify the impression of unspoiled nature.

short of the excesses of Le Nôtre).ʷ Even more important, the entire idea of a garden is by definition one of artificiality—of constructing an artifact using the stuff of nature as materials. In both the Chinese and the Western case, intellectual categories *are imposed upon natural forms to produce a desired impression*. The problem, therefore, ultimately devolves upon the diverging conceptions of nature in the two civilizations.

We have already seen in the preceding chapters that the Western tradition has generally viewed the natural universe as something ontologically separate from—significantly less than—the absolute truth of existence. Thus even when the opposition between human subject and natural object is minimized so that art and nature are no longer in conflict, the common ground thus reached remains an incomplete phase of the total picture, a veiled figure of true being.ˣ In the pre-modern Western tradition, nature exists to be transcended or to serve a higher purpose—whether that be religious or artistic in essence.

Within the Chinese spatialized conception of totality referred to throughout this study, the given universe contains within itself the entire ground of being. Just as the concept of ontological disjunction between created and uncreated existence has no place within such a world-view, so too the corresponding distinction between anthropomorphic will and spontaneous process is not emphasized. Instead, the continuum of possibilities between conscious creation and spontaneous generation takes its place among all the other polar coordinates that, taken together, constitute the universe of experience.ʸ Returning to the garden literature, we find that where one writer emphasizes unspoiled natural beauty (e.g. 不待人力而巧 "ingenious without human effort"),³³ another stresses the

---

ʷMost of the "artificial" features associated with such formal gardens as those of Le Nôtre at Versailles can be traced back to Medieval and even classical Western gardens, although not, of course, with the specific philosophical implications of the seventeenth and eighteenth centuries.

ˣAs we have seen in the concept of Natura in the *Romance of the Rose*, Chaucer's *Parlement of Foules*, and Spenser's "Mutabilitie Cantos."

ʸSee above, Chapter III.

importance of careful tending (e.g. 信其用力之多且久也 "clearly the result of extensive and prolonged effort").[34] In the same way, the author of *Fu-sheng Liu-chi* criticizes one garden for its intellectual stiffness: 此思窮力竭之為，不甚可取 "This was contrived with an expense of thought and effort, and was therefore not very attractive,"[35] and several pages later praises another for its fine harmony of artifice and nature: 此人功而 歸於天然者… "This proceeded from human effort to an ultimate naturalness."[36] The point is not that Chinese garden critics are inconsistent on this issue, but rather that they recognize as essentially complementary both poles of this range of possibilities.

This fact becomes even clearer when we note that the Chinese garden makes extensive use of the fantastic, the curious, and even the supernatural alongside of its natural elements. The grotesquely shaped *t'ai-hu* stones immediately come to mind in this regard, as do doorways in the shape of jars, gourds, or flower petals, or pavilions named for the islands of the immortals. Thus exceptionally fine examples of garden construction are conventionally praised for their unearthliness rather than their naturalness, as in Chuang Shao-kuang's island retreat in *Ju-lin Wai-shih*: 真如仙境 "as enchanting as fairyland,"[37] or Hsi-men Ch'ing's flower garden in *Chin P'ing Mei*: 天上蓬萊，人間閬苑 ("Like P'eng-lai in Heaven, a paradise among men"[38]). The point is, again, that both the familiar and the exotic are contained as viable alternatives within the total range of possibilities relevant to the garden landscape.[z]

The Chinese literary garden, then, is a mixed composition of elements that, taken together, comprise a synecdochical sampling of the infinite phenomena of the world beyond its gates. It is a place for solitude (e.g., Ssu-ma Kuang's Tu-leh Yüan) or casual companionship (e.g., T'ao Yüan-ming's retreat, Wang Wei's Wang-ch'uan), for family outings (e.g., P'an Yüeh's leisure estate)[aa] or more intimate human relations

---

[z]This is an example of the general confluence of physical and metaphysical phenomena within the monistic Chinese world-view.

[aa]Po Chü-i voices a similar ideal in "Ts'ao-t'ang Chi" 草堂記: 左手引

(e.g., the gardens in *Hsi-hsiang Chi, Mu-tan T'ing*, and *Chin P'ing Mei*). It provides a setting for serious study (Ssu-ma Kuang's Tu-leh Yüan, Po Chü-i's Ts'ao-t'ang), quiet drinking (T'ao Yüan-ming), lazy fishing (Ssu-ma Kuang), or the composition of poetry ("Lan-t'ing-chi Hsü," Li Po's "Ch'un-yeh Yen Tsung-ti T'ao-li-yüan Hsü" 春夜宴從弟桃李園序, Wang Wei's Wang-ch'uan poems). It can produce a means of livelihood (as the author of *Fu-sheng Liu-chi* and his young wife daydream),[40] and it can provide quiet occupations for leisure time (e.g., the old gardener in Chapter 55 of *Ju-lin Wai-shih*). Significantly, while the garden is conceived with an eye towards philosophical principles that demand serious contemplation, this enlightenment is ideally realized through the gradual process of performing the day-to-day activities of a quiet life, and not on the basis of abstract meditation. On the other hand, as we have seen, it is not these acts themselves to which the traditional garden is oriented, but rather the vision of totality that arises therein. What exactly is the nature of this total vision, and how it is evoked perceptually in what is a limited deployment of space will be the subject of the following pages.

Without making too much of the enclosure-radical present in several of the Chinese characters used to express the garden idea (園, 圃, 囿),[ab] we may still say that the enclosed landscape is intended to be apprehended as an entire world in miniature, in both the spatial and temporal sense.[41] There is little doubt that this impression is to a great extent attributable to the quality of fullness that naturally follows from the sheer variety of natural and architectural phenomena presented within a single limited space. One common literary device for evoking this sense of plenitude is that of extensive cataloguing of physical objects, such as we see as early as the *Ch'u Tz'u* poems

---

妻子, 右手抱琴書, 終老於斯 ("With my left hand leading my wife and children, and with my right hand carrying my lute and books, I will come to finish out my old age here").[39]

[ab]T'ung Chün (*ibid.*, p. 7) goes so far as to interpret the 土, 口, and 衣 elements (in 園) as representing buildings, ponds, and foliage, respectively.

163

and at its fullest development in the *fu* literature of the Han and Six Dynasties periods, including the "Shang-lin Fu" and P'an Yüeh's "Hsien-chü Fu." A later example of this impulse may be seen in Chuang Shao-kuang's royally bestowed pleasure ground in *Ju-lin Wai-shih*:

園裡合抱的老樹，梅花桃李芭蕉桂菊，四時不斷的花，又有一園
的竹子有數萬竿…

"In the garden were old trees, their trunks thicker than a man could encircle with his arms; and with plum, peach, pear, plantain, cassia, and chrysanthemums there were flowers at every season. There was also a grove of tens of thousands of bamboos . . ."[42]

Such an illusion of completeness is further advanced by the play of fantasy we have seen at work in the *t'ai-hu* stones and other capricious features by which the observer is invited to exercise his imagination beyond the physical bounds of the phenomena presented. Shen Fu's description of his youthful fantasies in a garden setting seem in this regard to indicate a more mature appreciation of this principle than might otherwise be suspected:

于土牆凹凸處，花臺小草叢雜處，常蹲其身使與臺齋. 定神細視，
以叢草為林，以蟲蟻為獸，以土礫凸者為邱，凹者為壑. 神遊其
中怡然自得.

"I used to crouch down by the hollows and protrusions of the mud wall or among the tangled grasses and bushes on the raised flower beds, so that I was on the same level as the flower beds. Then I would compose myself and look closely, until the clumps of grass became a forest, the ants and other insects 'became wild beasts, the clods and pebbles which jutted up were hills, and those which sank down were valleys. My spirit roamed freely in this world and I felt completely at ease."[43]

The attempt to achieve a sense of fullness based on rich variety is of course highly conditioned by the financial and natural resources available to the garden master. With this in mind, theorists of the Ming and Ch'ing periods often turn to the oblique device of "borrowing views" (*chieh-ching* 借景) in order to surmount their logistic limitations. The author of *Yüan Yeh*, for example, places great emphasis on site selection and careful planning with an eye toward capturing particularly prized scenic views—even from within a neighbor's garden— and making them a part of one's own composition: 晴巒聳 秀, 紺宇凌空, 極目所至, 俗則屏之, 嘉則收之 ("Bright-hued peaks looming forth with their intense color, purple-roofed mansions thrusting up into the sky, as far as the eye can see, in a vulgar composition all this is blocked off, but in a fine one it is taken in").[44] Li Yü makes a similar recommendation in a discussion of window designing: 開牖莫妙于借景, 而借景之法予能得其三昧 向猶私之 ("Windows should ideally open out onto a 'borrowed view,' and by the method of 'borrowing views' I have been able to attain the mystery, although hitherto I have kept it to myself").[45] But the evocation of a perception of plenitude on the basis of a wealth of detail, even with the aid of unbridled imagination and the ingenious incorporation of external views, is still a far cry from an actual vision of the totality of existence. In other words, the piling up of finite sensory images, as in the *fu* tradition, is never sufficient in itself to add up to a sum of infinity.

It is perhaps significant, therefore, that the Chinese garden tradition does not emphasize the presentation of panoramic views as a necessary element in its spatial extension from the finite to the infinite.[ac] Instead, it is sooner the idea of divided space: smaller prospects broken up by artificial hills, winding streams, and overhanging foliage, or framed by carefully designed windows, doorways, and railings, that characterize

[ac]While the essentially vertically oriented metaphors of the Western earthly paradise (cf. Eliade's "point of passage") would naturally have little use for a terrestrial panorama (Adam's mountaintop vision in Books XI and XII of *Paradise Lost* is significantly temporal rather than spatial), it would perhaps be expected that the panorama would accord nicely with the idea of synecdochical extension. But that, of course, would imply an overly literal interpretation of the trope of synecdoche.

the Chinese garden. When a tower or mountaintop pavilion is present within the confines of a garden, as in Ssu-ma Kuang's Tu-leh Yüan or in the Nanking Yao Yüan 姚園 visited by Tu Shao-ch'ing in Chapter 33 of *Ju-lin Wai-shih*, it is generally for the purpose of "borrowing" a view, as described above, and not for achieving a panoramic vista of the entire garden space.[ad]

But while the futility of a literal-minded effort to perceptually apprehend the vastness of the universe is implicit in the Chinese literary garden, the assumption that the entire range of existence is in fact intelligible, and hypothetically at least knowable, remains one of its most fundamental underpinnings. The notion that through a direct observation of phenomena and events (cf. 致知在格物 "Such extension of knowledge lay in the investigation of things")[47] the human mind may attain a state of great learning upon which to base the proper ordering of self and society: i.e., the intelligibility of all existence through its observable manifestations, is implicit in the Chinese garden as in many other facets of the civilization. Significantly, Po Chü-i seizes upon precisely this idea in the *Ta-hsüeh* text in order to explain the sense of cosmic harmony he experiences in his own garden:

今我為是物主, 物至致知, 各以類至, 又安得不外適內和, 體寧心恬哉.

"Now that I am the master of these things, and can extend my knowledge on the basis of the things through fully understanding each category, how can I help but feel in harmony with the outside world and at peace within myself, my body at ease and my heart content."[48]

It is at this point that the concept of allegory as a literary structure designed to render intelligible the ultimate nature of existence through the presentation of patterns of meaning on the level of visibilia may shed light on the gardens of Chinese

[ad]Cf. the bourgeois interpretation of this principle in *Chin P'ing Mei*: 登山頂一望, 滿園都可見到 ("Climbing to the top of the hill one could see the whole garden in a single view").[46]

literature. We have already seen in previous chapters that the Chinese tradition—as early as its recorded mythology and its canonic texts, and as late as the *Dream of the Red Chamber*—draws consistently upon archetypal patterns of two-term and five-term *alternation* as fundamental structural principles. It has further been suggested that these ritually oriented archetypes—like the narrative-oriented archetypes of the Western tradition—function as the patterns of intelligibility upon which the vision of allegory is grounded. Here the distinction raised earlier between the Western reliance on the trope of metaphor to link by analogy the level of fictional presentation to that of unseen truth, and the essentially synecdochichal nature of the unilevel Chinese allegorical structure, may become clearer. The *point is that the enclosed landscape in the latter case is related* to the given universe as the part to the whole, rather than as figure to truth. In other words, the bipolar and cyclical co-ordinates according to which the phenomena of the garden are presented do not refer obliquely to analogous configurations of truth, but simply *partake* of a totality of existence within which the coordinates actually presented in the text—and all other possible coordinates—are simultaneously contained within the whole. With this in mind, let us return now to investigate the specific coordinates that determine the range of meaning of the Chinese literary garden.

In one of the most well-known passages of Chinese garden aesthetics, the author of *Fu-sheng Liu-chi* sets forth several pairs of contrasting qualities as criteria for a successful composition:

若夫園亭樓閣，套室廻廊，疊石成山，栽花取勢，又在大中見小，小中見大，虛中有實，實中有虛，或藏或露，或淺或深，不僅在周廻曲折四字，又不在地廣石多，徒煩工費．

"In laying out garden pavilions and towers, suites of rooms and covered walkways, piling up rocks into mountains, or planting flowers to form a desired shape, the aim is to see the small in the large, to see the large in the small, to see the real in the illusory and to see the illusory in the real. Some-

times you conceal, sometimes you reveal, sometimes you
work on the surface, sometimes in depth. One need not waste
labor in vain merely in terms of the well-known formula:
'winding, deceptive intricacy,' or "a broad area with many
stones.' "[49]

Immediately following this passage, the author goes on to suggest certain specific devices by which these aesthetic principles
may be realized. The clear conformance of Shen Fu's discussion to the archetypal patterns outlined above in Chapter
III—bipolarity of form, ceaseless alternation, presence within
absence, and overlapping of polar pairs—alerts us to the fact
that we are dealing here with such qualities as large and small,
or solid and intangible, as abstract coordinates rather than as
quantifiable indices. In other words, it is more the interplay
between these paired concepts than the specific terms involved
that concerns Shen Fu. The same may be said of three axes
posited by the Sung author Li Ko-fei (李格非) in his *Lo-yang
Ming-yüan Chi*: 務宏大者少幽邃，人力勝者少蒼古，多水泉者
艱眺望 ("where open breadth is stressed suggestive depth is
diminished, where conscious artistry is dominant weatherworn
charm is less evident, and where there are many water courses
an expansive view is difficult").[50][ae]
One of the most characteristic of the polar axes perceived
within the Chinese landscape in general and garden in particular is that of "mountains and water," the *shan-shui* 山水,
which together comprise the continuum of terrestrial nature in
the Chinese view. It is if anything a "poetical requisite" of the
tradition that a garden be described in terms of its eminences
of piled earth or stone and its water-filled depressions, as in
Wang Hsi-chih's essay: 此地有崇山峻嶺，茂林修竹，又有清
流激湍 ("This place has towering peaks and steep cliffs with
dense woods and tended bamboo, as well as clear streams
swiftly flowing"),[51] or Su Tung-po's poetic description of

[ae]The complementary nature of these axes is confirmed by Li's praise
of a garden in which all six polar qualities are manifest.

Ssu-ma Kuang's Tu-leh Yüan: 青山在屋上，流水在屋下 ("Green hills above the house, a flowing stream below").[52] Given this complementary conception of physical features, the expression *ch'iu-ho* 丘壑 ("hills and valleys") often takes on a particular semantic function as an indicator of the all-encompassing breadth of vision present within the mind of the master and manifest within his landscape artifact. We have already seen, however, that the range of possibilities encompassed by the Chinese garden extends beyond the merely terrestrial, so that the polar coordinates of Heaven and Earth (*t'ien-ti* 天地 or *ch'ien-k'un* 乾坤) are often called into play. The vertical continuum of Heaven and Earth is generally reinforced by formulas such as above and below, high and low, and particularly looking up and looking down, e.g.: 仰觀宇宙之大，俯察品類之盛 ("Looking up one views the vastness of the universe; looking down one observes the profusion of species and classes"),[53] 仰觀山，俯聽泉，傍睨竹樹雲石 ("Turning my face up I see the mountain, turning down I hear the brook, at the side I catch sight of bamboos, trees, mist, and rocks").[54] By the same token, the spatial coordinates involved in the vertical frame of reference may be rotated to project the axis of nearness and distance, such as we have seen functioning in the alternation of panoramic and close-up views. Within the special context of the enclosed garden, the related concepts "inside" and "outside" take on particularly subtle significance, as the self-contained vision of the garden as a whole is set off as complementary to the logical implication of further existence beyond its sphere—thus raising the idea of self-containment to yet a higher power.

In addition to these more or less spatially conceived coordinates, the same aesthetic control of paired concepts may be applied to more strictly perceptual qualities as well. Examples of this type include light and darkness and density and openness: . . . 俯視園亭既曠且幽 (" . . . looking down one sees the pavilions and the garden, both wide-open and darkly remote at the same time"),[55] axes often interrelated in the positioning of buildings, artificial mounds, and foliage for a maximum effect of light and shadow.[af] Similarly, the subtle interplay of hardness and softness seen in the prized moss covering on rocks and the positioning of rocks in streams adds yet another dimension to the garden scene. Even in the area of color, which one might not expect to be subsumed within bipolar form, we find the same pairing at work as in the more pairable qualities. Especially common is the establishment of red and green as coordinates of color, in much the same manner as hard and soft constitute a continuum of texture: 一路朱紅欄杆, 兩邊綠柳掩映 ("The path [inside the gate was paved with white pebbles and] bordered by scarlet balustrades, shown off to advantage by green willows on either side").[56] In the plays *Hsi-hsiang Chi* and *Mu-tan T'ing*, as in much of Chinese "romantic" drama, the juxtaposition of red and green serves to set up the intangible continuum of sensuality (*se* 色) which is associated with the sensory continuum of color.

Passing from the perceptual to the conceptual, we arrive at pairs of coordinates involving increasingly greater degrees of abstraction. We may note first of all the qualities of solidity and emptiness (*shih-hsü* 實虛) referred to by Shen Fu in a previously cited passage. This axis often has particular application to the *t'ai-hu* stones that present limitless possibilities, through their impression of unsupported weight and in the many folds and openings within their surfaces, for subtle variation of mass and void. Another pair of abstract categories highly favored by Chinese garden artists is that of stillness and movement (*tung-ching* 動靜). The author of *Yüan Yeh* presents a fine, if somewhat stereotyped, example of interplay along this continuum in his description of ripples within the reflection of the moon on a still pond, and a calm breeze rustling the strings of a zither.[57] Earlier in the same text the author speaks of the contrasting qualities *p'ien* 偏 and *ch'i* 齊 in different garden scenes, referring specifically to the relative degree of accessi-

---

[af]Cf. Yüan Mei, *ibid.*, p. 18: 屋少不遮山, 池多不妨荷 ("The buildings are few and do not block the mountains; the ponds are many so as not to cramp the lotus").

bility of a spot, although apparently with the Ch'an correlatives of particularity and universality (*p'ien-cheng* 偏正) in mind. Finally, we may add the additional continuum of life and death, or more precisely animate and inanimate matter, involved in the juxtaposition of buildings, stones, and water, on the one hand, with flora and fauna, on the other.

The above list of polar pairs underlying the aesthetics of the Chinese garden is by no means exhaustive. Indeed, since it is the formal relation of bipolarity (with the logical implications of alternation, interpenetration, and overlapping) that is at issue here, nearly any pair of specific terms may be substituted. In Po Chü-i's "Ts'ao-t'ang Chi," for example, we find the following line: 廣袤豐殺一稱心力 ("East to west, north to south, rich harvest or poor, all are encompassed by the strivings of the mind"), in which the axis of north-south versus east-west (an axis of axes) and the qualities of bounty and blight provide interesting variations on the principle of complementary bipolarity.

It should be borne in mind here with reference to these various overlapping paired concepts that the notion of bipolarity by no means implies an ideal of symmetry. While all possible pairs of opposites, being mutually complementary, may be assumed to balance out in the sum total of existence, they remain by the same token necessarily unequal within any less-than-total enclosure of space. That is, the principle of closed-system alternation ensures that for all possible pairs of concepts one term must be dominant and one recessive at any given point in time. As a result, any attempt at compositional symmetry would run counter to the spirit and the letter of the bipolar aesthetics analyzed here.

As discussed in detail in Chapter III, an essential step in the logical method of deriving a sense of totality through the overlapping of polar coordinates consists in extending the same formal relations that hold in the two-term system into schemes of multiple correspondences. Typically, the entire range of extension from duality through multiplicity to infinity is telescoped into the various five-term structural patterns we have

171

considered. In the specific area of garden aesthetics, this archetypal principle is generally manifested in the cycle of seasons
to which literary descriptions (and personal enjoyment) of the
Chinese *locus amoenus* are inextricably linked. The most common device employed in this context is a direct enumeration
of the specific joys attendant upon each season of the year in a
given garden setting, as the following examples will demonstrate:

春有錦繡谷花，夏有石門澗雲，秋有虎谿月，冬有鑪峯雪，陰晴
顯晦昏旦含吐，千變萬狀不可殫紀.

"In spring there are the flowers in Brocade Valley; in summer the mist that rises over Stone-gate Stream; in autumn
the moon over Wildcat Gorge, and in winter the snow on
Lu Peak. Cloudy or clear, bright or dim, dusk or dawn,
subtle or obvious, their are a thousand changes, ten-thousand
shapes, such as cannot be fully recorded."[58]

野芳發而幽香，佳木秀而繁陰，風霜高潔，水落而石出者，山間
之四時也. 朝而往暮而歸. 四時之景不同，而樂亦無窮也.

"The remote fragrance of wild flowers, the dense shadows
of luxuriant trees, the noble purity of wind and frost, the rocks
which stand out as the water recedes: these are the four
seasons in the mountains. One can set out in the morning
and return with dusk; the scenery of the four seasons varies,
but its joys are limitless."[59]

春水滿四澤，夏雲多奇峯，秋月揚明暉，冬嶺秀孤松.

"The spring water fills the four lakes; the summer clouds
form numerous strange-shaped peaks; the autumn moon
raises shafts of light; on the winter ridge a lone pine
sparkles."[60]

Fan Ch'eng-ta cleaves even more faithfully to the five-term
scheme implicit in the four-season cycle by specifying five
distinct seasons in his own garden retreat, dividing the vernal
months into two seasons for this purpose.[61]
It may perhaps be objected at this point that the brilliance

and poignancy of seasonal change are essential elements in the garden aesthetics of all cultures. While this is of course true in practice—particularly in the four-season climate zones—it is a striking fact that the Western tradition of *literary* gardens is almost exclusively concerned with the ideal landscape *in springtime alone*. The cataloguing of *locus amoenus* delights includes flower-decked meadows, warm breezes, and twittering birds, but rarely if ever a turning leaf or a cicada's call. This fact may go a long way towards illuminating the essential distinction drawn in this study between Chinese and Western garden allegories. We have seen that the Western literary garden—for all its synecdochical reach to the limits of finite creation—remains necessarily incomplete with respect to the world of true being to which it can refer only obliquely through the trope of metaphor.[ag] Since, moreover, the nature of the transcendent truth is generally conceived in terms of warmth, light, and growth,[ah] it follows that the earthly paradise—the highest point of imperfection striving towards perfection—be represented or negatively adumbrated in figures of these attributes; hence, the constant springtime.

This is not to imply, of course, that the Chinese tradition does not provide examples of lovely spring gardens (e.g. Tu Fu's poem "Kan Yüan" 甘園,[62] "Lan-t'ing-chi Hsü, and particularly *Hsi-hsiang Chi* and *Mu-tan T'ing*), nor may we overlook the converse view of autumn in terms of foreboding and melancholy (cf. Tu Fu's "Autumn Meditations," Ou-yang Hsiu's "Sounds of Autumn" 秋聲賦, and a large chunk of the corpus of Chinese literature). The point is, however, that given the formal relations of seasonal alternation described in this study, a model of perfection within enclosed space—such as the Western tradition presents in figures of vernal amenities— can be realized in Chinese literature only on the basis of a *complete* presentation of seasonal change. This impulse occasionally appears in a slightly debased form in the conventional desideratum of having flowers in bloom through all four

---

[ag]As clearly allegorized on Spenser's Arlo Hill.
[ah]See above, Chapter v.

seasons, thus implying the retention of spring throughout the year. But the deeper significance of seasonal periodicity in the more philosophically oriented gardens remains evident. Sometimes it even seems as if the complementary inclusion of autumn and winter within the context of seasonal totality betokens an actual *preference* for the waning phases of the yearly cycle (e.g. 四運雖鱗次理化各有準, 獨有清秋日, 能使高興盡 "Although the four seasons are transformed in orderly sequence, each with its own standards, only a clear autumn day can push exhilaration to its limits").[63] In keeping with the idea of presence within absence implied by five-term periodicity, however, the presentation of autumnal motifs directly evokes a sense of the inevitable return of spring within the ceaseless rotation of the seasons.

The reader familiar with Chinese aesthetics will have noticed that the principles of bipolar coordinates and multiple periodicity here described as the underpinnings of garden art are in fact common to much of Chinese creativity, and to the genres of landscape poetry and painting in particular.[ai] It may even be argued that the aesthetic features analyzed here on the basis of evidence from literature are more representative of literary convention than garden practice, although that should not trouble us since that is precisely the subject of this essay. In any event, it is clear that such gardens as Wang Wei's Wang-ch'uan, Po Chü-i's Ts'ao-t'ang, Ssu-ma Kuang's Tu-leh Yüan, and Yüan Mei's Sui Yüan partake of a ground of philosophical depth that transcends the boundaries of genre and medium. Yüan Mei notes the philosophical seriousness of garden design:[aj] 惟夫文士之一水一石一亭一臺皆得之於好學深思之餘 ("But for the true scholar every stream, every rock, every pavilion, every tower derives from a love of learning and deep contemplation"),[64] while the Ming painter and art critic Tung Ch'i-

---

[ai]This common ground is described by J. D. Frodsham in another context as follows: "For both these groups, scenery provided the best evidence of the fundamental nature of the universe." ("The Origins of Chinese Nature Poetry," in *Asia Major*, VIII, 1, 1960, p. 103.)

[aj]In another place, Yüan states his preference for poetry over painting to convey the beauty of his garden (*ibid.*, p. 55).

ch'ang describes the natural extension of what Frankel has termed "the convertibility of poetry and painting" into the sphere of garden design: 蓋公之園可畫, 而余家之畫可園 ("That is, while other men's gardens can be painted, my paintings can be made into gardens").[65]

Given this essential "convertibility" of art forms, it is not surprising that many of the critical concepts developed with respect to poetry and painting may apply to gardens as well. The idea of subtle variation along axes of polar coordinates immediately brings to mind the varying degrees of parallelism and pseudo-parallelism at work in Chinese poetry, and particularly in the regulated verse form. Similarly, the notion of vague echoes or recurrent variation on a theme (e.g., *hu-ying* 呼應)[ak] also comes into play in the ordering of the innumerable details of a garden landscape. The quality of mysterious depth often applied to landscape poetry (*yu* 幽) is also used in connection with garden art, where it seems to refer more to the inaccessibility of the total vision (inaccessible due to vastness, not to ontological otherness), than to any perceptual quality of darkness or depth. Finally, the author of *Yüan Yeh* introduces two specific terms: *te-t'i* 得體 and *ho-i* 合宜 to account for the impression of internal coherence which sheds artistic unity on the successful garden composition.[al]

As implied in the *Yüan Yeh*'s choice of terms, the vision of cosmic completeness projected by the aesthetic completeness of the garden landscape may give rise to the illusion that its limited plot of space is in itself a self-contained totality. From this it is only one more step to the attribution of self-contained completeness to the mind—or more accurately, the self—of

[ak]Cf. Ch'ien Yung (錢梅溪): 造園如作詩文, 必使曲折有法, 前後呼應 ("Building a garden is like writing poetry or prose; it must be subtly varied but systematic, with recurrent motifs throughout the piece"), quoted in T'ung, *ibid.*, p. 7.

[al]In the discussion in question Chi Ch'eng seems to apply the former term to the suitability of a given architectural or natural feature to a given spot, and the latter to the compositional ensemble of elements in an entire scene, although his usage of the terms is not consistent throughout the treatise.

the beholder who comprehends by means of perceptual and conceptual vision the totality of the garden.[am] Without relying on Chuang Tzu's insight for support: 天地與我並生, 而萬物與我為一 ("Heaven and Earth came into being together with me, and the myriad things are one with me"),[66] we may note that the personal response of the persona of the Chinese literary garden is often one of self-sufficiency, or ultimately the identification of the self with the totality of its vision:

雖取舍萬殊, 静躁不同, 當其欣于所遇, 暫得于己, 快然自足.

"Despite the myriad subtleties of likes and dislikes and the differences of quietude and excitement, at the moment one takes pleasure in his environment he contains it for a time within himself. He is happy and self-content."[67]

It should be added that while the notion of personal self-containment remains a consistent ideal of the Chinese tradition, without the implications of blasphemy we have seen in Western allegory, still the point that self-containment may easily degenerate into self-centeredness and even selfishness was not missed by Chinese thinkers. Thus Po Chü-i notes the danger of complacency resulting from the achievement of a fine garden,[68] while Li Ko-fei bewails the indulgent garden extravagance: 放乎以一己之私自為 ("They abandoned themselves to their own selfish pursuits"), which, as he sees it, brought on the fall of the T'ang.[69]

In any event, it must be recognized that this self-contained vision of totality, being essentially an illusory approximation, cannot be sustained over an indefinite period of time and inevitably breaks down.[an] This is especially true in the syntactical (hence, temporal) medium of literature, and even Chuang Tzu goes on from the insight cited above to the corollary that the existence of an all-embracing self implies its own reduplication and hence relative diminution. With respect to garden art this fact is manifest in the often-noted tendency towards rapid

---

[am]Cf. the "paradise within thee" in the Western context, Chapter v, above.
[an]See above, Chapter iv.

decay—what Siren has termed "the impression of mouldering and impermanence." While Siren's comment, and those of T'ung Chün to the same effect, are based on personal observations conducted during a period of massive social and political upheavals in China—particularly in the cities where, as we have seen, garden art is necessarily concentrated—nevertheless we must recognize that the aging process is an integral feature of Chinese garden aesthetics even in the best of times. Chinese poets, like their counterparts elsewhere, enjoy mourning the passing of youth in a garden setting, but visible signs of aging are generally prized by garden masters. Yüan Mei, for example, states this principle quite succinctly: (老更佳 "the older the finer"),[70] as does the author of *Yüan Yeh* (久而後成 "it becomes complete only after a long time has elapsed"). Particularly prized evidence of garden age includes a luxuriant coat of moss on rocks, and trees bearing the scars and burdens of accumulated years.[ao] Of course, such evidence of age and deterioration must also be considered within the context of the formal relations of complementary bipolarity and presence within absence. A fine example of the presence of life-force within external deterioration is realized in Act 28 (Yu-kou 幽媾) of *Mu-tan T'ing*, where a garden heavy with age becomes the setting for one of the most youthful scenes in Chinese literature.

[ao]Cf. *Fu-sheng Liu-chi* (Taipei, 1963), p. 214: 老樹多極紆廻盤鬱之勢 ("There were a great many old trees whose intertwined [branches] wound into dense patterns").

CHAPTER VIII

A GARDEN OF TOTAL VISION:
THE ALLEGORY OF THE
TA-KUAN YÜAN

ON the basis of the preceding discussion, the significance of the name of the Chia family garden in *Dream of the Red Chamber* becomes quite clear. The idea of a grand view (or "total vision" as I have rendered it), evoked through patterns observed within finite space, seems without doubt to be behind Ts'ao Hsüeh-ch'in's choice of a name for the self-contained world he creates in his great novel. In order to demonstrate that this is indeed the proper interpretation of the term *ta-kuan* 大觀, let us adduce examples of its usage in the literary tradition carried forth by the novel. Our purpose is not to determine the original source (*ch'u-ch'u* 出處) of the term—although the authors themselves indulge in this literati exercise with a number of the key names in the work (Pao-yü, Tai-yü, Wang Hsi-feng, Hsi-jen)—but rather to define the range of meaning encompassed by it.

Probably the earliest extant use of the expression *ta-kuan* in Chinese literature is found in the *I Ching* under Hexagram 20 *kuan* 觀. Here, in the *t'uan* (彖) commentary we find the following passage:

大觀在上，順而巽，中正以觀天下，觀，盥而不薦，有孚顒若．下觀而化也．觀天之神道，而四時不忒，聖人以神道設教而天下服矣．

A great view is above. Devoted and gentle.
Central and correct, he is something for
the world to view.

Contemplation. The ablution has been made, but not yet the offering. Full of trust they look up to him.

Those below look toward him and are transformed.
He affords them a view of the divine way of heaven, and the four seasons do not deviate from their rule.
Thus the holy man uses the divine way to give instruction, and the whole world submits to him.[1]

The passage, according to Wilhelm, refers to "the moment of deepest inner concentration which occurs between the ablution and libation (盥而不薦)" of a sacrificial ritual performed on or near a ceremonial tower (*kuan* 觀).[a] Even if we may be wary of Wilhelm's pointedly religious interpretation of the text,[b] the connection made here between ritual centrality, four-seasons periodicity, and universal harmony cannot but be striking within the context of the present essay.

Passing quickly ahead in literary history, we may briefly note that Chuang Tzu makes use of the expression *ta-kuan* to contrast the greater insight of Hui-shih with the empty paradoxes of lesser logicians,[3] while Chia Yi applies the same turn of phrase in his discussion of narrow and expansive views of

[a] For another example of *kuan* as a sacrificial tower, see *Li Chi*: 昔者仲尼與於蜡賓，事畢出遊於觀之上 ("Once Confucius was present at the Cha ritual. Upon the conclusion of the rites he went out to take his ease on the tower").[2] Arthur Waley ("The Book of Changes," BMFEA, v, 1933, p. 132) relates the association between ritual and ocular vision in the character *kuan* with the Latin root *templum* in the word *contemplare*.

[b] The attention of the reader is called to the remaining line and image commentary on the hexagram, and particularly the lines: 初六童觀小人道也 ("The boylike contemplation of the six at the beginning is the way of inferior people"), 六二闚觀利女貞 ("Six in the second place: Contemplation through the crack of the door. Furthering for the perseverance of a woman"), 六三觀我生進退 ("Six in the third place: Contemplation of my life decides the choice between advance and retreat"), 觀其生志未平也 ("Contemplation of his life. The will is not yet pacified") (*Chou-i Che-chung*, pp. 277–282, 816–818, tr. Wilhelm), lines applicable to several aspects of the *Dream of the Red Chamber*. The point, of course, is not that the authors of the novel had this passage in mind, but rather that the "random" coincidences of situation and judgment that comprise the text of the *I Ching* continue to *coincide* in areas of Chinese literature that would seem to be entirely unrelated to ancient divination.

179

existence in the "Owl Fu": 小智自私兮賤彼貴我，達人大觀
兮物無不可 ("The witless takes pride in his being, scorning
others, a lover of self. The man of wisdom sees vastly and
knows that all things will do").[4] The possibility of Buddhist
resonance in the term—particularly in view of the recurrent
use of Buddhist terminology in the novel—should also not be
overlooked. For example, the writer may have such concepts
as *ta-yüan chüeh kuan* 大圓覺觀 or *ta-yüan-chüeh ching-chih*
大圓覺鏡智 in mind when he sums up the grand spectacle of
the work as follows in Chapter 120: 方知石兄下凡一次磨出光明
修成圓覺，也可謂無復遺憾了 ("Now we know that since our
friend the stone has descended to earth this time, thus polishing
his brightness and cultivating his 'full vision,' there should be
no further cause for regret").

Getting back closer to our garden literature, we may recall
Wang Hsi-chih's phrase: 仰觀宇宙之大 ("Looking up one
views the vastness of the universe") in "Lan-t'ing-chi Hsü,"
which seems to refer to the same idea of total vision through a
finite perception of landscape. For an even more explicit
rendering of the concept—and perhaps the *ch'u-ch'u* of Ts'ao
Hsüeh-ch'in's usage, judging by the standards of the editors of
the *P'ei-wen Yün-fu*—we may turn to Fan Chung-yen's famous
essay "Yüeh-yang-lou Chi," in which he describes the panoramic view of Tung-t'ing Lake afforded by Yüeh-yang Tower:

予觀夫巴陵勝狀，在洞庭一湖，銜遠山，吞長江，浩浩湯湯橫無
際涯. 朝暉夕陰，氣象萬千，此則岳陽樓之大觀也.

"I looked out over the unparalleled scenery of Pa-ling all
within the expanse of Tung-t'ing Lake: the distant mountains
were contained, the endless river swallowed up, vast and
expansive, with no bounds of breadth. The morning sunlight
and evening shadows, myriads upon myriads of manifest
forms: this is the great view of the Yüeh-yang Tower."[5]

Interestingly enough, Fan Chung-yen goes on to place his
literally broad view into the context of a discussion of the
mixed feelings that arise upon contemplation of the vastness of

space (and the unpredictability of human events) towards the close of the piece.

In any event, by the Ming and Ch'ing periods the use of combinations of the characters *ta* and *kuan* with respect to garden aesthetics and metaphysics seems to have become quite conventional. The author of *Yüan Yeh*, for example, uses the expression twice in his introductory chapters: 大觀不足, 小築 允宜 ("If a total view is not forthcoming, a smaller layout may be satisfactory"), and: 略成小築, 足徵大觀也 ("A smaller layout roughly formed, may be sufficient to evoke a total view")[6] to assert the principle that the ideal of compositional completeness may be evoked with limited resources, and need not rely on construction on a grand scale. In *Fu-sheng Liu-chi*, Shen Fu mentions a Ta-kuan Pavilion[7] in a garden outside Chungking, and himself uses the term to describe the yamen garden of a *tao-t'ai* near T'ung Kuan 潼關 in Shensi Province: 河之北山如屏列已屬山西界, 真洋洋大觀也 ("The mountains north of the river lined up like a screen, already over the Shanshi border. It was truly a boundlessly vast view").[8]

While none of the above citations may be identified as the source of Ts'ao Hsüeh-ch'in's usage, it is maintained that it is the idea of vast vision within enclosed space, and not a literal panorama, to which the author refers.[c] This may be affirmed by the fact that the Ta-kuan Yüan is explicitly described as being built on a circumscribed plot of land between two urban compounds, and that, though the garden is provided with an artificial mountain (Ta-chu Shan 大主山) and a multiple-story structure (Ta-kuan Lou 大觀樓[d]), nowhere in the text do its inhabitants enjoy a panoramic view in the literal sense. Although Chia Cheng seems to be interested in such a possibility at one point during his tour of the garden in Chapter 17 (I, 195): 到 底從那一邊出去, 也可略觀大概 ("If we go out from that side we

[c] The Chih-yen Chai commentator, at least, uses the expression in several places with this range of meaning in mind.

[d] A Ch'ing commentator writing under the name Ching-san-lu Yüeh-ts'ao-she Chü-shih stresses the allegorical meaning in this particular figure: 又顯寓萬物斫歸之義 ("... and it is clearly intended to bear the meaning of the ultimate conclusion of all worldly phenomena")[9].

should be able to get a general view of the entire composition"), the initial occurrence of the expression *ta-kuan* is voiced by Pao-yü in purely abstract terms in his famous discussion of garden aesthetics to which we will return below.

Before proceeding to consider the implications of the Ta-kuan Yüan in the allegorical structure of the novel, let us briefly review some of the more outstanding physical features of this memorable Chinese garden. We have already noted that the Ta-kuan Yüan is located within the city on a plot obtained by adding land between the Ning-kuo-fu and Jung-kuo-fu compounds to an already existing garden within the Ning-kuo-fu. This earlier tract is not explicitly named, but it seems clearly to be the Hui-fang Yüan[e] visited by Pao-yü in Chapter 5. The fact that the Hui-fang Yüan is again mentioned later in the novel (Chapter 75) would perhaps seem to deny this, but Pao-yü's embarrassed recognition of the site of his earlier vision of the Red Chamber dream-sequence in Ch'in K'o-ch'ing's suite[f] seems to indicate that the smaller garden has indeed been incorporated into the larger one. In any event, the decision of the Chia elders to reconstruct an existing garden rather than to select a new site elsewhere (Chapter 16) accords well with the advice of the *Yüan Yeh* treatise. The construction of the garden is left in the hands of craftsmen, since it is conceived with practical rather than artistic intent (Chih-yen Chai argues that Yüan-ch'un's visit is the pretext, not the inspiration for the garden), and is later said to have taken one year's labor (Chapter 42) at an expense of thousands of ounces of silver (Chapter 53). The extent of the garden plot is surveyed at three and one half li (in circumference?). While this measure is of course approximate at best,[g] it may be noted that the Ta-kuan Yüan is later estimated as more than twice the area of the

[e]The name Hui-fang Yüan 會芳園 may be derived from a line in Li Po's essay cited earlier: 會桃李之芳園 ("mingle in the garden with fragrances of peach and plum").
[f]Of course, it is his memory of the supernatural landscape of his dream rather than Ch'in K'o-ch'ing's bedroom that is at issue.
[g]This must be a stereotyped exaggeration, as a similar size is attributed to the garden visited by Liu Meng-mei in *Mu-tan T'ing*, Act 24.

bailiff Lai Ta's garden (Chapter 56), although the latter is described in another place as quite opulent in its own right (Chapter 47).

The layout of the Ta-kuan Yüan garden may be roughly described as follows.[h] Moving northward through the main gate in the southern wall, the observer is immediately confronted by an artificial mountain: 只見一帶翠嶂 ("All one could see was a deep green bluff") which blocks off all view of what lays beyond. After circling this initial obstruction by means of a winding, tunnel-like passageway 曲徑通幽 (ch'ü-ching t'ung-yu), one comes to an expanse of water of varying width spanned by a major bridge (Ch'in-fang Ch'iao 沁芳橋) leading to the richly landscaped central area in which the residences of the three major characters are located. Moving further inwards, the ground begins to rise to a central eminence (Ta-chu Shan 大主山) beyond which is located the "main hall" (Ta-kuan Lou 大觀樓) with its flanking structures. Off in the far (eastern, despite the artist's rendering in Appendix III) corner, nestled in this ridge, lies the model "village" Tao-hsiang Ts'un 稻香村.

Within this general layout we may visualize the specific features of the Ta-kuan Yüan, many of which are already familiar to us from the preceding discussion of the Chinese garden tradition as a whole. Among these details, we may note the whitewashed plaster walls, ornamental gate, moon gates in interior walls, winding pathways, and zigzag bridges.[i] While considerations of space will limit a full description of all the various pavilions, kiosks, and lodges half-hidden amidst the foliage, we may pause to take note of the dense bamboos, tortuous passageways, and rare artifacts that contribute to the remote elegance (yu 幽) of Tai-yü's Hsiao-hsiang Kuan 瀟湘舘,[j] the mysterious fragrances and pure simplicity (ch'ing-ya 清雅)

---

[h]See Appendix III for schematic diagram and Ch'ing artist's conception.

[i]The fullest passages of description occur in Chapters 17, 18, 23, 40–41, and 76.

[j]Thus striking the visitors in Chapter 17 as a perfect spot for a scholar's study.

that characterize Pao-ch'ai's Heng-wu Yüan 蘅蕪院, and the brilliant reds and greens and the lavish appointments of Pao-yü's I-hung Yüan 怡紅院.[k] Mention should also be made of the fourth principal garden spot (according to Yüan-ch'un's judgement in Chapter 18), the rustic "village" set by a green mountain and identified by such conventions of the recluse tradition as a wattled fence, mulberry trees, a well, and of course sown fields. Of the remaining inhabited structures,[l] including T'an-ch'un's Ch'iu-shuang Chai 秋爽齋, Ying-ch'un's Chui-chin Lou 綴錦樓, and Hsi-ch'un's Liao-feng Hsüan 蓼風軒, only the retreat of the nun Miao-yü Lung-ts'ui An 櫳翠菴 receives special attention.

One of the noteworthy features of the Ta-kuan Yüan is its elaborate handling of the element of flowing water. Brought in from an external source through a water-gate (Ch'in Fang Cha 沁芳閘), the water winds throughout much of the area of the garden, flowing occasionally in imitation of mountain streams and at times gathered in ponds broad and deep enough to permit pleasure boating.[m] The mountain element of the *shan-shui* landscape is manifest in the central hill and the miniature peak just inside the gate, as well as in ingeniously designed caves, grottoes, and even tunnels in the rock formations. Many of the rocks in the garden, in keeping with the fact that it is built on an older garden site, are covered with a luxuriant coat of moss. As for the flowers that we have seen to play so important a role in the allegorical structure of the novel, we may note that in addition to profuse growth throughout the area, the garden includes the conventional raised flower beds, parterres, and trellises: 過了荼蘼架入木香棚, 越牡丹亭

[k]The description of the brilliant hues in terms of *wu-se* 五色 is perhaps an oblique reference to Pao-yü's five-colored origin. Of particular interest in the I-hung Yüan is the hall of mirrors that confuses Chia Cheng (Chapter 17), and later Liu Lao-lao (Chapter 41). Cf. the maze of mirrors in the Ming novella *Hsi-yu Pu* 西遊補.

[l]We have noted above the unconventionality of turning a majority of the structures in the garden into permanent residences.

[m]E.g. Liu Lao-lao's tour in Chapter 40. Chih-yen Chai speaks repeatedly of the intricacy of the garden's water courses.

度芍藥圃到薔薇院 ("Passing by a trellis of *t'u-mi* flowers, they entered a booth of *mu-hsiang* roses; proceeding through a peony pavilion and crossing a *shao-yao* peony bed, they came to a hall of roses") (Chapter 17, I, 192).

In view of this last feature, it will be necessary to consider the question of the "naturalness" of the Ta-kuan Yüan garden, for although the issue was briefly set aside above as a function of varying concepts of nature, it does come up for discussion early in the novel, and indeed at the first mention of the *ta-kuan* idea, in the famous passage (I, 192):

却又來，此處置一田莊，分明是人力造作成的. 遠無隣村，近不負郭，背山無脈，臨水無源，高無隱寺之塔，下無通市之橋. 峭然孤出，似非大觀. 那及數處，有自然之理，自然之趣呢？ 雖種竹引泉，亦不傷穿鑿. 古人云「天然圖畫」四字，正恐非其地而強為其地，非其山而強為其山，即百般精巧，終不相宜.

"Come now, to put a country village in this spot is obviously an artifical construction. It neither has neighboring villages in the distance, nor does it sit close by a city-wall; its back is to a mountain with no ridges of rock, and it faces a stream with no source. Above there is no pagoda of a hidden temple, below there is no bridge leading to the marketplace. Standing out in stark isolation, it seems to deny a broader view. How can it compare to the natural intelligibility, the natural flavor, of the previous spots? Although the bamboo was planted and the streams directed, they did not suffer from over-precision. The ancients had an expression: 'A painting like nature,' which I think means if one tries to deliberately form terrain where there is no such terrain, or to deliberately make a mountain where a mountain is not meant to be, one will never have satisfactory results, even if he exercises great ingenuity."

Pao-yü is here speaking of the introduction of a country scene—the Tao-hsiang Ts'un "village" equipped with rustic wineshop—into the otherwise conventional garden landscape. His point is well-taken that since the Tao-hsiang Ts'un is not a

real village with roots in the soil, but has simply been inserted
with no organic connections into what is essentially an artistic
composition, its effect is one of artificiality in comparison to
the other more predictable examples of garden architecture.
It should be noted to Chia Cheng's credit that he himself
recognizes the inherent artificiality of the scene (I, 190):
雖係人力穿鑿，却入目動心，未免勾引起我歸農之意 ("Although
it is carved out by human effort, still it captivates the eye
and moves the heart, and cannot but arouse my desire to
return to a country life"), although he cannot help but be
moved by the recluse ideal it calls to his mind.[n] Ultimately,
however, it is not the inclusion of "naive" motifs in the otherwise sophisticated composition to which Pao-yü takes objec-
tion, but rather the fact that it is a forced statement, a deliberate
play for naturalness, and not the spontaneous such-ness to
which the Chinese term for naturalness (t'ien-jan 天然) so
aptly refers.[o] In the terminology of the Yüan Yeh treatise, it is
a violation of the principle of te-t'i 得體, which results in the
opposite of the desired impression of naturalness. Pao-yü may
perhaps be carefully restating his position two pages later,
when, in displaying his botanical erudition gained from studying sao and fu literature, he calls our attention to Tso Ssu's
"Wu-tu Fu" 吳都賦. The fact that the opening passage of this
difficult rhyme-prose work speaks of the same problem of
adjusting architectural design to the physical lay of the land
in very nearly the same wording as Pao-yü's remark cited
above: 齷齪而筭顧亦曲士之所歎也，旁魄而論都抑非大人壯觀也
("To conduct surveys in a cramped area is a source of frustration for the stubborn scholar, but to speak of building a
capital in a barren wilderness is also not the expansive view
of a great man")[10] is an extremely interesting coincidence, if
not necessarily a direct hint on the part of the author.

[n]Chia Cheng's reaction is based more on culture and education than
on personal experience, as seen in the association of the scene with Fan
Ch'eng-ta's poetry.

[o]Cf. the Neo-Platonist distinction between natura naturata and natura
naturans underlying some of Spenser's figures (Harry Berger, Jr., "The
Mutabilitie Cantos," p. 168).

In any event we find in the Ta-kuan Yüan the same tolerant hospitality towards artificial elements alongside of the natural, which we have described above as characteristic of the Chinese garden tradition. Particularly striking examples of this may be seen in the decking out of the Ta-kuan Yüan with ornamental lanterns, banners, and even artificial flowers for Yüanch'un's late-winter visit, or the tying of cloth streamers and willow-plaited horses to trees and shrubs in observance of the Mang-chung festival 芒種節, acts quite out of place in a purely "natural" landscape. Similarly, we also find descriptions of the garden couched in stereotyped expressions of supernatural beauty, thus adding another dimension to the total vision.

The reader will perhaps have noticed that what we have in the Ta-kuan Yüan is a summing up, a composite picture of the entire range of Chinese garden art. With this in mind, the ongoing search among *Hung-hsüeh* scholars for the true location of the Chia garden loses much of its significance (although not its interest). Although the identification of a historical site is entirely irrelevant to our archetypal analysis of the garden that exists only on the pages of the novel, let us pause here to review certain details uncovered in the course of this study that may have a bearing upon the issue. If we assume it to be true that Ts'ao Hsüeh-ch'in's grandfather (Ts'ao Yin) did indeed build an ornate private garden in Nanking to receive the K'ang-hsi Emperor during one or more Imperial tours to the South, and that Ts'ao Hsüeh-ch'in did grow up in this garden, as Spence asserts; and if we accept Yüan Mei's claim (repeated by Spence) that his own Sui Yüan was acquired from a certain Sui Ho-te 隋赫德 who had taken possession after the ruin of the Ts'ao family in 1728,[p] the question still remains as to whether or not the garden later described by Ts'ao Hsüeh-ch'in in *Dream of the Red Chamber* was, in fact, patterned after the Nanking tract. At least the fact that the Ta-

[p]Cf. Yüan Mei, *ibid.*, p. 77: 隨園為國初江寧織造隋公之園, 乾隆時園已坍廢 ("The Sui Yüan was the garden of a certain Mr. Sui, a textile manufacturer in Chiang-ning at the beginning of the dynasty. By the Ch'ien-lung period the garden was already in disrepair").

kuan Yüan is explicitly set within a city on relatively flat ground, while Yüan Mei's garden is clearly located on a hill, Hsiao-ts'ang Shan 小倉山 near Ch'ing-liang Shan 清涼山[q] (inside the Nanking city walls) with an explicitly mountainous terrain, would seem to deny any strict adherence to this model. On the other hand, the lush vegetation described in the novel would seem to indicate a more southern location, as would the whitewashed walls that T'ung Chün describes as more characteristic of South China gardens, while the importance placed upon ingenuity in devising the garden's water supply would point perhaps more to a drier northern setting. One interesting alternative theory offered by Wu Liu,[11] among others, would have the Ta-kuan Yüan modelled after the palace of Prince Kung 恭親王 (I-hsin 奕訢) of the nineteenth century, taken over from the infamous eunuch Ho Shen 和珅.[r] Wu argues that the location of the Kung-fu in northwestern Peking[s] accords precisely with descriptions in the novel of streets and back alleys outside the Chia compound (e.g., the house set up by Chia Lien for his affair with Yu Erh-chieh), and also accounts for certain details of the garden's water supply.

Most likely, if we assume all the above facts to be true, the author's conception of the Ta-kuan Yüan owes a certain amount to both the Ts'ao family garden of his youth in the South and the great palatial estate near which he may have lived in less happy days in Peking, as well as to many other gardens of his personal experience and cultural heritage. The point is,

[q]*Ibid.*, p. 80: 西行二里得小倉山，山自清涼胚胎，分兩嶺而下 ("Walking two *li* west [of the old North Gate Bridge in Chin-ling] one reaches Hsiao-ts'ang Shan, a mountain originally of one formation with Ch'ing-liang Shan, split into two separate ridges . . ."). Cf. the Yao Yüan 姚園 garden, also on Ch'ing-liang Shan 清涼山, in *Ju-lin Wai-shih*, Chapter 33.

[r]The fact that Ho Shen was born only about the time that Ts'ao Hsüeh-ch'in was already composing his novel is countered by architectural evidence cited to the effect that the garden in question dates from late Ming and early Ch'ing.

[s]Cf. the following line from Pao-ch'ai's poem in Chapter 18 (I, 207): 芳園築向帝城西 ("The fragrant garden was built westwards from the Imperial City").

as it is hoped this study has demonstrated, that the Ta-kuan Yüan is such a successful summation of Chinese garden art that nearly any other example of the tradition will bear a resemblance to it.

Since the Ta-kuan Yüan is so complete a rendering of Chinese garden aesthetics, nearly all of the two-term coordinates discussed in the preceding section appear in the *Dream of the Red Chamber* as well. Without reviewing here all of these, and the other axes of alternation set forth in our consideration of the archetypal structure of the novel in Chapter IV, let us note briefly some of the paired concepts of particular importance in the Ta-kuan Yüan. We have already mentioned the striking interplay of reds and greens that characterize the I-hung Yüan (c.f. 怡紅快緑 "Pleasure in red, joy in green"), and the emphasis on the intersection of mountain and water elements in the ubiquitous streams that wind through the complicated maze of rockery. An additional axis of alternation that repeatedly emerges in the course of the long novel is that of fullness and emptiness with respect to habitation. Thus we find the Ta-kuan Yüan described as too crowded in Chapter 58 and too vacant in Chapter 74. In Chapter 76 visitors are again jostling along its paths, but thereafter its population steadily dwindles, only to see a scene of reunion in the final chapter. One somewhat striking set of coordinates, that of "convex" and "concave" (凸凹), is presented in Chapter 76 when the Chia clan, intent on viewing the brilliant moonlight on an autumn-festival evening, moves from the T'u-pi T'ang 凸碧堂 to the Ao-ching Kuan 凹晶舘. Significantly enough, this scene provokes a lengthy comment by Shih Hsiang-yün on the entire range of aesthetic coordinates that together comprise the mastery of the garden (III, 982):

可知當日蓋這園子就有學問……可知這兩處，一上一下，一明一暗，一高一矮，一山一水，竟是特因玩月而設此處.

"You can see that when they built this garden, they truly had artistic mastery. . . . Obviously these two spots; one up, one down, one bright, one dark, one high, one low, one on

189

a mountain, one near water, were arranged with the specific purpose of enjoying the moon in mind."[t]

Even more important, however, is the sense of alternation between the enclosed state of the garden and the wide world outside that comprises a major structural pattern of the entire novel.[u] Perhaps in imitation of the absolute adherence to the distinction between inside and outside in the life of the Imperial court, of which we gain glimpses in Chapter 83 (Yüan-ch'un's illness) and Chapter 85 (Pei-ching Chün-wang's birthday celebration), the manners and regulations of the Chia compound also place great emphasis on this distinction. This is especially visible on formal occasions such as the Matriarch's final birthday celebration in Chapter 110, at which the formal inhibitions against mixed company are orchestrated in terms of precisely controlled seating arrangements. The complex but strictly preserved distinction between "inner" and "outer" clan members (*nei-tsu, wai-tsu* 內族外族), of course, has fateful repercussions in the intramural rivalries within the Chia compounds.[v]

With specific reference to the garden situation, the distinction between in and out centers about the walls that enclose the garden world. The theme of locking the gates appears at quite a few points in the novel, for example in Chapter 62, when Pao-ch'ai characteristically advises keeping the doors shut, and in Chapter 77, when Pao-yü visits the dying maid Ch'ingwen and is urged to hurry back lest he be locked out overnight. An extremely complex treatment of the inner-outer continuum is seen in Chapter 111, when the guard of the near-empty garden (himself an outsider) tries to bar admittance to the nun Miao-yü, who, though referred to as "beyond the thresh-

---

[t]In a note to Chapter 17, Chih-yen Chai discusses the entire garden composition in nearly identical terms.

[u]Scenes set outside the Chia compounds occur in no less than 23 of the novel's 120 chapters; 10 chapters are devoted almost exclusively to outside action (Chapters 4, 15, 24, 64–67, 99, 104, 112).

[v]Cf. Pao-yü's remark: 裏頭外頭都是一樣的 ("Inside, outside, it's all the same") during his disoriented state in Chapter 109 (IV, 1382).

old" (檻外人), is in this case anxious to get in. This sense of the fragility of the essential distinction, or the inevitable inter-penetration of the two poles, is perhaps most clearly revealed in the easy scaling of the wall by intruders.[w] The horror at-tached to this act is first felt in a rumor spread in Chapter 73, later suppressed in the ritual exorcism in Chapter 102, and finally materialized in the outrages of Chapters 111 and 112.

Passing on to the application of structural patterns of five-term alternation in the Ta-kuan Yüan, let us consider the dimension of seasonality discussed earlier. The periodicity and mutual implication of the five elements is of course one of the major archetypal patterns from which the allegorical meaning of the novel is projected (see Chapter IV), and the concomitant rotation of the cycle of seasons is particularly visible in the shifting hues of the enclosed landscape.[x] Throughout the first 80 chapters of the work Ts'ao Hsüeh-ch'in exercises masterful control over the correspondence of plot detail and seasonal moment (the hand of the continuer is noticeably looser on this point), in order to ensure that the inhabitants of the *locus amoenus* go fishing, chase butterflies, fly kites, roast a deer, or sweep fallen petals in accordance with the yearly sequence. Most memorable in this regard are the outdoor celebrations, with their inevitable poetry-bouts, in appreciation of the prized flowers and other specific delights of each season. As the novel moves ponderously through four years of calendar time[y] we witness a New Year's season (Chapters 8–22), refined autumn pleasures (Chapters 37–42), and a glistening winter scene (Chapters 49–50), after which the year turns and the cycle repeats (New Year in Chapters 53–54, Mid-Autumn Festival

[w]The theme of garden wall-leaping in Chinese literature appears as early as the *Shih Ching*: 将仲子兮無踰我園 ("I beg of you, Chung Tzu, do not climb into our garden"), "Chiang Chung-tzu" (tr. in Birch, *Anthology of Chinese Literature*, Vol. I, p. 10), and as late as Act 3 of *Hsi-hsiang Chi.*

[x]Within this context, we may note the author's careful attention to meteorological phenomena in general, and temperature shifts in particular.

[y]From Chapter 18 to Chapter 107. In the introductory and final chapters of the novel, however, additional years pass unannounced. See Appendix II.

in Chapters 75–76, etc.). Such occurrences as the opening of the garden at the beginning of spring, the first major attacks on garden innocence in the autumn season (the search of the garden, the marriage of Ying-ch'un), and the marriage of Pao-yü and Pao-ch'ai, with the simultaneous death of Tai-yü, at the height of spring (although the point is not emphasized and may easily escape notice)[z] make it clear that the orchestration of seasonality throughout the novel is far from arbitrary.

We have already seen that the thrust of seasonal periodicity in the Chinese garden tradition is towards the evocation of a sense of totality through the spatialized juxtaposition of phenomenological change. Thus one of Pao-yü's first acts after moving into the Ta-kuan Yüan (Chapter 23) is the composition of four poems, presumably in one sitting, for all of the seasons of the year. But as noted in the tradition in general, the season of autumn is singled out for particular attention in Pao-yü's garden. It is as if the necessity of including the seasons of decay and dormancy within the total garden vision is driven home by deliberately dwelling upon the particular beauties of the cooler months. Thus the crystal ethereality of the moonlit garden in Chapters 75 and 76 (III, 983):

只見天上一輪皓月，池中一個月影，上下爭輝，如置身於晶宮鮫室之內．微風一過，粼粼然池面皺碧疊紋，真令人神清氣爽．

"One was struck by the circle of the bright moon in the sky above and the shadow of the moon within the pond, vying vertically in brightness. It was as if one were transported to a crystal palace, the abode of mermaids. As a light breeze blew by, making rippling patterns in the dark green water, it made one feel that his soul was purified and his spirit refreshed"

and the poignant strains of Tai-yü's lute on an autumn night

[z]Wu Shih-ch'ang notes a comment by Chih-yen Chai that Pao-yü was to have revisited Tai-yü's house in late autumn" (*On the Red Chamber Dream*, Oxford, 1961, p. 170). But shortly before the wedding we are told that Chia Cheng received an Imperial order in the second month to leave without delay for an official assignment, thus necessitating the immediate consummation of the match (IV, 1232).

one year later (Chapter 87) rival the balmy spring afternoons in brilliance. The fact that this sensitivity to the autumnal season is not limited to Pao-yü and his unusually sensitive cousins is emphasized in Chapter 40, when gloomy shade and withered leaves "enhance an autumn scene" (助秋興) viewed by the Matriarch and her country relative Liu Lao-lao, and again in Chapter 89, when Chia Cheng and his intimates gather "to seek out the splendors of the fall season" (尋秋之勝).

As we have seen in the preceding discussion, the aesthetic values embodied in two-term coordinates and five-term periodicity lies neither in symmetrical balance nor simply in pleasing variety, but rather in a projected vision of spatial totality that, in turn, sheds a sense of coherent completeness upon the garden composition. As we recall the close interrelation of garden and painting art, it is significant that the fullest exposition of aesthetic principles within the novel occurs in connection with Hsi-ch'un's monumental project of encompassing the vast scope of the Ta-kuan Yüan in a single painting (II, 517):

如今畫這園子, 非離了肚子裏頭有些邱壑的, 如何成畫. 這園子却是像畫兒一般, 山石樹木樓閣房屋遠近疏密, 也不多, 也不少, 恰恰的是這樣. 你若照樣兒往紙上一畫, 是必不能討好的. 這要看紙的地步遠近, 該多該少, 分主分賓, 該添的要添, 該藏該減的要藏要減, 該露的要露. 這一起了稿子再端詳斟酌方成一幅圖樣.

"Now if you are going to paint this garden, unless you have some 'hills and valleys' within you, how can you expect to accomplish it? This garden is, you might say, like a painting: it has mountain rocks and trees, towers, pavilions, and dwellings with specific degrees of distance and density, not too great, not too little, but precisely as it is. If you try to set it down on paper according to each feature it will certainly not be satisfactory. For this you must consider the distance within the range of the paper, putting more in some places and less in others as required. You must distinguish between primary and subsidiary subjects, you must add where necessary, conceal or diminish where necessary, and reveal where necessary. Only in this way, by first drafting a rough copy and then paying careful attention to the details, will it become a complete canvas."[aa]

In this passage, Pao-ch'ai instructs Hsi-ch'un on the artistic necessity of an all-embracing vision (*tu-li ch'iu-ho* 肚裏邱壑), taking in subtle variations in distance and density before the numerous details of the garden may be incorporated into a coherent work. It may be suggested here that Pao-ch'ai's advice in the art of ordering a thickly populated canvas may be applied with equal weight to the narrative art of which the *Dream of the Red Chamber* is a prime example.[ab]

While it has been a central contention of this study that the *Dream of the Red Chamber* is concerned more with the creation than the dissipation of a vision of totality in the Ta-kuan Yüan,[ac] still it must be allowed that what the reader actually experiences as he makes his way through the pages of the novel is the slow but inexorable deterioration of the garden. The fact that the garden arises in the prosperous dawn of a new year and begins to break up noticeably in a poignant autumn season adds to the conclusion that the unilinear perspective of aging and death must be recognized—along with bipolar alternation and cyclical periodicity—as a fundamental structural element of the novel. The remainder of this chapter, then, will consider the steady breakdown of the Ta-kuan Yüan as it relates to the allegory of totality realized in the novel.

We have already seen in the preceding chapter that the process of physical alteration and deterioration is an essential element in Chinese garden aesthetics. In the Ta-kuan Yüan,

[aa]The idea for the project is suggested by the Matriarch at the request of Liu Lao-lao in Chapter 42, necessitating Hsi-ch'un's request for one or two years' exemption from her poetic responsibilities. In Chapter 82 we are told that the work is still unfinished.

[ab]Chih-yen Chai often uses the expression 邱壑 to describe the breadth of vision of his novelist friend.

[ac]In an extremely interesting note in Chapter 54, Chih-yen Chai asserts that this sense of plenitude is at times *excessive*, "like eating greasy crabs" (一部大觀園之文皆若食肥蟹).

hints of inevitable decay appear as early as Chapter 56,[ad] when the financial situation of the garden necessitates drastic administrative reforms on the part of T'an-ch'un and Li Wan (apportioning the land to individual caretakers for growing profitable crops), and from Chapter 81 on the changing atmosphere becomes dominant. Thereafter, we witness a continuing worsening of the situation until the garden becomes desolate, dirty (Chapter 108), and even haunted by vengeful flower spirits (Chapters 99–102). Finally, of course, the near-empty garden falls prey to thieves and rapists (Chapters 111–112) and cannot even be sold to frightened neighbors (Chapter 114).

Given the extreme importance of popular Buddhist conceptions of retribution in Chinese domestic fiction, we must pause here to consider the moral dimensions of the dissolution of the Ta-kuan Yüan. It has been noted earlier that while the Chinese literary garden is generally more concerned with evoking a vision of the totality of existence than with the tropological significance of human action in a setting of fulfilled desire, still the dimension of moral interpretation of garden phenomena is far from absent. Even more important, we have seen that the dramatic literature to which the authors of the *Dream of the Red Chamber* are so indebted—and particularly the dramas *Hsi-hsiang Chi* and *Mu-tan T'ing*[ae]— is deeply concerned with the essentially moral problem of reconciling the intensely personal emotion of *sao* and *fu* romanticism with the more balanced wisdom of the Confucian classics.

Reverberations of traditional associations of the joys and

[ad]Chih-yen Chai notes that the garden is dangerously overextended already in Chapter 45.

[ae]The debt of the novel to these dramas is deep and pervasive enough to merit separate treatment. In addition to direct quotes in Chapters 23, 26, 35, 36, and 40, we may note numerous borrowings of plot detail, including the mourning of fallen blossoms, broken marital-promises, and vicarious love-making through lute-music (*Hsi-hsiang Chi*), and obstructive flower spirits (*hua-shen* 花神), lost examination candidates, and parental beatings (*Mu-tan T'ing*).

dangers of earthly delights are undeniably present in the literary garden of the *Dream of the Red Chamber*. Throughout the novel, the concept of spiritual wandering (*yu* 遊), so important in visions of infinity in Chinese literature, is repeatedly associated with other expressions signifying amusements of a more mundane or immediate nature (*kuang* 迋, *shua* 耍, *wan* 玩). In Chapter 23 (I, 267), for example, the life of Pao-yü and his cousins in the garden is described as follows: 園中那些女孩子正是混沌世界, 天真爛漫之時, 坐臥不避嬉笑無心 ("Those girls in the garden lived in a true world of disorder. In their innocent and carefree moments, they sat and slept together without inhibitions, laughing happily without taking heed . . ."). Later in the same chapter, we find Pao-yü writing sybaritic poetry for the enjoyment of local dandies (*ch'ing-po tzu-ti* 輕薄子弟), reading prohibited erotic books, and encountering Tai-yü in a romantic scene that, though chaste, is not quite innocent. Even after he has suffered a serious beating at the hands of his father for associations with the sort of elegant rakes who appreciate his poetry, we still find Pao-yü engaged in the same type of play in Chapter 37 (II, 440): 每日在園中任意縱性遊蕩, 真把光陰虛度, 歲月空添 ("Every day in the garden he would run free, roaming at will wherever his spirit led him; he did truly pass his time in vain, idly counting the months and years"). This aspect of Pao-yü's life in the garden is given most explicit treatment in Chapter 79 (III, 1031), when, after Ying-ch'un's departure leaves him literally sick with grief, he is consigned to his apartments for one hundred days of what seems to be unrestricted play:

暫同這些丫鬟們斯鬧釋悶…這百日內只不曾拆毀了怡紅院, 和這些丫頭們無法無天, 凡世上所無之事都玩耍出來, 如今且不消細說.

"For the time being he made mischief with his maids to dispel his sorrow. . . . Within these hundred days they nearly tore down the I-hung Yüan. He carried on with his maids as if there were neither law nor Heaven. Things never before done in this world were all tried in their play, but we need not go into detail at this point."

Another example of the "use" of the Ta-kuan Yüan as a paradise of earthly delights occurs at the end of Chapter 71, when Yüan-yang unwittingly discovers the maid Ssu-ch'i and her cousin-lover engaged in a noteworthy exception to the observation made earlier about love in the Chinese garden. The resulting discovery and suicide of Ssu-ch'i (presumably, the erotically embroidered bag that brings about the search of the garden and the discovery of a love-letter among Ssu-ch'i's possessions in Chapters 73-74 was left behind on this or a similar occasion), as well as her multiple links with Ying-ch'un[af] who departs soon thereafter to a fatal marriage, add to the impression of punished wrongdoing. Significantly, Ssu-ch'i's original assignation in Chapter 71 (III, 921) is described as taking place, true to convention, behind a *t'ai-hu* stone: 因下了甬路找微草處走動, 行至一塊湖山石後大桂樹底下來, 剛轉至石邊只聽一陣衣衫響 ("Therefore she left the path and was looking for a less overgrown spot, when she passed under a large cassia tree behind a *t'ai-hu* stone. As soon as she had rounded the stone, she heard the rustle of clothing . . ."), the scene of many other acts of mischief in the course of the novel.[ag]

It should be noted here that repeated warnings as to the dangers of improper garden use are voiced throughout the work. For example, Yüan-ch'un's first words after entering the Ta-kuan Yüan in Chapter 18 (I, 202): 太奢華過費了 ("It is too extravagant, you have spent too much on it") echo the senti-

---

[af]She is Ying-ch'un's maid, and her maternal grandmother Wang Shan-pao's wife (whose overly eager search results in her discovery) is the personal servant of Ying-ch'un's mother (father's wife), Madame Hsing.

[ag]E.g. P'ing-erh eavesdrops on a conversation between Yüan-yang and Hsi-jen from behind a *t'ai-hu* stone in Chapter 46, Pao-yü corners a maid to ask about Ch'ing-wen's death in a similar spot in Chapter 78, and Pao-yü tosses a brick into the water to frighten four girls in Chapter 81 from the same hiding place.

ments of Mencius and Hsün Tzu cited earlier. Before Pao-yü is allowed to move in, moreover, his father summons him for serious admonition as to what is expected of his life there. Later, in Chapter 34, the maid Hsi-jen begs Madame Wang to have Pao-yü moved out of the garden before he gets into more trouble of the sort punished by beating shortly before, and in Chapter 85 we find Pao-yü's tutor reiterating the warning.[ah] When Pao-ch'ai decides to move out of the Ta-kuan Yüan in Chapter 78 (III, 1011), on the pretext of helping her mother prepare for her brother Hsüeh P'an's impending marriage, her explanation leaves little room for doubt that her motives are in fact related to the danger of excessive garden delights: 如今彼此都大了…倘有一時照顧不到的皆有關係 ("But now we have all grown up. . . . If at some time there should arise a situation beyond our control, it would have serious repercussions"). At times it seems that even the insentient objects of the garden are providing ominous reminders as to the wages of sin, as when the *hai-t'ang* tree in Pao-yü's yard blossoms (Chapter 77) and withers (Chapter 94) out of season, when the guests at a mid-autumn party hear a strange moaning noise in the garden[ai] (after which Chia She is tripped up by a stone and breaks his leg), and particularly in the mysterious attack on Wang Hsi-feng in Chapter 99, which can hardly be interpreted as other than retribution for her part in the deception of Pao-yü and Tai-yü.

At the same time, however, the possibility of a more proper use of natural bounty is kept before the reader's eyes in the person of the peasant Liu Lao-lao, who appears at several key points of the novel bringing with her the rustic air of honest labor that Chia Cheng finds so appealing in the model village in the garden.[aj] In addition, Ts'ao Hsüeh-ch'in seems to draw

[ah]Cf. the warnings of parents and teachers against garden play in *Hsi-hsiang Chi* and *Mu-tan T'ing*.

[ai]This is one of a whole series of strange noises (at least ten) in the final third of the novel. One is reminded of the sound of a snapping cable, with very similar implications, in Chekhov's *The Cherry Orchard*.

[aj]Liu Lao-lao's role in *Dream of the Red Chamber* seems to parallel that of "Camel" Kuo in *Mu-tan T'ing*.

special attention to the busy labors of the servants who are assigned by T'an-ch'un to grow profitable crops in the garden after Chapter 56:

因近日將園中分與衆婆子料理，各司各業. 皆在忙時. 也有修竹的. 也有剔樹的，也有栽花的，也有種豆的，池中間又有駕娘們行着船，夾泥的，種藕的.

"Since the garden had recently been divided up among the many married women-servants for tending, every section was just at its busiest time. Some were tending bamboos, some were pruning trees, some were planting flowers, some were planting beans. Even in the middle of the ponds some women were riding on boats planting lotuses in the mud" (Chapter 58, ii, 740).

In an extremely interesting passage—one that might have aroused considerable critical attention had it appeared in another cultural context—the maid Hsi-jen suggests to a servant in charge of peach trees beset by bees that she cover the fruit with gauze netting in order to protect them from damage. When the woman gratefully offers Hsi-jen a taste of the fruit, she sternly declines on the grounds that it is not her place to eat what rightly belongs to her masters (Chapter 88). In contrast to such scenes of productive labor, the young inhabitants of the garden are often depicted as bedridden by fatigue and illness brought on by a life of leisure. For example, in Chapter 36 Pao-yü is described as "weary of playing" 遊的膩煩 (ii, 436), and later we are told that Tai-yü "having played too much these last times, could not but exhaust herself" 多遊玩了兩次，未免過勞了神 (Chapter 45, ii, 552).

In spite of such obvious excesses and unheeded warnings, however, the deterioration of the Ta-kuan Yüan is ultimately not a tropological figure. For one thing, if any guilt may be assigned for the actual confiscation of the garden, it must fall on the masters who live outside its precincts (Wang Hsi-feng, Chia She, Chia Chen, Chia Lien), or perhaps the servants and hangers-on who cause mischief within, not on Pao-yü

199

and his cousins.[ak] But the philosophical problem at issue in
the Ta-kuan Yüan is far greater than one of guilt or logical
causality.[al] Instead, a sense of the inevitability of the dissolution of the ideal landscape of *Dream of the Red Chamber* gains
increasing momentum through the course of the long novel
until the bubble has clearly burst by the final chapters.

Without making too much of the recurrent refrain 各自散
"each went his way," which ends nearly every gathering of
people in the garden, we may note the theme of certain dispersal
(散) in passages such as the following (Chapter 77, III, 994f.).

想這園裡凡大的都要去呢？　依我説將來總有一散，不如各人去
罷.

> "If you think about it, I suppose anyone in the garden who
> grows up must leave. Mark my words, eventually there
> must be a final dispersal. Each of us might as well just go her
> own way."

The same observation, moreover, is repeatedly voiced as a
tenet of popular wisdom, in such proverbs as: 盛筵必散 ("The
most sumptuous feast must have its end") (Chapter 13),
or 千里搭長棚没有個不散的筵席 ("You can set up tents for a
thousand miles, but there will never be a banquet that does not
finally break up") (Chapter 26).[am] In Chapter 113 (IV, 1431),
after the bitterest breach of the garden walls, Pao-yü meditates
on Chuang Tzu's views on permanence, and concludes: 虛無縹
緲人生在世，難免風流雲散 ("Floating in the Void, man's life on
earth must be like the flow of the wind, the dispersal of the
clouds").[an]

[ak]But Chih-yen Chai does speak of the "guilt" (罪) of Pao-yü at certain
points (e.g. Vol. I, p. 823).

[al]Even in Dante or Milton, for that matter, the Boethian argument of
conditional necessity cannot be said to greatly soften the blow of the
essential inevitability of the loss of paradise, given the finite imperfection
of the created universe.

[am]Cf. Ch'in K'o-ch'ing's recitation of the proverb: 樹倒猢猻散 ("When
the tree falls, the monkeys scatter") in Chapter 13. Chih-yen Chai points
out the wider implication of this line, as well as the recurrent refrain:
各自幹各自的去了 ("everyone went his own way").

[an]The passage cited is not from the book of *Chuang Tzu*, although its
implications are certainly compatible with that work.

As is evident in the above passages, the idea of the inevitable deterioration of the Ta-kuan Yüan is most movingly manifested in the accelerating departure of its inhabitants. Here we come to perhaps the most fundamental and pervasive theme of the entire *Dream of the Red Chamber*: the absolute necessity of egress from the self-contained world of the garden. The concept of exit (*ch'u* 出) takes on many subtle variations in the course of the novel, most notably official service (*ch'u-shih* 出仕), marriage (*ch'u-ko* 出閣, *ch'u-chia* 出嫁), and Buddhist-Taoist renunciation (*ch'u-chia* 出家), all of which are referred to at one point or another by the general expression for departure (*ch'u-men* 出門).[ao] But although the possibility of forcible *expulsion* remains before us in the many dismissals of servants for various degrees of wrongdoing, and most vividly in the *exile* of Chia She, Chia Chen, and Chia Lien for crimes against the state, it must be repeated that the inevitability of egress from this earthly paradise is rooted in the very nature of things, and not in any specific human actions. More precisely, the configurations of change that take effect within the Ta-kuan Yüan partake of the same processes of creation, growth, decay, and dissolution that characterize the entire phenomenological universe beyond its walls. The analogy to the stages of human life—pre-natal self-containment, unselfconscious childhood, maturity, marriage, regeneration, aging, and death—needs no further elaboration.

The use of the figure of ceaseless exit to characterize the human condition from birth to death is, of course, common to many cultures.[ap] In the Chinese tradition, we may note examples in the writings of Lao Tzu: 出生入死 ("come forth to life, fall back into death"),[12] Chuang Tzu: 有乎生有乎死有乎出有乎入 ("There is life and there is death; there is a coming

---

[ao] A faint echo of this theme may be perceived in the outflow of unreplaced funds in the economy of the garden: 出多入少 ("too much outflow, too little inflow").

[ap] Cf. the "universal egg" motif associated in Chapter II with the *hulu* gourd of Chinese mythology. The word *hulu* seems to recur too many times in the novel to be altogether accidental. We read of the Hulu Temple in Chapter 1, and we hear the expressions 閬葫蘆 and 葫蘆提 repeated constantly, a point not missed by Chih-yen Chai.

forth and there is a falling back within"),[13] and, in a very loose sense, Confucius: 子在川上曰，逝者如斯夫，不舍晝夜 ("By the river Confucius said, 'This is the way things move inexorably on, never pausing day or night' ").[14]

The fact that Lao Tzu and Chuang Tzu see the processes of exit as complementary with those of entry within the totality of existence, however, is not necessarily comforting to those mortals who become aware that they themselves are in the former phase and are being swept relentlessly to the sea. As a result, the sense that each step in life is a step towards the grave inspires as a rule fear and anxiety in the inhabitants of the Ta-kuan Yüan as they move out from the self-contained innocence of childhood to the self-conscious vulnerability of maturity.[aq] The association between exit from the garden and steadily approaching death is made most consistently in the theme of marriage, its significance perhaps heightened by the tensions of patrilocal exogamy in traditional Chinese society. One by one we see the girls leave their maiden garden and meet their various fates: early widowhood (Li Wan, Pao-ch'ai. Shih Hsiang-yün), harsh treatment (Ying-ch'un), distant separation (T'an-ch'un), and death (Ying-ch'un, Yüan-ch'un)— in each case a swift lesson in the *eros-thanatos* link. The case of Yüan-ch'un is particularly poignant, for it is *within* the deepest chambers of the Forbidden City (*Ta-nei* 大內) that she is shut *out* from the happiness of her youth. In the marriage of Pao-ch'ai to Pao-yü, the motif of leaving home takes an even more subtle turn, as Pao-ch'ai's marriage exit (*kuo-men* 過門) occurs for all practical purposes under one roof,[ar] although with equally irreversible consequences. Finally, we may note the specific destination: a return to Yang-chou in the South, which is repeatedly associated with Tai-yü's in-

[aq]In Chapter 98, Tai-yü's entry into and exit from this life are described with the terms *chü* 聚 and *san* 散. But although she is said to prefer the latter phase of existence: 那黛玉天性喜散不喜聚 ("Tai-yü, by her nature, enjoyed separation more than union," Chapter 31, II, 370), her tenacious will would seem to belie this.

[ar]Pao-ch'ai had moved out of the Chia garden in Chapter 78, so that, in a sense, she is returning to it for her marriage.

evitable exit (in the maid Tzu-chüan's ill-considered jest in Chapter 57, in Tai-yü's dream in Chapter 82, and ultimately in the return of her coffin for burial).

In any event, the inhabitants of the garden are quite aware of this sad fact of the human condition and comment on it frequently in the course of the novel: 嫁出去的女孩兒潑出去的水 ("A girl married out is water spilled out") (Chapter 81, III, 1046). In the context of such a view of the sudden loss of self-contained beauty upon emerging from maiden seclusion, Chia Yü-ts'un's couplet composed in the first chapter of the novel and repeated to him by Chen Shih-yin 102 chapters later: 玉在匵中求善價, 釵於奩內待時飛 ("A jade within a box asks a fine price, A hairpin within its case waits for the flight of time") seems to take on additional meaning.[as] While the specific context of the original citation of the poem no doubt refers simply to Chia Yü-ts'un's as yet unlaunched career, the association between the value of undisplayed gems and sequestered maidenhood is affirmed in Chapter 59 (II, 750) when the maid Ch'un-yen quotes Pao-yü as follows: 女孩兒未出嫁是顆無價寶珠, 出了嫁不知怎麼就變出許多不好的毛病兒來 ("A girl who has not yet been married is a priceless pearl. Once she is married somehow a number of unpleasant flaws appear").[at]

The problem of mortal existence, however, is not restricted exclusively to young girls. Pao-yü's impatience with studying and his anxiety towards his father's insistence that he prepare for an official career must, therefore, be interpreted as signifying more than simply the self-indulgent whims of a spoiled heir. The overlapping associations between government service away from home, the loss of innocence, and accelerated death are clearly linked in the novel in the unfortunate events of Chia Cheng's several terms "abroad" (*wai-jen* 外任) in the prov-

[as]Of course, the couplet also sets up the complementary relation between Tai-yü (玉) and Pao-ch'ai (釵), as well as citing Chia's scholar-name: Shih-fei (時飛). The wording in Chapter 103 varies slightly.

[at]Cf. T'an-ch'un's remark about Pao-yü's lost jade in Chapter 94 (IV, 1214): 這件東西在家裡是寶, 到了外頭不知道的是廢物 ("This thing is a treasure here at home, but outside anyone who is not familiar with it would consider it worthless rubbish").

inces.[au] Even more significant, we have seen that it is Chia
Cheng's approaching departure that necessitates the hasty
conclusion of Pao-yü's marriage to Pao-ch'ai, a point again
emphasized by the fact that Chia Cheng indeed begins his
journey on the morning after the wedding.

Finally, we may note that of the many scenes in the novel
that depict excursions outside the Chia compound, a majority
are associated with death, suffering, or at least thwarted desire.
One of the most noticeable reasons for exit, of course, is the
conducting of the funerals that occur at periodic intervals
(Chapters 14–15, 64, 95, 112). This is particularly true with
reference to Pao-yü. In the course of the novel we see him
outside of the Ta-kuan Yüan no less than 14 times,[av] including
such memorable scenes as his stay at the Man-t'ou An 饅頭庵
Nunnery in Chapter 15 (leading to the fatal affair of Ch'in
Chung with the nun Chih-neng 智能, as well as Wang Hsi-
feng's involvement in the death of Chang Chin-ko 張金哥 and
her lover), his sacrifice to the memory of the expelled maid
Chin-ch'uan 金釧 in Chapter 43, his visit to the dying maid
Ch'ing-wen in Chapter 77, and finally his own disappearance
in Chapter 119. Even his lighthearted visit to Hsi-jen's home
in Chapter 19 takes a fateful turn, as it leads directly into a
discussion of marriage and death later in the chapter.[aw]

In considering the most extreme possibility of egress presented within the novel, we run into a paradox. That is, while
the term ch'u-chia (literally, "leaving home") would seem to
indicate an acceptance of the fact of the human condition
described above, in actuality it signifies quite the opposite: a
pulling back, a withdrawal from the outside world of temporal
flux. The authors of the *Dream of the Red Chamber* seem to

[au]We may also mention the conjunction of death and initiation into
the ways of the world in Chia Yü-ts'un's early post in Chapter 4.

[av]Chapters 15, 19, 24, 25, 28, 29, 43, 52, 77, 80, 93, 95, 119 (twice in
Chapter 77). By contrast he remains within his rooms for extended periods
in Chapters 34–36, 79, and 118–119.

[aw]And follows immediately upon Pao-yü's interruption of his page
Ming-yen in the middle of performing the rites of mortality. Chih-yen
Chai notes that the servant deliberately agrees to lead Pao-yü out of the
compound in order to cover his fault.

recognize this fact in their paradoxical use of the expression *ju-men* 入門 or *ju k'ung-men* 入空門 ("enter the gate") for this type of exit (Chapters 66, 119, 120), as well as in their depiction of the ambiguous state of those who actually take the tonsure within the text. Miao-yü, for example, is a resident of the garden, and though she styles herself "beyond the threshold," she is unwilling to leave her private retreat. Later, her departure from worldly concerns is called into question in her intimacy with Pao-yü, her prophetic dream in Chapter 87, and most sardonically in her ultimate fate. Similarly, Hsi-ch'un's defiant act of *ch'u-chia* betrays a force of will unbecoming to her new role, and she too accepts a compromise of "leaving home" by settling within the garden. Since Pao-yü's exit from the world of red dust is necessitated by the special conditions of his entry (while Liu Hsiang-lien's final decision is based on an immediate personal reaction rather than on deep contemplation of the nature of existence),[ax] it may be argued that the act of Buddhist renunciation is not presented as a viable solution to the human problem of exit within the text of the novel.

Since the inevitable breakdown of the self-contained garden world is not a question of guilt, either personal or cosmic, but simply a part of the nature of existence, it would seem to follow that the dimensions of creation and dissolution, entry and exit, must take their place among the other bipolar coordinates upon which the aesthetic totality of the novel is constructed. Even the perennial issue of official service versus personal freedom in the context of the Chinese Imperial system[ay]—the issue which ultimately drives Pao-yü *out* into irrevocable withdrawal—must properly be considered in terms of complementary phases of existence rather than a dialectical choice, as Su Tung-p'o observes in his discussion of one ideal garden situation:

[ax]Even Wang Kuo-wei admits that Liu Hsiang-lien's final solution is only "external" (他律) renunciation (in his essay "*Hung-lou Meng P'ing-lun*," in *Wang Kuo-wei Hsien-sheng San-chung*, Taipei, 1966).
[ay]Cf. Pao-yü's tutor's dictum: 成人不自在, 自在不成人 ("To become a man one cannot be free; if one is free he cannot become a man") in Chapter 82 (III, 1062f.).

古之君子不必仕，不必不仕，必仕則忘其身，必不仕則忘其君.
譬之飲食，適於饑飽而已……處者安於故而難出，出者扭於利而
忘返，於是有違親絕俗之譏，懷禄苟安之弊.

"The ancient sages did not necessarily serve, and did not necessarily refuse to serve. Those who feel compelled to serve forget themselves; those who must refuse service forget their sovereigns. It may be compared to eating and drinking. One need only conform to hunger and satiety. . . . He who stays put becomes settled in his ways and can no longer come forth. He who comes forth becomes entangled in profit and forgets to return. Thus people ridicule those who renounce their parents and leave the world, and condemn those who cherish reward and seek comfort."[15]

It should, however, be recognized to Pao-yü's credit that such a choice, though based on a misinterpretation of the significance of the enclosed landscape, is also confronted by as great a thinker as Han Yü: 出門各有道, 我道方未夷, 且於此中息, 天命不吾欺 ("Outside the gate each has his own way, but my way is not smooth. And so I will rest here [trusting that] the law of Heaven will not cheat me").[16]

As a result of this sort of dialectical understanding of the complementary phases of existence, the depiction of Pao-yü's life in an earthly paradise—for all its vast completeness—emerges as more a story of impatience and suffering than one of quiet contemplation. Thus, while the loss of paradise in the Ta-kuan Yüan is more a metaphysical than a tropological issue, still the inability or unwillingness of its inhabitants to make peace with this fact seems to be at least partially responsible for the uneasiness that hovers over the novel. More precisely, it is not the wrongful actions of Pao-yü and Tai-yü that cause the bitter passing of their dream, but it is through the sad fact of their apparent inability to grasp the complementary nature of joy and sorrow that the tragedy of inevitable loss is woven into the fabric of the work.

This idea is perhaps most clearly expressed in the theme of self-inflicted pain that recurs throughout the *Dream of the Red*

Chamber. Pao-yü in particular is rebuked several times for "seeking his own suffering" (自尋苦惱), an accusation voiced as early as Chapter 22 and later turned against Tai-yü in Chapter 49.[az] The repeated refrain of expressions of wasted beauty (*tsao-t'a* 糟蹋) or lost opportunities (*tan-ko* 耽擱, *tan-wu* 耽誤) also add to the sense of unnecessary suffering. The most striking example of this type is found after Chapter 89, when Tai-yü decides to end her life by refusing to eat (*chüeh-li* 絕粒), an act clearly labelled as self-destruction in Chapter 90 (III, 1160): 却說黛玉自立意自戕 "But let me say that Tai-yü made a deliberate decision to destroy herself. . ."

In a previous chapter it was suggested that the "tragedy" of the *Dream of the Red Chamber* lies more in a perceptual failure to attain a broader view of existence than in the frustration or consequences of human action. Within the context of the breakdown of the Ta-kuan Yüan, we must qualify the idea of a tragic failure of perception, since here it is not a question of blocked vision, but rather one of overhasty generalization. That is, the "mistake" of the tragic figures of the novel—the cause of their exaggerated suffering—lies in their going one step beyond the vision of totality evinced within their garden walls to the assumption that their finite enclosure is indeed a self-contained universe within itself, such that the temporal flux of finite space is no longer relevant. In terms of the distinction drawn earlier between the tropes upon which allegory is based in the Chinese and Western traditions, this may be described as a misinterpretation of the synecdochical relation of the garden to the universe as one of metaphorical identity.

It is in this sense that numerous references to the Ta-kuan Yüan as a complete world within itself[ba] take on further significance. This is not to say, of course, that Pao-yü does

[az] Cf. the verse cited upon the introduction of Pao-yü in Chapter 3: 無故尋愁覓恨 ("Seeking sorrow and bitterness for no reason"). We may perceive a grotesque exaggeration of the same theme in the ludicrous scene of apprehended wrongdoers slapping their own faces.

[ba] Cf. Pao-yü's incredulous question in Chapter 56 (II, 715): 除了我們大觀園竟又有這一個園子? ("Besides our Ta-kuan Yüan can there really be another garden like this?").

not occasionally leave the garden (see above), and even maintain personal relationships with people outside its precincts (Pei-ching Chün-wang, Liu Hsiang-lien, Chiang Yü-han, and the *ch'ing-po tzu-ti* of Chapter 23). Instead, what we are talking about is his consistent reluctance to accept the fact of emergence from self-contained innocence to social maturity. If Pao-yü's position here is somewhat ambiguous, or explainable as a common psychological phenomenon, we may see in the Chia compounds a whole range of more extreme examples of willful self-enclosure—from Chia Ching's drug-induced introversion and Chia She's desire to surround himself with more immediate consolations, to Chia Chen's assumed "overrating of personal relations" in the affair of Ch'in K'o-ch'ing. The fact that Chia She and Chia Chen are later subjected to the most violent expulsion of all—in the form of forced exile—further affirms the pervasiveness of the enclosure and exit structure of the novel. A particularly striking example of the overly literal interpretation of the self-contained fullness of the garden may be seen in the vain attempts of the Matriarch and her descendants to maintain an illusion of family completeness through a literal application of the expression *t'uan-yüan* 團圓 at contrived gatherings and celebrations. This is most masterfully depicted in Chapter 75 (III, 974), when the Chia clan deliberately sits down to round tables: 特取團圓之意 ("with the specific idea of fullness in mind") to view the roundest full-moon of the year, at a moment when all signs among seasonal phenomena and human events point towards the onset of a phase of decay and dissolution.[bb]

Although Pao-yü can scarcely be accused of literal-mindedness or of a failure to perceive the complementary nature of the aesthetic coordinates of his garden, he too, as suggested above, is subject to the delusion that the totality immanent in this enclosed world can withstand the temporal change that characterizes finite existence. He (but not he alone, as we have seen) seeks to treat his private realm of self as the sum total

[bb]E.g. the miniature search and confiscation (*ch'ao-chia* 抄家) in Chapter 73.

of existence rather than to emerge from this shell (his *hulu* egg) to redefine his self in relation to the outside world.[bc] In this context, the famous debate between Pao-yü and Pao-ch'ai in Chapter 118 shortly before his final "exit" into a state of insulation from time's flow may take on particular significance. In this scene, it will be recalled, Pao-yü's insistence on returning to the primary self-containment of a naked babe fresh from the womb (*ch'ih-tzu chih hsin* 赤子之心), in Lao Tzu's sense, is sharply contrasted with Pao-ch'ai's Mencian emphasis on the child's capacity for empathy (*pu-jen* 不忍), and hence interdependence. Significantly enough, it is upon hearing a line expressive of the former view from the dramatic act "Shan Men" 山門:[bd] 赤條條來去無牽掛 ("naked as a babe, free to come and go with no restraint") that Pao-yü first conceives of his final solution 96 chapters later (although, as we have noted, this decision is ultimately dictated by the frame of extra-human identity into which Pao-yü's story is set). Again, the philosophical issue confronted by Pao-yü and Pao-ch'ai in their "debate"— the relation between the enclosed garden of the self and the self-contained world of experience—is one that has troubled Chinese thinkers long before and after its particular appearance here. Ssu-ma Kuang, for example, in a description of his aptly named garden of self-enjoyment, Tu-leh Yüan, seems fully aware of the implications of this issue (the same issue discussed in the passage in Mencius from which he takes the name of the garden) as he carefully defends his self-imposed isolation as a fact determined by others:

或咎迂叟曰：吾聞君子所樂必與人共之，今吾子獨取足於己不以及人其可乎？迂叟謝曰．叟愚何得比君子？自樂恐不足，安能及人？

"Perhaps someone will rebuke me ('the stubborn old man'),

[bc]Pao-ch'ai notes the basic selfishness of Pao-yü's position in Chapter 100 (ɪv, 1287): 天下就是你一個人愛姐姐妹妹呢？ ("Are you the only one in the world who loves his sisters?").

[bd]From the play "Hu-nang Tan" 虎囊彈. It is perhaps significant that Pao-yü's inspiration is derived from a scene describing Lu Chih-shen's 魯智深 un-monkish behavior and subsequent *expulsion* from a monastery.

saying: 'I hear that the sage's joy must be shared with others. But now you seek satisfaction alone within yourself, and do not extend it to others. Is this valid?' I can only apologize: 'I am a simple man, how can I be compared to a sage? I am afraid I don't even have enough joy for myself, so how can I extend it to others?'"[17]

Pao-yü's final act, then, may be interpreted as an illusory exit from the red dust of illusion by means of a withdrawal into the self. It is based on an equation of the finite frame of reference of the individual mind with the infinite vastness of all existence. In terms of the concepts of *yin* 淫, *ch'ing* 情, and *hsing* 性 that come up for serious discussion in Chapters 1, 5, 111, 120 (see above, Chapter IV), it is this type of exaggeration of individual sensitivity into a private world of total significance that makes feeling (*ch'ing* 情) synonymous with sensual excess (*yin* 淫), rather than simply indicating the temporal (particularized) manifestation of the non-particular nature of things (*hsing* 性).[be]

We have noted earlier that Chih-yen Chai affirms the possibility of attaining enlightenment through the path of human feeling (以情悟道), but that he points out that at the time of Pao-yü's first intimation of his ultimate renunciation (in the discussions of Chuang Tzu and Ch'an in Chapters 21 and 22) he is still too attached to the "poison of excessive emotion" (情極之毒) to be capable of the leap to equanimity. It is particularly interesting for our purposes that in describing Pao-yü's irreverent treatment of his symbolic stone—during his first exit from the enclosed garden in Chapter 19—Chih-yen Chai uses the following expression: 玉原非大观者也 ("because Pao-yü was still not in possession of the total vision").[18] As late as Chapter 77, he again takes up the same philosophical problem:

所以此(始)于情終于語(悟)者，既能絡(終)于悟而止，則情不得濫漫而涉于淫佚之事矣．一人前事一人了法，皆非棄竹而復惆箏之意．

[be]As implied in the *Chung Yung* 中庸 passage cited above in Chapter IV.

"And so when one begins in feeling and ends in enlightenment, and has been able to cease after having arrived at the final enlightenment, then feeling cannot become excessive and spill over into instances of sensual abandon. It is a case of a single individual's prior experience and a single individual's ultimate state, which may never mean discarding the bamboo yet still coveting the bamboo shoots."[19]

The point here is not that Chih-yen Chai is inconsistent in his very personal response to the character of Pao-yü, or that Pao-yü's final act is necessarily right or wrong, but, on the contrary, that the apparent oppositions of self and other, integration and detachment, and even being and non-being that mark out this central issue of Chinese thought must ultimately also fall into a pattern of complementary alternation within the overall allegorical vision of the novel. When Paoyü's career in the red dust is viewed from the perspective of the five-elements totality of the existential universe, his final exit emerges as simply an integral part of the harmonious whole. But when this same story is apprehended from the point of view of the mortal sensitivity of the individual character and reader, despite the fact that it cannot fail to engage our sympathies, it nevertheless remains something less than the total vision (非大观者也) evoked by the structural fullness of the allegorical text.

CHAPTER IX

ENDINGS AND CONCLUSIONS

THE preceding chapter subtitled "The Allegory of the Ta-kuan Yüan," following upon a lengthy excursus into the area of European garden allegory, promised to set forth in detail something of the meaning projected in the central figure of *Dream of the Red Chamber*. But at this late point the reader may still rightly ask where that meaning lies. If we assume that the argument may stand that Ts'ao Hsüeh-ch'in carefully framed his semi-autobiographical text to convey an intelligible vision of existence through its patterns of narrative structure, the question remains as to precisely what significance he intends to figure forth in the gathering of the twelve "gold-hairpin" maidens in an earthly paradise and the subsequent dissolution of the garden world. Are the protestations of emptiness voiced by K'ung-k'ung Tao-jen and echoed by Pao-yü throughout the text meant to be the oracular pronouncements of the author's vision, so that the entire edifice of existential plenitude erected in the pages of the novel serves only to mock the reader's desire to grasp the meaning of it all? Is the dream only meaningful after we wake up from it?

In proposing answers to these questions, let us recall the above discussion of the manner in which allegorical fiction refers obliquely to a non-mimetic dimension of truth. We have seen that in the Western tradition the "meaning" of such texts as *The Divine Comedy* and *The Faerie Queene* is conveyed by means of the trope of metaphorical reference from particular figure to hypothetical fulfillment, which in turn sheds a measure of intelligibility on the specific figure. For example, Dante's crossing of the Styx, and his emergence from the reeds on the shores of the Purgatorial Mount, fall into a meaningful typological pattern only in the ultimate context of his baptism and conversion in the waters of the Earthly Paradise. By very definition the final fulfillment is unattainable, since it is held aloft by the same ontological dualism that delineates the two-level structure of the allegorical mode. But at the same time, the central thrust of Western allegory consists in moving towards the hypothetical end-point, adumbrating it, stripping away the *integumenta* that veil it from view. Even in allegorical romances such as Spenser's great work, where the inexorable forward motion of epic structure is deflected into lateral paths and byways, we may perceive the presence of a *logical* conclusion— a Sabaoths sight at the end—that renders the wandering chaos of the text ultimately meaningful.

Since each of the allegorical texts we have considered directly reflects the Christian foundation of medieval and renaissance civilization, it might be explained that this emphasis on logical unilinearity grows out of the eschatological thrust of that system of thought. But whether Scholastic and Neo-Platonized Christianity represent the cause or the effect of this end-oriented character of Western allegory, we may also note that the impulse towards logical finality remains a consistent underpinning of the aesthetics of the entire tradition. As Chaucer's Pandarus points out in his *Troilus and Criseyde*: "th' ende is every tales strengthe."[1] In other words the same aesthetic sense that propels us through the figural typology of medieval allegory also emerges in what Kermode has termed "the sense of an ending"[2]—the end-oriented dialectics that underlie so many cultural forms in the West.

In a work such as *Dream of the Red Chamber,* by way of contrast, we cannot properly say that the specific characters and events of the narrative move steadily towards a final, conclusive vision of truth. Often it seems that Ts'ao Hsüeh-ch'in is only playing a literati game—a game that he learned from Wu Ch'eng-en and passed on to Li Ju-chen, Liu T'ieh-yün, and other "scholar-novelists" of the Ch'ing period—when he injects hints of yin-yang and five-elements correspondences into his text. But I believe that the sum total of all such hints and correspondences does add up to a certain dimension of meaning when we follow the author's most obvious signpost and look for a level of overall significance—total vision—in the figure of the Ta-kuan Yüan garden. Where the specific incidents that make up the narrative texture of the novel are most often idle, petty, anything but monumental, these individual elements may be seen to fall together into a total that is more than the sum of its parts. That is, the association of Tai-yü with the element wood and Pao-ch'ai with metal is patently meaningless, but the sense that the experience of young maidens maturing in an enclosed garden does in fact manifest the same structural models as those used to conceptualize the flux of the universe as a whole is in the final analysis an affirmation of the faith that human experience, in its totality, is intelligible.

Here we must restate our earlier characterization of this vision of totality as somehow "spatialized," in the sense that the sum total of human experience is conceived therein not as a unilinear process of historical development, but as an ever-present ground of flux that has neither beginning nor end. Where the entire sphere of natural mutability in the Western allegorical texts is clearly ordered to a First Cause and an apocalyptic end, in the Chinese literary vision the universe of experience is by definition endless. As a result, the attempt to reduce the intelligibility of the entire system to a mimetic narrative form by means of allegorical composition must necessarily embody the principle of ceaseless alternation in its own aesthetic structure.

This general aesthetic principle produces a particularly knotty problem in dealing with the *ending* of an encyclopedic work such as *Dream of the Red Chamber*. Ts'ao Hsüeh-ch'in, like Spenser, is conveniently relieved of this onus by virtue of having left what is generally considered to be an unfinished text; but the student of the novel must eventually come to terms with the manner in which whatever version he chooses to work with takes shape as a complete literary unit. The fact that the 120–chapter version of *Dream of the Red Chamber* has captured the imagination of nearly two hundred years of

214

readers indicates that—despite the internal inconsistencies pointed out by various commentators and endless polemics regarding the conclusion of the work—the book in its traditional form comprises a successful unit within the aesthetics of the Chinese literary system.

As we have already indicated, it will be suggested here that the sense of aesthetic completeness that has made *Dream of the Red Chamber* one of the classic Chinese novels is based more on the principle of compositional inclusiveness than that of logical conclusiveness. Given this general statement, it will be necessary to consider here the strong sense of *finality* which seems to accrue to the final denouement of the nearly interminable narrative. From the *Hao-liao Ko* 好了歌 song in oblique praise of finality in Chapter 1 to the end of Pao-yü's sojourn 1300 pages later (夙緣完了, "his preordained destiny was concluded"), a sense of weariness at the seeming endlessness of temporal change, and impatience for the final solution held out by the Taoist priest and Buddhist monk at several key points[a] (Chapters 1, 2, 5, 12, 25, 66, 104, 116, 117, 119, 120) follow the reader at every step. As the course of the tale moves towards its actual terminal point, echoes of this desire (one might call it a death wish) occur with increasing frequency, most movingly in Chia Cheng's anguished cry: 完了完了 ("It is finished, finished") after the confiscation of the family property in Chapter 105 (IV, 1336), in the Matriarch's quiet resignation on her deathbed: 這就是我的事情完了 ("With this my affair has ended"), and in Hsi-ch'un's search for a personal solution (*liao-chü* 了局). In the paragraphs leading up to Pao-yü's final exit, the expression *wan-le* 完了 appears no less than six times in a veritable coda of approaching finality, culminating in his last words of farewell in Chapter 119 (IV, 1495): 走了走了,不用胡鬧了,完了事了 ("I'm going, I'm going. There's no need to make a fuss. The story is over)." Finita la commedia.

It of course may not be denied that the attainment of a state of temporal completeness remains an attractive alternative in

---

[a]The Buddhist impulse towards finality may perhaps be seen in the expression of the Ch'an master Hui-neng quoted in Chapter 22: 美則美矣, 了則未了 ("Yes, it is beautiful, but it is not yet complete").

the Chinese (as the Western) tradition, or, for that matter, that Pao-yü's final solution may be read with profound admiration and even envy. This is particularly true in periods of breakdown and chaos in the external world, as Wang Kuo-wei's masterful essay "*Hung-lou Meng* P'ing-lun" demonstrates.[b] But it is here maintained that in Chinese literature in general, and within the context of the archetypal vision under consideration here in particular, the aesthetic principle of ceaseless alternation far outweights that of end-oriented finality.

Given the fact that the aesthetic patterns of structure upon which the *Dream of the Red Chamber* is based are ordered to a "goal" of endless totality rather than one of eschatological finality, we must reconsider the concluding forty chapters of the traditional text. We may assume for argument's sake that the final third of the work derives primarily from the hand of Kao E, the "editor" of the 1791 and 1792 120-chapter versions, although recent scholarship has begun to come around to the possibility that Kao's somewhat stereotyped claim of having "discovered" and collated an original manuscript of Ts'ao Hsüeh-ch'in's need not necessarily be false.[c] Like Jean de Meun and any other continuer of a great literary work, Kao E has come under critical fire on a number of points, although there is a general consensus that this "continuation" is of a quality that is beyond comparison with other less successful attempts at cashing in on the manifest greatness of the original work.

The first and most common criticism of the final section—the fact that a number of inconsistencies of detail have been allowed to slip by the "editor's" attention—may be quickly dismissed. Such inconsistencies are undeniably present in the last forty chapters, but they are also far from absent in the "original" eighty chapters, which, after all, were in a process of constant revision from the circulation of the first manuscripts up to the author's untimely death.[d] Even in the area of linguistic

---

[b]One is reminded of similar sentiments in an age of comparable dissolution one millenium earlier: 春花秋月何時了? ("Spring flowers, autumn moons: when will it all end?").

[c]Viz. C. T. Hsia, *The Classic Chinese Novel* (New York, 1968), p. 252f.

[d]Chih-yen Chai frequently points out discrepancies between the

216

discrepancies, the two sections of the text cannot be summarily distinguished. Wu Shih-ch'ang seems to be correct in questioning Karlgren's hasty conclusion that the underlying grammatical consistency of the first eighty and last forty chapters proves that they were the work of one hand, but, again, the occasional intermixing of Northern and Southern linguistic variants and the artificial overemphasis of Pekingese forms cited by Wu to disparage the latter section are significantly pointed out by Chih-yen Chai within the first eighty chapters alone.[3]

The real question, therefore, in evaluating the assumed role of Kao E in the formation of this masterwork of the Chinese tradition, devolves upon the manner in which he has brought the "endless" volume to a conclusion. We may immediately note the evident concern of the continuer with tying up loose ends, particularly through the device of explicit recapitulation of earlier details (as many as 64 times in the last forty chapters). He is, after all, finishing the book. Some of his efforts in this direction leave certain threads noticeably dangling (e.g., the possibly significant later role of Chia Yün and Hsiao-hung, upon whom a great deal of narrative time was expended in the early chapters of the work), or fail to take up hints planted in earlier passages (e.g., the ultimate fate of Hsi-jen, the manner of the death of Hsiang-yün's husband, etc.). But in general Kao E has been granted at least the credit for a meticulous reading of the first eighty chapters and a painstaking attention to following through on many of the prior foreshadowings of ultimate ends.[e]

---

manuscripts he is working with and what he knows to be the "original" version of the story.

[e]Much of the traditional condemnation of Kao E's work has centered around the issue of Chia Cheng's image as a stern Confucian enforcer, and Pao-yü's final decision to sit for the much-maligned state examinations. Without getting involved in these outdated polemics, we may note that at several points in the first section Chia Cheng betrays the possibility of warm sympathy beneath his stern commitment to Confucian values (e.g. Chapter 22, 78)—and for that matter even his famous beating of Pao-yü might be read as a symptom of his deeply felt concern for his son's welfare, provoked by seemingly irrefutable evidence of the dangerous consequences of Pao-yü's behavior. By the same token, the precise circumstances and motivations of Pao-yü's return to the Confucian classics in the continuation can scarcely be interpreted as any sort of capitulation to the Confucian system.

We should not overlook, in this regard, the fact that the last ten or so chapters of the first eighty, where we witness in rapid succession the miniature "raid" on the garden, Tai-yü's advancing illness, Ch'ing-wen's death, and Ying-ch'un's tragic marriage, already evince a sharp turn in the direction taken by the subsequent section. When we consider the general pattern within which the Ta-kuan Yüan garden-world arises in Chapters 17 to 19, attains its greatest fullness with the integration of several new maidens in Chapters 49 to 52 (significantly in winter), and then moves on to a masterfully depicted phase of emptiness within fullness such as we have seen in the autumn rituals of Chapters 75 and 76, the manner in which the continuation takes us on through further phases of desolation and renewed hope must merit a certain measure of critical appreciation.

What is of particular importance to us here, therefore, is not whether or not Kao E has done justice to every characterization or foreshadowing in the "original" manuscripts, but more specifically whether or not he has conformed to the basic aesthetic patterns that we have seen to underlie the allegorical structure of the work. In the critical terminology of Chih-yen Chai, the question is: does Kao E's handling of the alternation between union and separation or joy and sorrow fall into a "stereotyped mold" (窠臼) of juxtaposed scenes, or does it manifest a deep aesthetic sense of the complex interrelation of logical categories of experience, such as we have isolated as an archetypal underpinning of the Chinese literary tradition? As must be evident by this point, it is the opinion of this writer that Kao E's performance in this area marks out a positive contribution to Chinese literary history. That is to say, the common criticism of Kao E as a writer of simplistic happy endings seems to miss the point of the final chapters. Even if we were to accept the final scenes of the novel as a happy reunion and restoration of the glory of the family (although it takes place under circumstances that are only barely joyful, and anything but permanent), we cannot help but interpret them in the context of the ceaseless alternation of union and separation, prosperity and ruin, that we have observed in capsule form in the prologue-frame of Chen Shih-yin and Chia Yü-ts'un, and witnessed in the unsteady fortunes of the Chia clan through 120 chapters.[f] A traditional commentator who writes under the name Ming-chai Chu-jen (明齋主人)[g] sums up his own evaluation of the work as follows: 小説家結構大抵由悲而歡由離而合, 是書則由歡而悲, 由合而離 ... ("Where novelists generally structure their works from sadness to joy and from separation to union, this book moves from joy to sadness, from union to separation").[4] Within the context of this study, we may expand on this comment to state that the great novel that Ts'ao Hsüeh-ch'in began and Kao E finished follows in its entirety an aesthetic pattern that moves from sadness-within-joy (歡中悲) to joy-within-sadness (悲中歡), with the understanding always that both of these aspects of human experience are in the final analysis logically interrelated.

The implications of the aesthetics of ceaseless alternation are important not only for our appreciation of the greatness of *Dream of the Red Chamber,* but also because they account for a central critical dimension of the Chinese narrative fiction tradition as a whole. We may note that each of the "classic" Chinese novels evinces a comparable tendency to present a gradual gathering of the forces and figures that make up its particular mimetic world, culminating in a series of episodes marking the point of greatest fullness of this world, followed by an extended treatment of the dissolution or disillusionment of the central vision. In effect, what we observe is a "climax" long before the actual denouement of the works, with the corollary assumption that the cycle presented in the text has not been a unilinear pattern of rise and fall, but rather one cyclical sweep in the ceaseless recurrence of existential flux. Significantly, the Chinese dramatic literature to which we have

[f] See Appendix II for the fluctuations of the Chia family fortunes during the course of the novel.
[g] In *Hung-lou Meng Chüan* 紅樓夢卷 (Peking, 1963), I-su 一粟 attributes this commentary to Chu Lien 諸聯, a Ch'ing writer known for the *pi-chi* collection *Ming-chai Hsiao-shih* 明齋小識.

seen *Dream of the Red Chamber* to be deeply indebted, is often structured more in terms of the sort of unilinear, end-oriented patterns that we have associated with the dialectics of the Western tradition than in terms of the aesthetics of endlessness under consideration here. Thus we see in many plays (including *Mu-tan T'ing* and *Hsi-hsiang Chi*, etc.) an initial situation of separation or otherwise frustrated desire followed by trials of the hero's physical or intellectual prowess, leading to a final scene of joyful union or reunion. In view of Chih-yen Chai's comment that Ts'ao Hsüeh-ch'in originally intended to write a dramatic version of his autobiographical narrative (傳奇),[5] we may interpret his explicit disparagement of the *ts'ai-tzu-chia-jen* 才子佳人 romanticism of the popular stage and chapbook fiction in Chapter 1, as well as the Matriarch's restatement of this position in Chapter 54, as indicating that he was interested in a vision with broader implications than the particular fulfillment or frustration of youthful dreams.

In any event, this subtle balance between temporal finality and spatial completeness may help to explain why, in spite of the sense of infinite plenitude that arises out of the finite phenomena of the Ta-kuan Yüan, a recurrent theme of incompleteness runs like a minor mode through the course of the novel. Despite descriptions of the self-sufficiency and self-satisfaction of Pao-yü's life in the garden early in the work: 寶玉自進園來心滿意足, 再無別項可生貪求之心 ("From the time Pao-yü entered the garden, he was perfectly content, there was nothing else for which his heart could seek") (Chapter 23, I, 266),[h] consistent evidence of economic insufficiency (Chapter 56), financial insolvency, and health deficiency begins to pile up from the earliest chapters. One is reminded of Tai-yü's medical problem, *pu-tsu chih cheng* 不足之症, which later serves as a pretext for denying the fulfillment she seeks. The fact that all three of the major heroines: Tai-yü, Pao-ch'ai, and Shih Hsiang-yün, are full or partial orphans reveals a further dimension of the idea of incompleteness, as do the themes of

[h]Reminiscent of the idea of self-contentment (*tzu-tsu* 自足) we have seen earlier in connection with the garden tradition in general.

loss and forgetfulness considered above in Chapter IV. Moreover, a negative transformation of the same idea may be perceived in the themes of insatiability (*pu chih tsu* 不知足) or self-aggrandizement (*pu an pen-fen* 不安本分, *pu shou-chi* 不守己) which characterize a major portion of the static (*tung chung ching* 静中動) phases of existence in the garden. Perhaps the most explicit treatment of the theme of incompleteness appears in recurring statements as to the futility of seeking perfect contentment in individual existence, wisdom voiced ironically enough by Tai-yü in Chapter 76 (III, 983): 事若求全何所樂 ("If you seek completeness in life, how can you ever be happy").[i] The vanity of the desire for simultaneous fulfillment in all aspects of life (*liang-ch'üan* 兩全) seems to be implicit in the apparent attempt of Pao-yü to have his timeless totality and enjoy its temporal pleasures too, to combine the ideal virtues of Tai-yü and Pao-ch'ai (*chien-mei* 兼美, the childhood name of Ch'in K'o-ch'ing revealed to Pao-yü in his dream vision in Chapter 5) in a single love object. Here again, the aesthetics of plenitude not only do not rule out figures of mortal incompleteness, but in fact necessitate their inclusion, so that the very desire to attain a state of self-contained completeness in individual experience is in itself symptomatic of incomplete vision.

Finally, let us note the fact that the perception of incompleteness naturally arouses in the beholder the desire to fill in the gap, to repair the missing section. Significantly, the Chinese word for such a concept: *pu* 補, occurs at many points in the text, its meaning varying from economic measures (T'an-ch'un's austerity program in Chapter 56) and bodily reconstitution (cf. Tai-yü's medicine described in Chapter 45), to the literal mending of clothing (Chapter 52, 勇晴雯病補孔雀裘 "The brave Ch'ing-wen, though sick, mends the peacock

---

[i]Cf. Shih Hsiang-yün's use of the proverbial expression for insatiability: 得隴望蜀 ("Take Lung, and look towards Shu") in her reply to Tai-yü. The fact that Shih Hsiang-yün's seemingly perfect husband, blessed with both good looks and talent, dies leaving her a young widow, further bears out this sense.

cloak"). In what is perhaps a minor detail in Chapter 89, it is reported that Chia Cheng is kept away from home for an extended period of time in order to supervise the repair of dikes breached in local flooding. This insignificant passage is here singled out for particular attention, for it brings us back to the starting point of this essay: a mythological act of wall-repair (Nü-kua pu-t'ien 女媧補天) on a cosmic scale. We may recall that the 118-chapter story of Pao-yü's loss of paradise begins when his precious jade is rejected by Nü-kua in repairing the breach of Heaven, and that it is Nü-kua's partial solution to the problem of mortality which ultimately drives Pao-yü to terminate his sojourn in the red dust.

The preceding paragraphs may perhaps have left the impression that the allegory of the *Dream of the Red Chamber* is primarily concerned with the dialectics of innocence and experience, in much the same manner as we have seen in the garden allegories of the Western tradition. In a sense this is true, but it has been the purpose of this study to point out that the archetypal form of complementary bipolarity described in Chapter III may also be applied to such cosmic opposites as innocence and experience, self and other, creation and dissolution, being and non-being. As a result, even the unilinear progress of inexorable dissolution (on the model of human aging and death) must be envisioned in terms of ceaseless alternation rather than dialectically final acts of loss and recovery.

It is on this level of abstraction that the author's consistent emphasis on the interpenetration of truth and falsity, or reality and illusion (真假), within his "red-chamber dream" may take on a specific dimension of meaning. As mentioned at the start of this chapter, the possibility of interpreting the entire "red-chamber dream" as a false illusion—the opposite of the "true" vision of the Buddhist monk, the Taoist priest, and the pre-incarnate stone—presents itself repeatedly in the course of the long novel.[j] But it will be argued in conclusion that within the

[j]The traditional commentators of course dwell at length on the idea of the dream vision in their allegorical readings. Significantly, of the four-

breadth of vision that characterizes the work as a whole, even truth and falsity, reality and illusion, must be treated as complementary possibilities rather than dialectical antitheses. That is, if we follow the formula offered in Chapter 1 and repeated in Chapter 5: 假作真時真亦假 ("When the false is taken to be the true, then the true is also false") and thereby recognize the illusory nature of the vision of existential plenitude in the Ta-kuan Yüan, we must also go on to consider the obverse wisdom that the patently "false" story of Chia Pao-yü may still manifest a certain degree of positive truth regarding the human condition in the world of experience. In other words, we must understand the professed interrelation of truth and falsity, as allegorized in the *doppelgänger* mutual implication of the true and the false Pao-yü, as essentially a two-way street.

Thus when Chih-yen Chai explains the Ta-kuan Yüan as an allegorical figure for "the illusory land of the Void" (太虚玄境),[6] I believe his point is not to be taken in the sense of a literal protestation of the Buddhist doctrine of emptiness, but instead in the sense of the infinite totality of existential flux, the ground wherein such expressions as *t'ai-chi* 太極 or *wu-chi* 無極 tend to merge in meaning. Significantly, the same verse concerning truth and falsity which we have just considered goes on to remind us that: 無為有處有還無 ("Where non-being turns into being, being reverts to non-being"). That is, the spatial totality of the allegorical vision of the novel is of an order that includes both being and non-being within its scope, so that the apparent opposition of being and non-being emerges as an example of the sort of interpenetration of reality and illusion for which the dream is the nearest analogue in human experience.[k]

In the slow temporal process of reading this huge novel, the reader naturally tends to choose between Tai-yü and Pao-ch'ai, between the commitment of the "true" Chen Pao-yü and the

---

teen dreams presented in the course of the novel, all are sooner personal fantasies than mystic visions. Perhaps the most interesting occurrence is Pao-yü's non-dream: his failure to have a dream of Tai-yü in Chapter 109.

[k] After all, even the wit of Chuang Tzu's butterfly dream cuts two ways.

renunciation of the "false" Chia Pao-yü, between the illusory nature of reality and the affective real-ness of the illusion. But when weighed in the balance, in terms of the fullness of the work as a whole, all these potentially dramatic or even dialectical choices seem to emerge rather as complementary alternatives within a single, intelligible ground of being. It is as an example of this breadth of vision that the *Dream of the Red Chamber* takes its place as a major achievement of the Chinese literary tradition.

SOURCE NOTES

CHAPTER I

[1] Ernst Cassirer, *Language and Myth* (New York, 1946), p. 87.

[2] Northrop Frye, *Fables of Identity* (New York, 1963), p. 33.

[3] Derk Bodde, "Myths of Ancient China" (in *Mythologies of the Ancient World*, ed. Samuel Noah Kramer, Garden City, New York, 1961), p. 370.

[4] Robert Graves, *The Greek Myths* (New York, 1957), p. 10.

[5] Northrop Frye, *Anatomy of Criticism* (Princeton, 1957), p. 136.

[6] Bernhard Karlgren, "Legends and Cults in Ancient China" (in *BMFEA*, XVIII, 1946), p. 342.

[7] Bodde, "Myths," p. 405.

[8] Claude Lévi-Strauss, "The Structural Study of Myth" (in *Journal of American Folklore*, LXVIII), p. 430.

[9] Bodde, "Myths," p. 376.

[10] Lu Hsün, "Chung-kuo Hsiao-shuo Shih-lüeh" 中國小說史略 in *Lu Hsün San-shih-nien Chi* 魯迅三十年集, Vol. III, p. 28.

[11] Karlgren, "Legends and Cults," p. 201.

[12] *Ibid.*, p. 240.

[13] Henri Maspero, "Légendes Mythologiques dans le Chou King," *Journal Asiatique*, CCIV (1924), p. 99n.

[14] Karlgren, "Legends and Cults," p. 356.

[15] Chang Kwang-chih, *The Archaeology of Ancient China* (New Haven, 1968), p. 251f.

[16] Frye, *Anatomy*, p. 136f.

CHAPTER II

[1] Liu An 劉安, *Huai-nan Tzu* 淮南子 (Taipei, 1965), ch. 6, p. 7a; trans. Derk Bodde, "Myths of Ancient China," in *Mythologies of*

the Ancient World, ed. S. N. Kramer (Garden City, 1961), p. 386f.

[2]Yüan K'o 袁珂, Chung-kuo Ku-tai Shen-hua 中國古代神話 (Peking, 1960), pp. 54–58.

[3]Lo Pi 羅泌, Lu Shih 路史 (Taipei, 1965), 後紀, ch. 2, p. 1b.

[4]Lieh Tzu 列子 (Taipei, 1965), ch. 5, p. 3b.

[5]E.g. Shen Hsiang-jo 沈湘若, Shih-ch'ien Shen-hua 史前神話 (Kaohsiung, 1955), p. 2f.

[6]Ying Shao 應劭, Feng-su T'ung-i 風俗通義 (Taipei, 1968), p. 83 (trans. Derk Bodde, ibid., p. 388f.).

[7]Ch'u Tz'u 楚辭 (Taipei, 1962), "T'ien Wen" 天問, p. 28a (trans. Derk Bodde, ibid., p. 389).

[8]Karlgren, "Legends and Cults," p. 229.

[9]Liu An, Huai-nan Tzu, ch. 17, p. 4a.

[10]Shan-hai Ching Chien-shu 山海經箋疏 (Taipei, 1965), ch. 16, p. 1a.

[11]Ssu-ma Chen 司馬貞, Pu Shih Chi 補史記, p. 1b.

[12]Ying Shao, Feng-su T'ung-i, p. 49.

[13]Lo Pi, Lu Shih, 後紀, ch. 2, p. 2a.

[14]Chou-li Chu-shu chi Pu-cheng 周禮注疏及補正 (Taipei, 1967), ch. 14, p. 10a.

[15]Ssu-ma Ch'ien, Shih Chi, ch. 2, p. 16b.

[16]Wen I-to 聞一多, "Kao-t'ang Shen-nü Ch'uan-shuo chih Fen-hsi" 高唐神女傳說之分析, in Wen I-to Ch'üan-chi 聞一多全集 (Shanghai, 1949), Vol. 1, p. 102ff.

[17]T'ai-p'ing Kuang-chi 太平廣記 (Peking, 1959), pp. 2407 and 3115.

[18]Lo Pi, Lu Shih, 後紀, ch. 1, p. 7b.

[19]Ibid., ch. 2, p. 1b.

[20]Sung Chung 宋衷, Shih Pen 世本, cited in Wen I-to, Ch'üan-chi p. 3.

[21]Lu T'ung 盧仝, "Yü Ma I Chieh-chiao Shih" 與馬異結交詩 in Ch'üan T'ang-shih 全唐詩 (Peking, 1960), Vol. 6, p. 4383.

[22]Li Jung 李冗, Tu-i Chih 獨異志, in Pai-hai 稗海 (Taipei, 1965), ch. 下, p. 19a.

[23]Yüan K'o, Shen-hua, p. 42ff.

[24]Liu An, Huai-nan Tzu, ch. 6, p. 7b.

[25]Ssu-ma Chen, Pu Shih Chi, p. 1a.

[26]Yüan K'o, Shen-hua, p. 45.

[27]Wen I-to, "Fu-hsi K'ao" 伏羲考, in Ch'üan-chi, p. 59f.

[28]Pan Ku 班固, Po-hu T'ung 白虎通 (Taipei, 1967), ch. 1 上, p. 21.

[29]Bodde, "Myths," p. 386.

[30]Chuang Tzu 莊子, comm. Kuo Hsiang 郭象 (Taipei, n.d.), pp. 89, 141, 206, 311, 400.

[31] *Chou-i Che-chung* 周易折中, "Hsi-tz'u Chuan" 繫辭傳 (Taipei, 1971), p. 980 tr. R. Wilhelm, *The I Ching*, p. 296.

[32] Sir James George Frazer, *The Golden Bough* (New York, 1928, abridged edition), p. 324.

[33] Yüan K'o, *Shen-hua*, p. 48.

[34] Frazer, *The Golden Bough*, p. 109.

[35] Cheng Hsüan 鄭玄, *I Wei Pa-chung* 易緯八種 (Taipei, 1966), pp. 34, 45; and Werner, *Dictionary*, p. 334.

[36] Marcel Granet, *Danses et Légendes de la Chine Ancienne* (Paris, 1959), p. 46n; Wolfram Eberhard, "Lokalkulturen im Alten China," in *T'oung Pao*, Ser. 2, No. 37 (1942, supplement), pp. 138, 281, 359.

[37] Wolfram Eberhard, *Chinesische Volksmärchen* (Jena, 1927), pp. 29–31.

[38] Eduard Erkes, "The God of Death in Ancient China" (in *T'oung Pao*, Ser. 2, 35, 1939), p. 187.

CHAPTER III

[1] Eduard Erkes, "Die Dialektik als Grundlage der Chinesischen Weltanschauung" (in *Sinologica*, II, 1950), p. 36.

[2] Joseph Needham, cited in Frederick W. Mote, *The Intellectual Foundations of China* (New York, 1971), p. 20.

[3] *Lieh Tzu*, ch. 1, p. 4b.

[4] *Chou-i Che-chung*, "Hsi-tz'u Chuan," 下, p. 1062.

[5] *Ch'un-ch'iu Fan-lu* 春秋繁露 (Taipei, 1967), ch. 13, no. 59.

[6] *Chou-i Che-chung*, "Hsi-tz'u Chuan," 上, p. 1026.

[7] *Lao Tzu* 老子 (Taipei, 1965), p. 53.

[8] *Chou-i Che-chung*, p. 700, trans. Richard Wilhelm, *The I Ching* p. 575.

[9] Erkes, "Die Dialektik," p. 37f.

[10] Cf. Georges Poulet, *Les metamorphoses du cercle* (Paris, 1961), *passim*.

[11] Janusz Chmielewski, "Notes on Early Chinese Logic" (in *Rocznik Orientalistyczny*, XXVIII, XXIX, XXX, 1965–66).

CHAPTER IV

[1] Cf. Donald A. Mackenzie, *Myths of China and Japan* (London,

SOURCE NOTES

1923), p. 211f.; Henry Doré, *Recherches sur les superstitions en Chine* (Shanghai, 1915), *passim*.

2 *Chih-yen Chai Ch'ung-p'ing Shih-t'ou Chi* 脂硯齋重評石頭記 (1760 ms., Peking, 1955), Vol. II, p. 1874.

3 *Ibid.*, Vol. I, p. 405.

4 *Ibid.*, p. 856.

5 Ts'ao Hsüeh-ch'in 曹雪芹, *Tseng-p'ing Pu-t'u Shih-t'ou Chi* 增評補図石頭記 (Shanghai, 1930), ch. 22, p. 13.

6 E.g. *Chih-yen Chai Ch'ung-p'ing Shih-t'ou Chi*, Vol. I, p. 343; Vol. II, p. 1004.

7 *Ibid.*, pp. 297, 304, 405, etc.

8 *Ch'ien-lung Chia-hsü Chih-yen Chai Ch'ung-p'ing Shih-t'ou Chi*, 1754 ms. (甲戌), p. 21.

9 *Chih-yen Chai Ch'ung-p'ing Shih-t'ou Chi*, Vol. II, p. 1149.

10 Ts'ao Hsüeh-ch'in, *Tseng-p'ing Pu-t'u Shih-t'ou Chi*, Introductory Chapter: "Tu-fa" 讀法, p. 2f. (Sun K'ai-ti, p. 124f, cites this as part of an edition he designates *Chiao-ch'uan Ta-mou Shan-min Chia-p'ing Hung-lou Meng* 蛟川大某山民加評紅樓夢, and identifies Ta-mou Shan-min as Yao Hsieh 姚燮, but the editor of *Hung-lou Meng Chüan* attributes the same text to a certain Chang Hsin-chih 張新之.) It was printed in a number of different Ch'ing editions.

11 *Ch'ien-lung Chia-hsü Chih-yen Chai Ch'ung-p'ing Shih-t'ou Chi*, p. 24.

12 *Chih-yen Chai Ch'ung-p'ing Shih-t'ou Chi*, Vol. I, p. 513.

13 *Ibid.*, Vol. II, p. 1941.

14 *Ibid.*, Vol. I, p. 349.

15 Ts'ao Hsüeh-ch'in, *Tseng-p'ing Pu-t'u Shih-t'ou Chi*, "Tu-fa," p. 2.

16 K'ung Ling-ching 孔另境, *Chung-kuo Hsiao-shuo Shih-liao* 中國小說史料 (Shanghai, 1957), p. 198.

17 See C. T. Hsia, *The Classic Chinese Novel* (New York, 1968), p. 268.

18 *Ch'ien-lung chia-hsü Chih-yen Chai Ch'ung-p'ing Shih-t'ou Chi*, p. 55.

19 *Ibid.*, p. 244; and *Chih-yen Chai Ch'ung-p'ing Shih-t'ou Chi*, Vol. I, p. 639.

20 *Ibid.*, Vol. I, p. 468.

21 *Ibid.*, Vol. II, p. 1046.

22 *Ibid.*, Vol. II, p. 959.

23 *Ibid.*, Vol. I, p. 639.

[24] *Ch'ien-lung Chia-hsü Chih-yen Chai Ch'ung-p'ing Shih-t'ou Chi*, p. 63.

[25] *Ibid.*, p. 124.

[26] *Ibid.*, p. 106.

[27] *Ibid.*, p. 171.

[28] *Ibid.*, p. 101.

[29] *Chih-yen Chai Ch'ung-p'ing Shih-t'ou Chi*, Vol. I, p. 472.

[30] *Chou-i Che-chung*, p. 728, trans. Wilhelm, p. 664.

[31] Joseph Campbell, *The Hero with a Thousand Faces* (New York, 1956), p. 114.

[32] Claude Lévi-Strauss, *The Raw and the Cooked* (New York, 1969), p. 246.

[33] *Ibid.*, p. 320.

[34] *Ibid.*, p. 287.

CHAPTER V

[1] Ts'ao Hsüeh-ch'in, *Tseng-p'ing Pu-t'u Shih-t'ou Chi*, introductory sections; *Chih-yen Chai Ch'ung-p'ing Shih-t'ou Chi, passim.*

[2] E.g. St. Augustine, *On Christian Doctrine* (Indianapolis, 1958), III/29.

[3] Kenneth Burke, *A Grammar of Motives* (New York, 1945), p. 34.

[4] C. S. Lewis, *The Allegory of Love* (Oxford, 1936), p. 42.

[5] Heraclitus, *Homeric Questions*, 5/1, in Héraclite, *Allégories d'Homère* (Paris, 1962), trans. Félix Buffière, p. 4.

[6] Quintilian, Book VIII, Part VI, Section 44 (Loeb Classical Library, Cambridge, Massachusetts, 1943), Vol. III, p. 326.

[7] Lewis, *Allegory*, p. 44.

[8] Harry Berger Jr., *The Allegorical Temper* (New Haven, 1957), p. 166.

[9] Rosemond Tuve, *Allegorical Imagery* (Princeton, 1966), p. 18.

[10] Robert Hollander, *Allegory in Dante's Commedia* (Princeton, 1969), p. 52.

[11] D. W. Robertson Jr., *A Preface to Chaucer* (Princeton, 1962), p. 79.

[12] William Empson, *The Structure of Complex Words* (London, 1951), p. 346.

[13] Charles S. Singleton, *Dante Studies 2: Journey to Beatrice* (Cambridge, Mass., 1958), p. 96.

[14] Frye, *Anatomy*, p. 90.

[15] Dante Alighieri, Epistola X, in *The Latin Works of Dante* (Edinburgh, 1914), p. 348.

[16] Singleton, *Journey*, p. 73.

[17] Allen Tate, "The Symbolic Imagination" (in *Kenyon Review*, 1952), p. 259.

[18] Frye, *Anatomy*, p. 89; Lewis, *Allegory*, p. 44f; Bernard F. Huppé, *A Reading of the Canterbury Tales* (State University of New York, 1964), p. 34.

[19] Berger, *Temper*, p. 182ff.

[20] Marc-Rene Jung, "Études sur le poéme allégorique en France au Moyen Age" (in *Romanica Helvetica*, Vol. 82, 1971), p. 20.

[21] Frye, *Anatomy*, p. 71.

[22] Cicero, *De Oratore*, Book III, Section 166 (Loeb Classical Library, Cambridge, Massachusetts, 1948), p. 131.

[23] Lewis, *Allegory*, p. 60.

[24] C. K. Ogden and I. A. Richards, *The Meaning of Meaning* (New York, 1927), p. 213.

[25] Frye, *Anatomy*, p. 123.

[26] W. K. Wimsatt and Monroe Beardsley, *The Verbal Icon* (University of Kentucky Press, 1954), p. 217.

[27] Tuve, *Imagery*, p. 22.

[28] Marc-René Jung, "Études," p. 19.

[29] Max Black, *Models and Metaphors* (Ithaca, New York, 1962), p. 241.

[30] Edmund Spenser, *The Faerie Queene*, in *The Complete Poetical Works of Edmund Spenser* (Cambridge, Mass., 1908), Commendatory Verses, "Ignoto."

[31] C. S. Lewis, *Spenser's Images of Life* (Cambridge, 1967), *passim*.

[32] Boethius, *The Consolation of Philosophy* (ed. Richard Green, Indianapolis, 1962), p. 79.

[33] A. Bartlett Giamatti, *The Earthly Paradise and the Renaissance Epic* (Princeton, 1966), p. 237.

[34] Spenser, *Faerie Queene*, I:ii:10.

[35] *Ibid.*, III:viii:41.

[36] *Ibid.*, IV:i:18.

[37] *Ibid.*, III:vi:11.

[38] John Milton, *Paradise Lost and Paradise Regained*, ed. Christopher Ricks (New York, 1968), II:666.

[39] Arthur O. Lovejoy, *The Great Chain of Being* (New York, 1936), p. 90.

[40]Cf. A. S. P. Woodhouse, "Nature and Grace in *The Faerie Queene*" (in *ELH*, XVI, pp. 194–225), *passim.*

[41]Thomas Aquinas, quoted in Singleton, *Journey*, p. 134.

[42]Dante, Epistola x, *Latin Works*, p. 351.

[43]Singleton, *Journey*, p. 4.

[44]Northrop Frye, "The Structure of Imagery in *The Faerie Queene*" (in *University of Toronto Quarterly*, XXX), p. 117.

[45]Milton, *Paradise Lost*, V:383.

[46]Erich Auerbach, *Mimesis* (Princeton, 1953), p. 200.

[47]C. S. Lewis, *A Preface to Paradise Lost* (Oxford, 1942), p. 125.

[48]Milton, *Paradise Lost*, V:573.

[49]Lovejoy, *Great Chain*, p. 42.

[50]Milton, *Paradise Lost*, III:373, 375, 377.

[51]Thomas P. Roche Jr., *The Kindly Flame* (Princeton, 1964), p. 198.

[52]Tuve, *Imagery*, p. 98.

[53]Burke, *Grammar*, pp. 503, 508.

[54]Frye, *Anatomy*, p. 322.

[55]Spenser, *Faerie Queene*, VII:viii:2.

[56]Frye, *Anatomy*, p. 162.

[57]Geoffrey Chaucer, "The Nun's Priest's Tale," in *The Works of Geoffrey Chaucer*, ed. F. N. Robinson (Cambridge, Mass., 1957), ll. 4189–4190.

[58]Milton, *Paradise Lost*, II:550–551.

[59]Boethius, *Consolation*, p. 24

[60]*Ibid.*, p. 118.

[61]Georges Poulet, *Studies in Human Time* (Baltimore, 1956), p. 9.

[62]Lovejoy, *Great Chain*, p. 49.

[63]Edmund Spenser, "An Hymne of Heavenly Love," l. 95.

[64]Robertson, *Preface to Chaucer*, p. 374.

[65]Harry Berger Jr., "Spenser's Garden of Adonis: Force and Form in the Renaissance Imagination" (in *University of Toronto Quarterly*, XXX), p. 132.

CHAPTER VI

[1]Mircea Eliade, *The Sacred and the Profane* (New York, 1957), p. 63.

[2]Ernst Robert Curtius, *European Literature and the Latin Middle Ages* (New York, 1953), p. 197.

[3]*Ibid.*, p. 195.

[4] Mircea Eliade, "The Yearning for Paradise in Primitive Tradition" (in *Daedalus*, Spring 1959), p. 264.

[5] Lewis, *Allegory*, p. 75.

[6] St. Augustine, *Confessions* (New York, 1963), VIII:viii.

[7] John V. Fleming, *The Roman de la Rose* (Princeton, 1969), p. 224.

CHAPTER VII

[1] *Chou-i Che-chung*, p. 294, trans. Richard Wilhelm, *The I Ching*, p. 93.

[2] *Shih Ching Shih-i* (Taipei, 1961), p. 143.

[3] *Ch'u Tz'u* 楚辭, ed. Chiang Chi (Shan-tai-ko) (Taipei, 1962), ch. 1, p. 10b.

[4] *Ibid.*, ch. 4, p. 6b.

[5] *Ibid.*, ch. 6, pp. 7b, 8a, 20a; trans. David Hawkes, *Ch'u Tz'u* (Oxford, 1959), pp. 106, 107, 113.

[6] *Shan-hai Ching Chien-shu* 山海經箋疏 (Taipei, 1965), ch. 2, p. 17b.

[7] *Mu-t'ien-tzu Chuan* 穆天子傳 (Taipei, 1967), p. 6.

[8] *Liu-ch'ao Ssu-chia Ch'üan-chi* 六朝四家全集 (Taipei, 1968), p. 494; trans. Burton Watson, *Chinese Rhyme-Prose* (New York, 1971), pp. 103, 106.

[9] *Wen Hsüan* 文選 (Taipei, 1959), p. 149, trans. Watson, *ibid.*, p. 66.

[10] *Chin Shu* 晉書 (Taipei, 1965), ch. 33, p. 12a.

[11] "Chin-ku Shih-hsü" 金谷詩序, quoted in Ni Hsi-ying 倪錫英, *Lo-yang* 洛陽 (Shanghai, 1939), p. 57.

[12] Wang Shih-fu 王實甫, *Hsi-hsiang Chi* 西廂記 (Shanghai, 1955), p. 112.

[13] *Ibid.*, p. 124.

[14] T'ang Hsien-tsu 湯顯祖, *Mu-tan T'ing* 牡丹亭 (Shanghai, 1959), p. 151.

[15] *Ssu-shu Chi-chu* (Taipei, 1965), ch. 3, p. 21a, tr. D. C. Lau, *Mencius* (London, 1970), p. 113.

[16] *Hsün Tzu Chi-chieh* (Taipei, 1962), p. 148.

[17] *Wen Hsüan*, p. 86; trans. Burton Watson, in Cyril Birch, *Anthology of Chinese Literature* (New York, 1965), Vol. I, p. 152.

[18] *Lo-yang Ch'ieh-lan Chi* 洛陽伽藍記, quoted in *Kuang-po Wu-chih* 廣博物志 (Taipei, 1972), Vol. 5, p. 3054.

[19] Wang Hung-hsü 王鴻緒, *Shih Ching Chuan-shuo Hui-tsuan* 詩經傳說彙纂 (Taipei, 1967), pp. 154, 183, 279.

[20] *Liu Ch'ao Ssu-chia Ch'üan-chi*, p. 494; trans. Watson, *Chinese Rhyme-Prose*, p. 103.

[21]T'ao Yüan-ming 陶淵明, *T'ao Yüan-ming Shih Chien-chu* 陶淵明詩 箋註 (Taipei, 1964), p. 110.

[22]Chi Ch'eng 計成, *Yüan Yeh* 園冶, in *Hsi-yung-hsüan Ts'ung-shu* 喜咏軒叢書, Vol. 5, ch. 1, p. 3a.

[23]Li Yü 李漁, *Li Yü Ch'üan-chi* 李漁全集 (Taipei, 1970), p. 2429.

[24]Chi Ch'eng, *Yüan Yeh*, ch. 1, p. 2a.

[25]T'ung Chün 童寯, *Chiang-nan Yüan-lin Chih* 江南園林志 (Peking, 1963), p. 12.

[26]Shen Fu 沈復, *Fu-sheng Liu-chi* 浮生六記 (Taipei, 1963), p. 306.

[27]Oswald Siren, *Gardens of China* (New York, 1943), p. 4.

[28]Liu Tsung-yüan 柳宗元, *Liu Tsung-yüan Ch'üan-chi* 柳宗元全集 (Hong Kong, n.d.), p. 208; trans. Cyril Birch, *Anthology of Chinese Literature*, Vol. I, p. 258.

[29]Siren, *Gardens*, p. 17.

[30]*Ibid.*, p. 62.

[31]Li Yü, *Li Yü Ch'üan-chi*, p. 2429.

[32]Chi Ch'eng, *Yüan Yeh*, ch. 1, p. 3a.

[33]Li Ko-fei 李格非, *Lo-yang Ming-yüan Chi* 洛陽名園記 (Peking, 1955), p. 9.

[34]Su Shih 蘇軾, "Ling-pi Chang-shih Yüan-t'ing Chi" 靈壁張氏園 亭記, in *Su Tung-p'o Chi* 蘇東坡集 (Taipei, 1967), Vol. 2, pt. 6, p. 34.

[35]Shen Fu, *Fu-sheng Liu-chi*, p. 222.

[36]*Ibid.*, p. 230.

[37]Wu Ching-tzu 吳敬梓, *Ju-lin Wai-shih* 儒林外史, p. 349; trans. Yang Hsien-yi and Gladys Yang, *The Scholars* (New York, 1972), p. 450.

[38]*Chin P'ing Mei* 金瓶梅, quoted in T'ung, *Chiang-nan Yüan-lin Chih*, p. 41.

[39]Po Chü-i 白居易, "Ts'ao-t'ang Chi" 草堂記, in *Po-shih Ch'ang-ch'ing Chi* 白氏長慶集 (in *Ssu-pu Ts'ung-k'an*, Shanghai, 1919), *t'ao* 71, *ts'e* 9, ch. 26, p. 5b.

[40]Shen Fu, *Fu-sheng Liu-chi*, p. 54.

[41]E.g. Wang Hsi-chih 王羲之, "Lan-t'ing-chi Hsü" 蘭亭集序, in *Wang Yu-chün Chi* 王右軍集 (Taipei, 1971), p. 336.

[42]Wu Ching-tzu, *Ju-lin Wai-shih*, p. 349; trans. Yang and Yang, *The Scholars*, p. 450.

[43]Shen Fu, *Fu-sheng Liu-chi*, p. 78.

[44]Chi Ch'eng, *Yüan Yeh*, ch. 1, p. 1b.

[45]Li Yü, *Li Yü Ch'üan-chi*, p. 2367.

[46]*Chin P'ing Mei*, quoted in T'ung, *Chiang-nan Yüan-lin Chih*, p. 41.

[47]James Legge, *The Four Books* (New York, 1966), p. 312.

⁴⁸Po Chü-i, "Ts'ao-t'ang Chi," p. 5a.

⁴⁹Shen Fu, *Fu-sheng Liu-chi*, p. 92f.

⁵⁰Li Ko-fei, *Lo-yang Ming-yüan Chi*, p. 11.

⁵¹Wang Hsi-chih, *Wang Yu-chün Chi*, p. 335.

⁵²Su Shih 蘇軾, "Ssu-ma Chün-shih Tu-leh-yüan" 司馬君實獨樂園 in *Su Shih Shih* 蘇軾詩 (Hong Kong, 1965), p. 90.

⁵³Wang Hsi-chih, *Wang Yu-chün Chi*, p. 335.

⁵⁴Po Chü-i, "Ts'ao-t'ang Chi," p. 3b.

⁵⁵Shen Fu, *Fu-sheng Liu-chi*, p. 216.

⁵⁶Wu Ching-tzu, *Ju-lin Wai-shih*, p. 327; tr. Yang and Yang, p. 419.

⁵⁷Chi Ch'eng, *Yüan Yeh*, ch. 1, p. 5a.

⁵⁸Po Chü-i, "Ts'ao-t'ang Chi," p. 5a.

⁵⁹Ou-yang Hsiu 歐陽修, "Tsui-weng T'ing Chi" 醉翁亭記 in *Ou-yang Yung-shu Wen* 歐陽永叔文 (Taipei, 1964), p. 118.

⁶⁰T'ao Yüan-ming, "Ssu-shih i-shou" 四時一首 in *T'ao Yuan-ming Shih Chien-chu*, p. 133.

⁶¹Fan Ch'eng-ta 范成大, "Ssu-shih T'ien-yüan Tsa-hsing Liu-shih-shou" 四時田園雜興六十首 in *Fan Shih-hu Chi* 范石湖集 (Peking, 1962), p. 372.

⁶²Tu Fu 杜甫, "Kan Yüan" 甘園 in *Tu Shih Ch'ien-chu*, p. 276.

⁶³Yin Chung-wen 殷仲文, "Nan-chou Huan-kung Chiu-ching Tso I-shou" 南州桓公九井作一首 in *Wen Hsüan*, p. 206.

⁶⁴Yüan Mei 袁枚, "Sui-yüan Hou-chi" 隨園後記, in *Sui-yüan Ch'üan-chi* 隨園全集 (Hong Kong, n.d.), p. 81.

⁶⁵Tung Ch'i-ch'ang 董其昌, *T'u-ch'ai Chi* 兎柴記, quoted in T'ung, *Chiang-nan Yüan-lin Chih*, p. 44.

⁶⁶*Chuang Tzu*, p. 51.

⁶⁷Wang Hsi-chih, *Wang Yu-chün Chi*, p. 336.

⁶⁸Po Chü-i, "Ts'ao-t'ang Chi," p. 5a.

⁶⁹Li Ko-fei, *Lo-yang Ming-yüan Chi*, p. 13f.

⁷⁰Yüan Mei, "Ta-jen Wen Sui-yüan" 答人問隨園, in *Sui-yüan Ch'üan Chi*, p. 56.

CHAPTER VIII

¹*Chou-i Che-chung* 周易折中 (Taipei, 1971), pp. 661f., tr. R. Wilhelm, *The I Ching*, p. 486.

²*Li Chi Chang-chü* 禮記章句 (Taipei, 1967), ch. 9, p. 1.

³*Chuang Tzu*, p. 583.

⁴Chia Yi 賈誼, "Fu-niao Fu" 鵩鳥賦, in *Wen Hsüan*, p. 131; trans. Burton Watson, *Chinese Rhyme-Prose*, p. 27f.

SOURCE NOTES

[5]Fan Chung-yen 范仲淹, "Yüeh-yang-lou Chi" 岳陽樓記 in *Fan Wen-cheng Kung-chi* 范文正公集 (Taipei, 1968), ch. 7, p. 95.

[6]Chi Ch'eng, *Yüan Yeh*, ch. 1, pp. 2a, 4a.

[7]Shen Fu, *Fu-sheng Liu-chi*, p. 306.

[8]*Ibid.*, p. 320.

[9]Ching-san-lu Yüeh-ts'ao-she Chü-shih 晶三盧月草舍居士, "*Hung-lou Meng* Ou-shuo" 紅樓夢偶說, in I-su 一粟, *Hung-lou Meng Chüan* (Taipei, 1971), p. 125.

[10]Tso Ssu 左思, "Wu-Tu Fu" 吳都賦, in *Wen Hsüan*, p. 56.

[11]Wu Liu 吳柳, "Ching-hua Ho-ch'u Ta-kuan Yüan?" 京華何處大觀園, in Wu Shih-ch'ang 吳世昌, *San Lun Hung-lou Meng* 散論紅樓夢 (Hong Kong, 1963), pp. 186–200.

[12]*Lao Tzu* 老子 (Taipei, 1965), p. 61.

[13]*Chuang Tzu*, p. 433.

[14]*Lun Yü* 論語, IX:16.

[15]Su Shih, *Su Tung-p'o Chi*, Vol. 2, pt. 6, p. 34.

[16]Han Yü, "Ch'u-men" 出門, in *Han Ch'ang-li Chi*, ch. 1, p. 49.

[17]Ssu-ma Kuang 司馬光, "Tu-leh Yüan Chi" 獨樂園記, in *Ssu-ma Wen-kung Wen-chi* 司馬溫公文集 (Taipei, 1967), p. 305.

[18]*Chih-yen Chai Ch'ung-p'ing Shih-t'ou Chi*, Vol. I, p. 416.

[19]*Ibid.*, Vol. II, p. 1880.

Chapter IX

[1]Geoffrey Chaucer, *Troilus and Criseyde*, II, 260.

[2]Frank Kermode, *The Sense of an Ending* (New York, 1967), *passim*.

[3]*Chih-yen Chai Ch'ung-p'ing Shih-t'ou Chi*, Vol. I, p. 894; Vol. II, p. 1224.

[4]Ts'ao Hsüeh-ch'in, *Tseng-p'ing Pu-t'u Shih-t'ou Chi*, introductory chapters, "Ming-chai Chu-jen Tsung-p'ing" 明齋主人總評, p. 6.

[5]*Chih-yen Chai Ch'ung-p'ing Shih-t'ou Chi*, Vol. I, p. 502.

[6]*Ibid.*, p. 339.

235

APPENDIX I

Pictorial representations of Nü-kua and Fu-hsi (Wen I-to, *Wen I-to Ch'üan-chi* [Shanghai, 1948], pp. 6–7)

東漢武梁祠石室畫象 Stone relief in mausoleum of Wu-liang Tombs, Eastern Han period

238

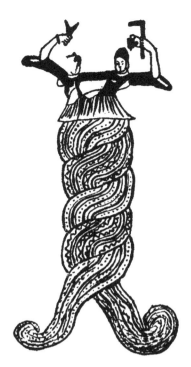

隋高昌故址阿斯塔那 (Astana) 墓室彩色絹畫 Silk painting (in color) from Astana mausoleum at ancient site of Kao-ch'ang, Sui period

東漢石刻 Stone relief from Eastern Han period

APPENDIX II

Chapter	Time	Movement	Stillness	Elegance	Baseness	Joy	Sorrow	Union	Separation	Harmony	Conflict	Prosperity	Decline
1	Mid-autumn New Year	•					•		•			•	•
2	Many years		•					•				•	
3	Late winter	•		•				•				•	•
4		•			•			•				•	•
5				•	•			•					
6	Early winter			•	•			•			•		•
7	"			•	•	•		•			•	•	•
8	"			•	•			•		•			
9	Months later	•		•				•				•	
10	Autumn	•		•				•				•	
11	9th mo., 11/30, 12/2	•		•	•			•				•	
12	Spring	•		•					•				
13		•		•			•		•		•		•
14	49 days			•			•					•	•
15		•		•			•		•			•	•
16	Spring	•		•	•		•					•	
17	Mid-spring			•	•	•						•	
18	10th mo., 1/15	•		•			•	•	•	•	•		
19			•								•	•	
20			•									•	
21			•	•	•						•		•
22	1/21	•		•	•		•			•	•		•
23	3rd mo.			•	•			•		•		•	
24				•	•						•		
25		•		•			•				•		
26				•				•		•			
27	4/26			•	•	•		•					
28		•		•	•		•	•					
29	5/3	•		•			•					•	•
30	5/5	•					•					•	
31		•											
32	Summer			•			•			•			
33		•									•		
34				•		•							
35				•	•						•		
36		•											•
37	8/20	•		•			•			•	•		•
38		•		•			•			•	•		•
39				•	•		•			•	•		•
40		•		•	•		•			•	•		•

✦ = turning year

Chapter	Time	Movement	Stillness	Elegance	Baseness	Joy	Sorrow	Union	Separation	Harmony	Conflict	Prosperity	Decline
41			•	•	•		•			•			
42	8/25		•	•			•			•			
43	9/2		•	•				•					
44		•			•							•	
45			•	•			•			•			
46			•	•								•	
47	9/14	•		•	•							•	
48	10/14		•	•					•	•			
49	10/17	•		•		•	•		•	•		•	
50			•	•						•	•		
51	Winter		•	•		•		•					
52			•	•									
53	12/29	•		•			•		•				•
54	1/15, 1/17	•		•			•		•		•		
55	1/18	•											•
56			•						•				•
57		•					•		•				
58	Ch'ing-ming Festival	•							•			•	
59			•									•	
60			•									•	
61			•									•	
62		•		•			•			•			
63			•	•						•			•
64	7th mo.	•		•	•		•	•					
65			•	•		•					•		
66	8th mo.	•											
67			•				•					•	
68	8/14, 8/15	•								•			
69		•								•	•		
70	Spring, 3/2, 3/3	•	•	•		•	•		•	•		•	
71	8/3, 8/5	•	•	•	•	•				•			
72	8/12	•										•	•
73			•	•									•
74		•		•								•	•
75	8/15	•					•			•			•
76	8/16		•	•				•		•			
77			•					•		•	•		•
78			•	•						•			
79	(100 days)		•					•		•		•	
80			•	•									

Chapter	Time	Movement	Stillness	Elegance	Baseness	Joy	Sorrow	Union	Separation	Harmony	Conflict	Prosperity	Decline
81			•	•							•		•
82			•	•			•						
83			•		•						•		•
84			•	•							•		
85		•		•	•	•	•				•	•	•
86			•	•	•								•
87	9th mo.		•	•							•		
88	Ch'ung-yang Festival		•	•	•						•		
89	10th mo.		•	•						•	•		
90			•		•						•		
91	Late winter		•	•	•						•		
92	11/1		•	•						•			•
93			•	•	•								•
94		•	•						•	•			•
95	12/18	•							•		•	•	
96	1/17	•	•	•						•			
97		•		•				•	•	•	•		
98		•		•				•		•		•	
99	1 month	•							•		•		•
100			•				•		•	•			
101		•										•	•
102	Several months	•										•	•
103			•				•		•				
104			•				•	•					
105	One year	•					•					•	•
106			•									•	•
107			•									•	•
108			•	•					•	•	•		
109			•	•				•	•				
110		•						•	•				•
111		•					•		•				•
112	3 years	•					•		•			•	
113				•			•			•	•		
114				•						•			•
115				•	•					•			
116				•									
117			•								•	•	•
118	8/3	•		•	•								•
119		•					•		•	•			•
120		•								•		•	

APPENDIX III

Ch'ing artist's conception of the Ta-kuan Yüan garden in *Dream of the Red Chamber* (From *Tseng-p'ing Pu-t'u Shih-t'ou-chi*, Shanghai, 1930)

Location of principal garden structures in Ch'ing artist's conception

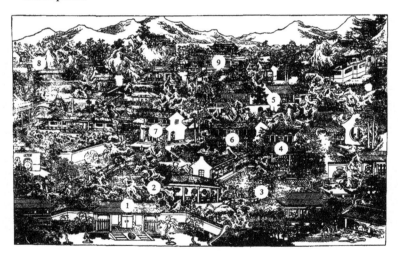

1	正門 Main gate	6	怡紅院 I-hung Yüan
2	曲徑通幽 Ch'ü-ching T'ung-yu	7	蘅蕪院 Heng-wu Yüan
3	沁芳橋 Ch'in-fang Ch'iao	8	稻香村 Tao-hsiang Ts'un
4	沁芳亭 Ch'in-fang T'ing	9	大觀樓 Ta-kuan Lou
5	瀟湘館 Hsiao-hsiang Kuan		

246

大觀園總圖

BIBLIOGRAPHY

Western Language Sources

Auerbach, Erich. *Mimesis*. Princeton, Princeton University Press, 1953.
——. "Typological Symbolism in Medieval Literature," *Yale French Studies*, IX (1952), p. 3–10.
Saint Augustine. *On Christian Doctrine*. Indianapolis, Bobbs-Merrill Library of Liberal Arts, 1958.
Bennett, Josephine Waters. "Spenser's Garden of Adonis," *PMLA*, XLVII, pp. 46–80.
Berger, Harry Jr. *The Allegorical Temper*. New Haven, Yale University Press, 1957.
——. "*The Mutabilitie Cantos*: Archaism and Evolution in Retrospect," in *Spenser: A Collection of Critical Essays*. Englewood Cliffs, New Jersey, Prentice-Hall, 1968.
——. "Spenser's Garden of Adonis: Force and Form in the Renaissance Imagination," *University of Toronto Quarterly*, XXX, pp. 128–149.
Berrall, Julia S. *The Garden*. Thames and Hudson, 1966.
Black, Max. *Models and Metaphors*. Ithaca, Cornell University Press, 1962.
Bloom, Edward A. "The Allegorical Principle," *ELH*, XVIII (1951), pp. 163–190.
Bodde, Derk. "Harmony and Conflict in Chinese Philosophy," in *Studies in Chinese Thought*. ed. Arthur F. Wright. Chicago, University of Chicago Press, 1963.
——. "Myths of Ancient China," in *Mythologies of the*

Ancient World. ed. Samuel Noah Kramer. Garden City, New York, Anchor Books, 1961.

Boethius. *The Consolation of Philosophy.* ed. Richard Green. Indianapolis, Bobbs-Merrill Company, 1962.

Brooke-Rose, Christine. *A Grammar of Metaphor.* London, Secker and Warburg, 1958.

Burke, Kenneth. *A Grammar of Motives.* New York, Prentice-Hall, 1945.

Campbell, Joseph. *The Flight of the Wild Gander,* New York, Viking Press, 1951.

————. *The Hero with a Thousand Faces.* New York, Meridian Books, 1956.

Cassirer, Ernst. *Language and Myth.* New York, Harper and Brothers, 1946.

Chang, H. C. *Allegory and Courtesy in Spenser: A Chinese View.* Edinburgh University Press, 1955.

Chang Kwang-chih. *The Archaeology of Ancient China.* New Haven, Yale University Press, 1968.

Charity, A. C. *Events and their Afterlife.* Cambridge University Press, 1966.

Chaucer, Geoffrey. *The Works of Geoffrey Chaucer.* ed. F. N. Robinson. Cambridge, Massachusetts, Houghton-Mifflin Company, 1957.

Ch'en, H. S. and Kates, G. N. "Prince Kung's Palace and its Adjoining Garden in Peking," *Monumenta Serica,* v (1940), pp. 1–80.

Cheney, Donald. *Spenser's Image of Nature.* New Haven, Yale University Press, 1966.

Cheng Te-k'un. "Yin-Yang and Wu-Hsing in Han Art," *Harvard Journal of Asian Studies,* xx (1957), pp. 31–45.

Chmielewski, Janusz. "Notes on Early Chinese Logic," in *Rocznik Orientalistyczny,* xxvi–xxvii (1962–69).

Christie, Anthony. *Chinese Mythology.* Middlesex, England, Hamlyn House, 1968.

Clifford, Derek. *A History of Garden Design.* London, Faber and Faber, 1962.

Crisp, Frank. *Medieval Gardens.* London, John Lane, 1924.

Curtius, Ernst Robert. *European Literature and the Latin Middle Ages.* Bollingen Series 36. New York, Pantheon Books, 1953.

Dante Alighieri. *La Divina Commedia,* ed. G. Vandelli: Milan, Società Dantesca Italiana, 1938.

————. *The Divine Comedy.* Modern Library, 1932.

————. *The Latin Works of Dante.* trans. A. G. Ferrers-Howell and Philip H. Wicksteed. Edinburgh, Temple Classics, 1914.

Doré, Henry. *Recherches sur les superstitions en Chine.* Shanghai, T'ou-se-we, 1915.

Dunbar, H. Flanders. *Symbolism in Medieval Thought and its Consummation in the Divine Comedy.* New York, Russell and Russell, 1961.

Duncan, Joseph Ellis. *Milton's Earthly Paradise.* Minneapolis, University of Minnesota Press, 1972.

Eberhard, Wolfram. *Chinesische Volksmärchen.* Jena, Diederichs, 1927.

————. "Lokalkulturen im Alten China," *T'oung Pao,* Ser. 2, No. 37 (1942), supplement.

Eliade, Mircea. *The Sacred and the Profane.* New York, Harcourt Brace and Co., 1957.

————. "The Yearning for Paradise in Primitive Tradition," *Daedalus,* Spring 1959, pp. 255–267.

Empson, William. *The Structure of Complex Words.* London, Chatto, 1951.

Erkes, Eduard. "Die Dialektik als Grundlage der chinesischen Weltanschauung," *Sinologica,* II (1950), pp. 31–45.

————. "The God of Death in Ancient China," in *T'oung Pao,* Ser. 2, 35 (1939), pp. 185–210.

Ferguson, John C. "Chinese Mythology," in *The Mythology of All Races.* Volume 8. ed. Canon John Arnot MacCulloch. Boston, Marshall Jones, 1928.

Fleming, John V. *The Roman de la Rose.* Princeton, Princeton University Press, 1969.

Fletcher, Angus. *Allegory, the Theory of a Symbolic Mode.* Cornell University Press, 1964.

Forke, Alfred. *The World-Conception of the Chinese*. London, Arthur Probsthain, 1925.

Frazer, Sir James George. *The Golden Bough*. New York, Macmillan, 1928 (abridged edition).

Frodsham, J. D. "The Origins of Chinese Nature Poetry," *Asia Major*, VIII, 1 (1960), pp. 68–103.

Frye, Northrop. *Anatomy of Criticism*. Princeton, Princeton University Press, 1957.

———. *Fables of Identity*. New York, Harcourt Brace, 1963.

———. *The Return of Eden*. University of Toronto Press, 1965.

———. "The Structure of Imagery in *The Faerie Queene*," *University of Toronto Quarterly*, XXX, pp. 109–127.

Fung Yu-lan. *A History of Chinese Philosophy*. Derk Bodde. Princeton, Princeton University Press, 1952.

Giamatti, A. Bartlett. *The Earthly Paradise and the Renaissance Epic*. Princeton, Princeton University Press, 1966.

Giles, Herbert A. *A Chinese Biographical Dictionary*. London, Bernard Quaritch, 1898.

Granet, Marcel. *Danses et Légendes de la Chine Ancienne*. Paris, Presses Universitaires de France, 1959.

———. *Festivals and Songs of Ancient China*. London, George Routledge, 1932.

Graves, Robert. *The Greek Myths*. New York, George Braziller, 1957.

Greene, Thomas. *The Descent from Heaven*. New Haven, Yale University Press, 1963.

Gunn, Alan M. F. *The Mirror of Love*. Lubbock, Texas, Texas Tech Press, 1952.

Hawkins, Sherman. "Mutabilitie and the Cycle of Months," in *Form and Convention in the Poetry of Edmund Spenser*. ed. William Nelson, New York, Columbia University Press, 1961.

Hollander, Robert. *Allegory in Dante's Commedia*. Princeton, Princeton University Press, 1969.

Howard, Edwin L. *Chinese Garden Architecture*. New York, Macmillan Co., 1951.

Hsia, C. T. *The Classic Chinese Novel*. New York, Columbia University Press, 1968.

Huppé, Bernard F. *A Reading of the Canterbury Tales*. Albany, State University of New York, 1964.

———and Robertson, D. W. Jr. *Fruyt and Chaf*, Port Washington, New York, Kennikat Press, 1963.

Inn, Henry. *Chinese Houses and Gardens*, Honolulu, Fong Inn's Ltd., 1940.

Jacobi, Jolande. *Complex, Archetype, Symbol in the Psychology of C. G. Jung*. Bollingen Series LVII, Princeton, Princeton University Press, 1971.

Jakobson, Roman and Halle, Morris. *Fundamentals of Language*, 's-Gravenhage, Mouton and Company, 1956.

Jung, Marc-René. "Études sur le poème allégorique en France au moyen age," in *Romanica Helvetica*, Vol. 82, 1971.

Karlgren, Bernhard. "Legends and Cults in Ancient China," *BMFEA*, XVIII (1946), pp. 199–365.

Ker, W. P. *Epic and Romance: Essays on Medieval Literature*. London, Macmillan and Company, 1908.

Kermode, Frank. *The Sense of an Ending*. New York, Oxford University Press, 1967.

Lau, D.C. *Mencius*. London, Penguin Books, 1970.

Legge, James. *The Four Books*. New York, Paragon Book Reprints, 1966.

———. *The Li Ki*. Sacred Books of the East, XXVII, Oxford, Clarendon Press, 1885.

———. *The Yi-King*. Sacred Books of the East, XVI, Oxford, Clarendon Press, 1882.

Lévi-Strauss, Claude. *The Raw and the Cooked*. New York, Harper and Row, 1969.

———. "The Structural Study of Myth," *Journal of American Folklore*, LXVIII, pp. 428–444 (1955).

Levin, Harry. *The Myth of the Golden Age in the Renaissance*. Bloomington, Indiana University Press, 1969.

Lewis, C. S. *The Allegory of Love*. Oxford, Clarendon Press, 1936.

———. *The Discarded Image*. Cambridge University Press, 1964.

———. *A Preface to Paradise Lost*. Oxford University Press, 1942.

————. *Spenser's Images of Life.* Cambridge University Press, 1967.

————. *Studies in Medieval and Renaissance Literature.* Cambridge University Press, 1966.

Lovejoy, Arthur O. *The Great Chain of Being.* New York, Harper and Brothers, 1936.

Mackenzie, Donald A. *Myths of China and Japan.* London, Gresham Publishing Company, 1923.

Maspero, Henri. *Le Chine Antique.* Paris, Presses Universitaires de France, 1965.

————. "Légendes Mythologiques dans le Chou King," *Journal Asiatique*, CCIV (1924), pp. 1–100.

Milton, John. *Paradise Lost and Paradise Regained.* ed. Christopher Ricks. New York, New American Library, 1968.

Mogan, Joseph J. Jr. *Chaucer and the Theme of Mutability.* The Hague, Mouton and Company, 1969.

Mote, Frederick W. *The Intellectual Foundations of China.* New York, Alfred A. Knopf, 1971.

Needham, Joseph and Wang Ling. *Science and Civilization in China.* Volumes I and II. Cambridge University Press, 1954.

Ogden, C. K. and Richards, I. A. *The Meaning of Meaning.* New York, Harcourt Brace and Company, 1927.

Panofsky, Erwin. *Studies in Iconology.* New York, Harper and Row, 1939.

Patch, Howard R. *The Goddess Fortuna in Medieval Literature.* Harvard University Press, 1927.

————. *The Other World, According to Descriptions in Medieval Literature.* Harvard University Press, 1950.

Poulet, Georges. *Les metamorphoses du cercle.* Paris, Libraire Plon, 1961.

————. *Studies in Human Time.* Batimore, Johns Hopkins Press, 1956.

Propp, Vladimir. *Morphology of the Folktale.* Austin, Texas, University of Texas Press, 1968.

Richards, I. A. *The Philosophy of Rhetoric.* London, Oxford University Press, 1936.

252

Robertson, D. W. Jr. "Chaucerian Tragedy," *ELH*, XIX (1952), pp. 1–37.

————. "The Doctrine of Charity in Medieval Literary Gardens," *Speculum*, XXVI (1952), pp. 24–49.

————. *A Preface to Chaucer*. Princeton, Princeton University Press, 1962.

Roche, Thomas P. Jr. *The Kindly Flame*. Princeton, Princeton University Press, 1964.

Le Roman de la Rose. ed. Félix Lecoy. Paris, Librairie Honoré Champion, 1974.

The Romance of the Rose. trans. Charles Dahlberg. Princeton, Princeton University Press, 1971.

Samuel, Irene. *Dante and Milton*. Cornell University Press, 1966.

Seznec, Jean. *The Survival of the Pagan Gods*. Bollingen Series 38, New York, Pantheon Books, 1953.

Singleton, Charles S. *Dante Studies 2: Journey to Beatrice*. Harvard University Press, 1958.

Siren, Oswald. *China and the Gardens of Europe*. New York, The Ronald Press, 1950.

————. *Gardens of China*. New York, The Ronald Press, 1943.

Spence, Jonathan D. *Ts'ao Yin and the K'ang-hsi Emperor*. New Haven, Yale University Press, 1968.

Spenser, Edmund. *The Complete Poetical Works of Edmund Spenser*. Cambridge, Massachusetts, Houghton-Mifflin Company, 1908.

Stambler, Bernard. *Dante's Other World*. New York University Press, 1957.

Tate, Allen. "The Symbolic Imagination," *Kenyon Review*, Vol. 14 (1952), pp. 256–277.

Tindall, William York. *The Literary Symbol*. Bloomington, Indiana University Press, 1965.

T'ung Chuin. "Chinese Gardens, Especially in Kiangsu and Chekiang," *T'ien Hsia Monthly*, III, 3 (1936), pp. 220–245.

Tuve, Rosemond. *Allegorical Imagery*. Princeton, Princeton University Press, 1966.

Vernon, John. *The Garden and the Map*. Urbana, University of Illinois Press, 1973.

Waley, Arthur. "The Book of Changes," *BMFEA*, v (1933), pp. 121–142.

Weng, Wango H. *Gardens in Chinese Art*. New York, China House Gallery, 1968.

Werner, E. T. C. *A Dictionary of Chinese Mythology*. Shanghai, Kelley and Walsh, 1932.

Wilhelm, Richard. *The I Ching*, trans. Cary F. Baynes. Bollingen Series XIX, Princeton University Press, 1950.

Wimsatt, W. K. Jr. and Beardsley, Monroe. *The Verbal Icon*. University of Kentucky Press, 1954.

Woodhouse, A. S. P. "Nature and Grace in the Fairie Queene," *ELH*, XVI (1949), pp. 194–225.

Wu Shih-ch'ang. *On the Red Chamber Dream*. Oxford, Clarendon Press, 1961.

CHINESE SOURCES

Cheng Te-k'un 鄭德坤. *Shan-hai Ching chi-ch'i Shen-hua* 山海經及其神話. n.p., n.d.

Chi Ch'eng 計成. *Yüan Yeh* 園冶. in *Hsi-yung-hsüan Ts'ung-shu*, Vol. 5.

Chin Shu 晉書. *Ssu-pu Pei-yao*. Taipei, Chung-hua Shu-chü, 1965.

Chou Ch'un 周春. *Yüeh Hung-lou Meng Sui-pi* 閱紅樓隨筆. Shanghai, Chung-hua Shu-chü, 1958.

Chou-i che-chung 周易折中. ed. Li Kuang-ti 李光地. Taipei, Chen-shan-mei Ch'u-pan-she, 1971.

Chou-li Chu-shu chi Pu-cheng 周禮注疏及補正. ed. Yang Chia-lo 楊家駱. Taipei, Shih-chieh Shu-chü, 1969.

Ch'u Tz'u 楚辭. ed. Chiang Chi 蔣驥 (Shan-tai Ko 山帶閣). Taipei, Kuang-wen Shu-chü, 1962.

Chuang Tzu 莊子. comm. Kuo Hsiang 郭象. Taipei, I-wen Shu-chü, n.d.

Fan Ch'eng-ta 范成大. *Fan Shih-hu Chi* 范石湖集. Peking, Chung-hua Shu-chü, 1962.

Fan Chung-yen 范仲淹. *Fan Wen-cheng Kung-chi* 范文正公集. *Kuo-hsüeh Chi-pen Ts'ung-shu* 278. Taipei, Commercial Press, 1968.

Fu Sheng 浮生. *P'ing Hung-lou Meng Wen-i* 評紅樓夢文藝. n.p., n.d.

Han Yü 韓愈. *Han Ch'ang-li Chi* 韓昌黎集. Taipei, Commercial Press, 1967.

Hsieh Ling-yün 謝靈運. *Hsieh Ling-yün Shih-hsüan* 謝靈運詩選. Shanghai, Ku-tien Wen-hsüeh Ch'u-pan-she, 1957.

Hsü Fu-kuan 徐復觀. *Yin-yang Wu-hsing chih Yen-pien chi jo-kan yu-kuan Wen-hsien ti Ch'eng-li Shih-tai yü Chieh-shih ti Wen-t'i* 陰陽五行之演變及若干有關文献的成立時代與解釋的問題. Hong Kong, Min-chu P'ing-lun She, 1961.

Hsün Tzu Chi-chieh 荀子集解. Taipei, Shih-chieh Shu-chü, 1962.

Hu-hua Chu-jen 護花主人. "Tsung-p'ing" 總評, in *Tseng-p'ing Pu-t'u Shih-t'ou Chi*, see below.

Huang-fu Mi 皇甫謐. *Ti-wang Shih-chi chi-ts'un* 帝王世紀輯存. Peking, Chung-hua Shu-chü, 1964.

Hui-t'u Feng-shen Yen-i 繪図封神演義. Shanghai, Chin-chang T'u-shu-chü, 1923.

Hung-lou Meng Chüan 紅樓夢卷 (reprinted under title *Hung-lou Meng Yen-chiu Tzu-liao Hui-pien*). ed. I-su 一粟, Taipei, Ming-lun Ch'u-pan-she, 1971.

Ku Chieh-kang 顧頡剛. "Chou-i Kua-yao-tz'u chung ti Ku-shih" 周易卦爻辭中的故事, in *Ku-shih Pien*, Vol. III, pp. 1–44.

Ku-shih Pien 古史辨. Volume 5. ed. Ku Chieh-kang 顧頡剛. Volume 7. ed. Lü Ssu-mien 呂思勉 and T'ung Shu-yeh 童書業. Taipei, Ming-lun Ch'u-pan-she, 1960.

K'ung Ling-ching 孔另境. *Chung-kuo Hsiao-shuo Shih-liao* 中國小説史料. Shanghai, Ku-tien Wen-hsüeh Ch'u-pan-she, 1957.

Kuang-po Wu-chih 廣博物志. Volume 5. Taipei, Hsin-hsing Shu-chü, 1972.

Lao Tzu 老子. Taipei, Hsin-hsing Shu-chü, 1965.

Li Chi Chang-chü 禮記章句. Taipei, Kuang-wen Shu-chü, 1967.

Li Jung 李冗. *Tu-i Chih* 獨異志, in *Pai-hai* 稗海, *han* 1, *ts'e* 8,

Pai-pu Ts'ung-shu Chi-ch'eng V. 14. Taipei, 1965.

Li Ko-fei 李格非. *Lo-yang Ming-yüan Chi* 洛陽名園記. Peking, Wen-hsüeh Ku-chi K'an-hsing-she, 1955.

Li Po 李白. "Ch'un-yeh Yen Tsung-ti T'ao-li-yüan Hsü" 春夜宴從弟桃李園序, in *T'ang-wen Hsüan* 唐文選. ed. Hu Yün-i 胡雲翼. Shanghai, Chung-hua Shu-chü, 1940.

Li Yü 李漁. *Li Yü Ch'üan-chi* 李漁全集. Taipei, Ch'eng-wen Ch'u-pan-she, 1970.

Lieh Tzu 列子. *Ssu-pu Pei-yao*. Taipei, Chung-hua Shu-chü, 1965.

Liu An 劉安. *Huai-nan Tzu* 淮南子. *Ssu-pu Pei-yao*. Taipei, Chung-hua Shu-chü, 1965.

Liu-ch'ao Ssu-chia Ch'üan-chi 六朝四家全集. Taipei, Hua-wen Shu-chü, 1968.

Liu Tsung-yüan 柳宗元. *Liu Tsung-yüan Ch'üan-chi* 柳宗元全集. Hong Kong, Kwong-chi Book Co., n.d.

Lo Pi 羅泌. *Lu Shih* 路史. *Ssu-pu Pei-yao*. Taipei, Chung-hua Shu-chü, 1965.

Lu Hsün 魯迅. *San-shih-nien Chi* 三十年集. Hong Kong, Hsin-i Ch'u-pan-she, 1968.

Lu T'ung 盧仝. "Yü Ma I Chieh-chiao Shih" 與馬異結交詩, in *Ch'üan T'ang-shih* 全唐詩. Peking, Chung-hua Shu-chü, 1960.

Ma Su 馬驌. *I Shih* 繹史. Taipei, Kuang-wen Shu-chü, 1969.

Ming-chai Chu-jen 明齋主人. "Tsung-p'ing" 總評, in *Tseng-p'ing Pu-t'u Shih-t'ou Chi*, see below.

Mu-t'ien-tzu Chuan 穆天子傳. *Ssu-pu Ts'ung-k'an Ch'u-pien So-pen*. Taipei, Commercial Press, 1967.

Ni Hsi-ying 倪錫英. *Lo-yang* 洛陽. Shanghai, Chung-hua Shu-chü, 1939.

Nien-wu-shih T'an-tz'u 廿五史彈詞. ed. Yang Sheng-an 楊升庵. Taipei, Te-chih Ch'u-pan-she, 1963.

Ou-yang Hsiu 歐陽修. *Ou-yang Yung-shu Wen* 歐陽永叔文. Taipei, Commercial Press, 1964.

Pan Ku 班固. *Po-hu T'ung* 白虎通. in *Ts'ung-shu Chi-ch'eng Chien-pien*, V. 98–99. Taipei, Commercial Press, 1967.

Po Chü-i 白居易. "Ts'ao-t'ang Chi" 草堂記, in Po-shih Ch'ang-ch'ing Chi 白氏長慶集, in *Ssu-pu Ts'ung-k'an*, Shanghai, Commercial Press, 1919, *t'ao* 71, *ts'e* 9, ch. 26.

Shan-hai Ching Chien-shu 山海經箋疏. *Ssu-pu Pei-yao.* Taipei, Chung-hua Shu-chü, 1965.

Shang Shu Shih-i 尚書釋義. ed. Ch'ü Wan-li 屈萬里. Taipei, Chung-hua Wen-hua Ch'u-pan-she, 1956.

Shen Fu 沈復. *Fu-sheng Liu-chi* 浮生六記. Taipei, Hsin-lu Shu-chü, 1963.

Shen Hsiang-jo 沈湘若. *Shih-ch'ien Shen-hua* 史前神話. Kaohsiung, Pai-ch'eng Shu-tien, 1955.

Shih Ching Shih-i 詩經釋義. ed. Ch'ü Wan-li 屈萬里. Taipei, Chung-hua Wen-hua Ch'u-pan-she, 1961.

Shih-hsi San-jen 石溪散人. *Hung-lou Meng Ming-chia T'i-k'ao* 紅樓夢名家題考. Taipei, P'ei-wen Shu-she, 1961.

Ssu-ma Chen 司馬貞. *Pu Shih Chi* 補史記; in Ssu-ma Ch'ien 司馬遷. *Shih Chi* 史記. *Ssu-pu Pei-yao.* Taipei, Chung-hua Shu-chü, 1965.

Ssu-ma Kuang 司馬光. *Ssu-ma Wen-kung Wen-chi* 司馬溫公文集. Taipei, Commercial Press, 1967.

Ssu-shu Chi-chu 四書集注. Ssu-pu Pei-yao, Taipei, Chung-hua Shu-chü, 1965.

Su Shih 蘇軾. *Su Shih Shih* 蘇軾詩. Hong Kong, Lü-ch'uang Shu-wu, 1965.

———. *Su Tung-p'o Chi* 蘇東坡集. Taipei, Commercial Press, 1967.

T'ai-p'ing Kuang-chi 太平廣記. Peking, Jen-min Ch'u-pan-she, 1959.

T'ai-p'ing Yü-lan 太平御覽. Taipei, Commercial Press, 1967.

T'ang Chün-i 唐君毅. *Chung-kuo Wen-hua chih Ching-shen Chia-chih* 中國文化之精神價值. Taipei, Cheng-chung Shu-chü, 1953.

T'ang Hsien-tsu 湯顯祖. *Mu-tan T'ing* 牡丹亭. Shanghai, Chung-hua Shu-chü, 1959.

T'ang-wen Hsüan 唐文選. ed. Hu Yün-i 胡雲翼. Shanghai, Chung-hua Shu-chü, 1940.

T'ao Yüan-ming 陶淵明. *T'ao Yüan-ming Shih Chien-chu* 陶淵明詩箋註. ed. Ting Chung-hu 丁仲祜. Taipei, I-wen Yin-shu-kuan, 1964.

——. *T'ao Yüan-ming Chi* 陶淵明集. Peking, Tso-chia Ch'u-pan-she, 1956.

Ts'ao Chih 曹植. *Ts'ao Tzu-chien Chi* 曹子建集. *Ssu-pu Pei-yao*. Taipei, Chung-hua Shu-chü, 1965.

Ts'ao Hsüeh-ch'in 曹雪芹. *Ch'ien-lung Chia-hsü Chih-yen Chai Ch'ung-p'ing Shih-t'ou Chi* 乾隆甲戌脂硯齋重評石頭記. Taipei, Chung-yang Yin-chih-ch'ang, 1961.

——. *Chih-yen Chai Ch'ung-p'ing Shih-t'ou Chi* 脂硯齋重評石頭記. Vols. I and II. Peking, Wen-hsüeh Ku-chi K'an-hsing-she, 1955.

——. *Hung-lou Meng* 紅樓夢. Taipei, Yüan-tung T'u-shu Kung-ssu, 1959.

——. *Hung-lou Meng* 紅樓夢. Peking, Jen-min Wen-hsüeh Ch'u-pan-she, 1972.

——. *Tseng-p'ing Pu-t'u Shih-t'ou Chi* 增評補圖石頭記. Shanghai, Commercial Press, 1930.

Tu Fu 杜甫. *Tu Shih Ch'ien-chu* 杜詩錢注. Taipei, Shih-chieh Shu-chü, 1968.

T'ung Chün 童雋. *Chiang-nan Yüan-lin Chih* 江南園林志. Peking, Chung-kuo Kung-yeh Ch'u-pan-she, 1963.

Tung Yüeh 董説. *Hsi-yu Pu* 西遊補. Peking, Wen-hsüeh Ku-chi K'an-hsing-she, 1955.

Wang Hsi-chih 王羲之. *Wang Yu-chün Chi* 王右軍集. Taipei, Hsüeh-sheng Shu-chü, 1971.

Wang Hsi-lien 王希廉. See Hu-hua Chu-jen 護花主人, above.

Wang Hung-hsü 王鴻緒. *Shih Ching Chuan-shuo Hui-tsuan* 詩經傳説彙纂. Taipei, Chung-ting Wen-hua Ch'u-pan Kung-ssu, 1967.

Wang Kuo-wei 王國維. "Hung-lou Meng P'ing-lun" 紅樓夢評論, in *Wang Kuo-wei Hsien-sheng San-chung* 王國維先生三種. Taipei, Kuo-min Ch'u-pan-she, 1966.

Wang Shih-fu 王實甫. *Hsi-hsiang Chi* 西廂記. Shanghai, Hsin Wen-i Ch'u-pan-she, 1955.

Wang Wei 王維. *Wang Yu-ch'eng Chi Chien-chu* 王右丞集箋注. Shanghai, Chung-hua Shu-chü, 1961.

Wen Hsüan 文選. Taipei, I-wen Yin-shu-kuan, 1959.

Wen I-to 聞一多. *Wen I-to Ch'üan-chi* 聞一多全集. Shanghai, K'ai-ming Shu-tien, 1949.

Wen K'ang 文康. *Hui-t'u Cheng-hsü Erh-nü Ying-hsiung-chuan* 繪圖正續兒女英雄傳. n.p. 1878.

Wu Ching-tzu 吳敬梓. *Ju-lin Wai-shih* 儒林外史. Hong Kong, Chung-hua Shu-chü, 1972.

Wu Shih-ch'ang 吳世昌. *San-lun Hung-lou Meng* 散論紅樓夢. Hong Kong, Chien-wen Shu-chü, 1963.

Ying Shao 應劭. *Feng-su T'ung-i* 風俗通義. Chung-fa Han-hsüeh Yen-chiu-so T'ung-chien Ts'ung-k'an. Taipei, 1968.

Yü P'ing-po 俞平伯. *Chih-yen Chai Hung-lou Meng Chi-p'ing* 脂硯齋紅樓夢輯評. Shanghai, Ku-tien Wen-hsüeh Ch'u-pan-she, 1957.

Yüan K'o 袁珂. *Chung-kuo Ku-tai Shen-hua* 中國古代神話. Peking, Chung-hua Shu-chü, 1960.

Yüan Mei 袁枚. *Sui-yüan Ch'üan-chi* 隨園全集. Hong Kong, Kwong Chi Book Co., n.d.

INDEX

Adam, 24, 100, 133, 136n, 140,
   144, 165n
adumbration, 107f
A-fang Palace, 149
allegory, 4, 7f, 73, 80, 84–126,
   88f, 166,˙178–212, 222f;
   allegorical gardens, 127–146;
   four-fold, 89; reading versus
   composition, 86, 90, 105
alternation, 6f, 9, 45–52, 55, 57f,
   61, 66, 69, 73, 79, 81, 83, 109f,
   114f, 167f, 171, 189, 194, 214,
   216, 218, 222
anagnorisis, 104, 104n
anagogical figures, 89f, 129,
   136–145, 146
archetype, 4–8, 11–16, 20f, 25–27,
   35, 37f, 40, 43, 47, 52f, 55, 66,
   81, 94, 167f, 187, 189, 216,
   218, 222; psychological, 13n,
   94
Aristotle, 15, 72
Auerbach, E., 89n
St. Augustine, 86, 118, 132, 135
axes of alternation, 6, 44–46, 169,
   171, 189; elegance and
   baseness, 55; fullness and
   emptiness, 189, 195, 218;
   harmony and conflict, 55, 61;
   inside and outside, 169, 190;
   joy and sorrow, 55f, 58, 60f,
   72, 206, 219; movement and
   stillness, 6, 46, 55, 59, 170,

221; prosperity and decline,
   6, 55, 219; truth and falsity,
   60, 222f; union and
   separation, 6, 14, 55f, 115,
   218f

being and becoming, 8, 102f, 113;
   and non-being, 46, 87n, 97,
   211, 222
Berger, H., 135n, 139n, 145,
   186n
binary opposition, 43, 94, *see
   also* dualism
bipolarity, complementary, 6, 8,
   26, 40, 44f, 47, 53, 55, 58–60,
   68, 70f, 78, 95, 109, 162, 167f,
   168n, 170f, 174, 177, 189, 194,
   202, 205f, 208, 222, 224
Black, M., 94n
Bodde, D., 16, 18f, 39
Boethius, 96, 113, 116f, 125,
   200n
borrowing views, 165f
breakdown, 8, 17, 176, 194–211,
   222
Buddhist elements, 180, 195, 201,
   204f, 215, 222f
Burke, K., 87n, 110n

Camel Kuo, 158, 198n
Camoens, 128
Campbell, J., 13, 15, 80
Cassirer, E., 14

261

INDEX

"Kao-t'ang Fu," 32, 82, 151, 160
Karlgren, B., 17, 19, 20, 21n, 30,
217
Ken-yüeh, 149
Kermode, F., 213
Ku, Chieh-kang, *Ku-shih Pien,*
20n, 23n
K'uei, 17
Kuei Yu-kuang, 153n
Kung Kung, 5, 17, 29, 36n, 39,
42, 54, 75
Kung, Prince, 156n, 188
K'ung-k'ung Tao-jen, 212
K'un-lun Mountains, 36, 148,
148n
Kuo P'u, 148n

Ladder of Heaven, 36, 41, 99
lantern riddles, 63, 65
Lao Tzu, 11, 201f, 209
lawns, 158
Leng Tzu-hsing, 54, 60
Levin, H., 128n
Lévi-Strauss, C., 19, 39, 43, 81ff
Lewis, C. S., 90, 92n, 96, 131,
142
Li Chi, 22, 32, 52, 179n
Li Ko-fei, 168, 176
Li Po, 158n, 163, 182n
Li Wan, 70, 195, 202
Li Yü, 155, 159, 165
Lieh Tzu, 29, 45
Liu Hsiang-lien, 205, 208
Liu Lao-lao, 57, 74, 184n, 193,
194n, 198n
Liu Tsung-yüan, 158
locus amoenus, see garden
"Lo-shen Fu," 35, 151
loss, 75
love, divine, 102, 122–125, 139,
143; earthly, 130, 132ff, 151,
158, 197
Lovejoy, A. O., 99, 106n, 125
Lo-yang Ch'ieh-lan Chi, 153

Lu Hsün, 19
Lu T'ung, 32, 34
Lucretius, 118n, 145
Lun Heng, 16

Madame Wang, 198
marriage, 5, 35, 39f, 48, 80, 100,
122, 125, 141, 143, 192, 197,
201ff; cosmic, 37, 43, 78
Martianus Capella, 86
Maspero, H., 17, 20
Matriarch, 190, 193, 194n, 208,
215
meaning, 6–8, 74, 85ff, 89f, 94,
109, 125, 146, 166f, 191, 212,
214, 222
medicine, 55, 57, 63f, 66, 68, 81,
220f
Mencius, 11, 152, 198, 209
metaphor, 8, 91–93, 106, 122, 125,
128, 144, 146, 167, 167n, 173,
207, 212; radical metaphor, 13
Miao-yü, 57, 184, 190, 205
Milton, J., 11, 95, 101, 106, 127,
130, 200n; *Paradise Lost,* 8,
85, 88, 104, 111, 120, 131ff,
134, 135n, 136, 141, 165n;
Adam, 104f; Eve, 98, 105;
Father and Son, 106; Garden
of Eden, 140–42;
pandemonium, 123; Raphael,
141; Satan, 99, 101, 104, 121,
124, 136n; Sin and Death, 91,
97, 108, 124
Ming-chai Chu-jen, 219n
mirrors, 65, 159, 184n
Mote, F. W., 155n
motion, ceaseless, 119; with
direction, 102ff, 105, 122
mutability, 7, 111, 113, 115, 117,
119, 145
Mu-tan T'ing, 69, 76, 151, 160,
163, 170, 173, 177, 182n, 195n,
198n, 220

265

psychomachia, 135f
pu, 221. *See also* Nü-kua
Pu-chou Shan, 29, 42n

quest, 103, 106. *See also* journey
Quintilian, 88

rainbow, 28, 81ff
recluse ideal, 149f, 151, 155, 186
recurrence, cyclical, 5, 6, 111,
  114f, 118f, 219
ritual, 5, 21–25, 32, 54, 179, 191
Robertson, D. W., 116
romance, 12, 86, 103, 117, 213
Romance of the Rose, 8, 85f, 88,
  103, 108, 113, 117-121, 127n,
  138, 161n; Jean de Meun, 97,
  102, 134n, 216; Amant, 104,
  132, 134, 136; Garden of
  Deduit, 132; Genius, 99, 136,
  136n; Narcissus, 97, 114, 123,
  132, 134; Pygmalion, 123, 134;
  La Vielle, 99

Sang Lin, 30ff
San-kuo Chih Yen-i, 60n
self-containment, 110f, 120, 122,
  124, 163, 169, 178, 201, 203,
  207ff; self-love, 122f, 141;
  self-sufficiency, 123f, 139, 141,
  176, 220
sense and *sententia*, 87, 125
Shang P'ien, 30
"Shang-lin Fu," 149, 153, 164
Shan-hai Ching, 16, 31, 148
"Shan-men," *Hu-nang Tan*, 209,
  209n
Shih Ching, 36n, 82, 147, 153f,
  191n
Shih Ch'ung, 150f
Shih Hsiang-yün, 55, 65, 69, 189,
  202, 217, 220, 221n
Shu Ching, 17, 20, 22, 29n, 52
Shui-hu Chuan, 31n

Shun, 15, 17, 25, 152
Shuo-wen Chieh-tzu, 27, 31
Singleton, C., 135n, 143
Siren, O., 154, 157, 177
Song of Songs, 130, 130n, 132, 134
Spenser, E., 95–97, 107n, 213f;
  The Faerie Queene, 8, 85ff,
  100, 102–108, 118, 123, 125,
  133, 135n, 212; Acrasia, 134f,
  145; Arlo Hill, 130, 173;
  Bower of Bliss, 113; Calidore,
  107; Cupid, 97f; Duessa, 97,
  99, 104; Florimell, 99; Garden
  of Adonis, 98, 120, 130, 141,
  144f; Guyon, 93, 98, 107, 113,
  135; Gyant, 99, 102;
  Mammon, 93, 119;
  Mutabilitie Cantoes, 111f,
  119f, 123, 124, 161n; Prince
  Arthur, 100, 113; Phaedria,
  131, 134f, 145; Red Cross
  Knight, 91; Sabaoths sight,
  108, 136, 144, 213;
  Scudamour, 102, 118n, 138;
  Temple of Venus, 102, 131f,
  138ff; Una, 104, 113
Ssu-ch'i, 71, 197
Ssu-ma Ch'ien, 149n
Ssu-ma Kuang, 152, 152n, 157ff,
  162f, 166, 169, 174, 209
stone, five-colored, 28, 39, 42, 54,
  78, 84, 210; *t'ai hu*, 159f,
  160n, 162f, 170, 184, 197
Su Shih, 155, 168, 205f
suffering, 8, 58, 59n, 74, 77f, 206f
Sui Yang-ti Yen-shih, 151n
Sui-jen, 33, 40
symbol, 90–93, 105f, 110, 131
synecdoche, 8, 110, 141, 146, 162,
  165n, 167, 173, 207
system of knowledge, 12, 16, 87;
  of literature, 12, 14, 15, 43, 55
systematizing, 5, 12, 19f, 24, 41n
Ta hsüeh, 166

82, 213; *see also* dualism
Ying-ch'un, 184, 192, 196f, 197n,
  202
Yu Sisters, 58, 68, 71, 188
Yü, 15, 17, 25, 32n, 34n
Yü Hsin, 150, 154
Yüan Mei, 147n, 157n, 170n,

174, 177, 187, 187n, 188,
  188n
Yüan Yeh, 154ff, 156n, 159, 165,
  170, 175, 175n, 177, 181f, 186
Yüan-ch'un, 60, 71, 80, 80n, 182,
  190, 202
Yüan-yang, 197n

Library of Congress Cataloging in Publication Data

Plaks, Andrew H   1945–
    Archetype and allegory in the Dream of the red chamber.

    Bibliography: p. 247
    Includes index.
    1.   Ts'ao, Chan, 1717(ca.)–1763. Hung lou meng.
    2.   Allegory. I. Title.
    PL2727.S2P5   895.1'3'4   75–3469
    ISBN   0–691–04616–6

Made in the USA
Middletown, DE
29 April 2022

64986777R00156